Climbing Colorado's Thirteeners

T0346438

Help Us Keep This Guide Up to Date

Every effort has been made by the author and editors to make this guide as accurate and useful as possible. However, many things can change after a guide is published—trails are rerouted, regulations change, techniques evolve, facilities come under new management, etc.

We appreciate hearing from you concerning your experiences with this guide and how you feel it could be improved and kept up to date. While we may not be able to respond to all comments and suggestions, we'll take them to heart and we'll also make certain to share them with the author. Please send your comments and suggestions to the following address:

FalconGuides
Reader Response/Editorial Department
246 Goose Lane, Suite 200
Guilford, CT 06437

Thanks for your input, and happy trails!

Climbing Colorado's Thirteeners

The Best Hikes and Scrambles over 13,000 Feet

James Dziezynski

GUILFORD, CONNECTICUT

FALCONGUIDES®

An imprint of The Rowman & Littlefield Publishing Group, Inc.
4501 Forbes Blvd., Ste. 200
Lanham, MD 20706
www.rowman.com

Falcon and FalconGuides are registered trademarks and Make Adventure Your Story is a trademark of The Rowman & Littlefield Publishing Group, Inc.

Distributed by NATIONAL BOOK NETWORK

Photos by James Dziezynski unless otherwise noted
Maps by Melissa Baker

British Library Cataloguing-in-Publication Information available

Library of Congress Control Number: 2021930957
ISBN 978-1-4930-4620-1 (paper : alk. paper)
ISBN 978-1-4930-4621-8 (electronic)

∞™ The paper used in this publication meets the minimum requirements of American National Standard for Information Sciences—Permanence of Paper for Printed Library Materials, ANSI/NISO Z39.48-1992.

Overview

Contents

Acknowledgments

Big thanks to my wife Sheila and our timeless hiking dogs, Mystic and Fremont. After thirteen years of big mountain adventures, the pups are enjoying a fine retirement at our home in Boulder, Colorado.

Also thanks to the friends who have joined the fun (and sometimes the misery) in the mountains during this project: Richard Harvey, Meredith Knauf, David Tanguay, Daniela Tanguay, Janet Seston, Jenny Salentine, Paul Lenhart, Paul Perea, and Bart DeFerme.

Additional thanks to Jessica d'Arbonne and the team at FalconGuides, Jon Bradford, Liba Kopeckova, Senad Rizvanovic, Chris Tomer, Marie Willson, Thomas Lunt, Doug Schnitzspahn, Nancy Coulter-Parker, Laura Keresty, and Paul Retrum.

Finally, thanks to Cathy Herbstler and the team and Leki Poles, Suzanne Loring, Jeff Banowetz, Marcus Woolf, Blaine Bachelor, Abbie Lang, Jeff Bartlett, Wendy Cranford, and Candice Blodgett.

Introduction

There are 584 ranked 13er summits in Colorado and another 220 recognized as significant peaks. That is a whopping 804 mountains—a *lot* of terrain to explore! The majority of 13ers are less traveled than Colorado's wildly popular 14,000-foot mountains (of which there are 58 . . . or 53, or 54, or 56, depending on whom you ask). Many 13ers miss out on bragging rights due to their relative obscurity. "I just climbed Unnamed Peak 13,580!" just does not resonate as powerfully as well-known Rocky Mountain classics like Longs Peak or the Maroon Bells. Perhaps because of their low profile compared to 14ers (no pun intended), 13ers offer a uniquely intimate mountain experience for those bold enough to seek their summits.

The 13ers offer the full spectrum of alpine challenge. Some are straightforward hill walks, but many more require strong navigational skills, solid route-finding, and bone-jarring 4x4 access roads to reach non-signed trailheads. The collection of hikes in this guide do their best to avoid "suffering for suffering's sake," such as slogs through willow-riddled swamps or miles of unstable scree fields. However, it is the nature of 13ers that there will be occasional river crossings or requisite bashing through patches of alpine shrubbery. Good thing you're tough.

Narrowing down the field to 40 primary routes containing roughly 100 13ers was no easy task. Besides my own personal experience of summiting more than 500 13ers, I consulted many respected Colorado climbers, including 13er completers, to come up with a list of excellent, nontechnical hikes and scrambles. Those that made the cut were chosen using objective criteria: their natural beauty, the quality of the rock, the wildlife, the presence of thrilling ridgewalks. Added to those rational measures was an emotional element, one that beats in the heart of every mountaineer. The feelings that great adventures evoke are not to be dismissed when evaluating mountains.

I see it in the eyes of those who have made the journey to the remote top of 13,825-foot Rio Grande Pyramid or braved the riveting traverse to 13,501-foot North Arapaho Peak. Even as I write these words, I can summon the electrified feeling of being high on those mountains, the depth of the camaraderie with my hiking partners (both human and canine), and the unique sensations that can only be found on high mountains.

It is my honor to share with you some of the very best Colorado 13ers. Whether you are following faint trails deep into the mysterious Gore Range or scaling the airy ridges above I-70, these mountains will reveal the character and challenge of the Rocky Mountains' wildest side. May your summits be sunny, your blisters few, and your adventures legendary!

Hiking in Colorado's Mountains

Even though Colorado's 13ers aren't the highest peaks in the state, they still carry the same risks and challenges of higher summits in the Rocky Mountains. Each of these factors could be separate books on their own, so the overview that follows here is by no means comprehensive. For more details on all these subjects, consider picking up *Mountaineering: The Freedom of the Hills* by The Mountaineers. This guide is updated regularly and is the definitive mountain safety manual.

Weather

Early starts can make all the difference when it comes to weather safety in the mountains. Being on-trail by 5 a.m. is a good habit, especially in the prime hiking season from June to September. Leaving summits by 11:30 a.m. or earlier is the counterpart to early starts. On most summer days, thunderstorms can be expected to roll in by around 1 p.m., even on days where there may be no storms in the forecast. Getting trapped above tree line when storms hit is no fun. Mountain storms can burn themselves out in 20 minutes or rage for hours.

It's worth noting that storms are not beholden to any schedule. I've seen violent storms roll in at 9 a.m. on days with clear forecasts, blow out, and then return as usual around 1 p.m. Basic weather skills such as using a barometer and knowing what types of clouds are most likely to develop into storms are important. Snow and hail can happen in any month of the year.

Storms aren't the only weather events to pay attention to. Sunny days, especially in the summer, can accelerate dehydration, sunburn, and eye fatigue. Covering exposed skin—ideally with clothing first, sunblock second—can stave off UV light that can manifest itself as fatigue or headaches later in the day from sunburn. Invest in a good pair of UVA/UVB-blocking sunglasses to help mitigate eye strain, another common cause of headaches.

Depending on the year, hiking in autumn can provide optimal conditions in the mountains. Thunderstorms are far less likely to develop thanks to lower temperatures, and there is often enough daylight to still get in a full day of hiking before darkness rolls in. Early season snowstorms can effectively cut hiking seasons short, but in dry years the months of September through November can be perfect for summit hikes.

As soon as seasonal snow sticks to the mountains (which can happen anywhere from early September to early December), consider the higher country to be winter hiking conditions. Winter hiking can be especially difficult on remote 13ers and requires an advanced skill set including snow travel gear (crampons, ice axes, pickets, ropes), avalanche gear (and the knowledge how to use it), how to read snow conditions, warmer gear, and insulating footwear. Elevations over 12,000 feet regularly stayed locked below zero and winds can howl. Winter summits can be wonderful

A look at the exciting ridge leading to the summit of UN 13,001, Colorado's lowest officially ranked 13er. This humble 13er is also known as Lost Man Peak due to its proximity to Lost Man Lake and Lost Man Pass.

experiences when you are properly prepared by being aware of the unique dangers present in the coldest months.

Spring is an interesting season in the Rocky Mountains. Much like autumn, conditions can vary greatly year to year. Late spring hiking can be perfect for snow climbing routes or traversing snow-covered ground over tedious talus fields. When conditions stabilize enough to minimize (but not eliminate) avalanche danger, there is a sweet spot in the spring where the sun is bright, storms are unlikely, and the footing is solid. As spring degrades into summer, the nightmare of post-holing through soggy snowfields and miles of mud begins. Runoff fuels rivers that can make normally benign water crossings quite dangerous. Access roads may seem clear, only to be decorated with careless 7-foot-high snowdrifts blocking an otherwise passable road. Spring can be a wildcard underfoot, but rarely do thunderstorms factor into the equation.

Altitude

At sea level, the effective oxygen rate is 20.9 percent. At 13,000 feet, this level drops to 12.7 percent. Our bodies are great at acclimating to high elevations, but it's a process that takes time. Acute Mountain Sickness (AMS) is always a threat at altitude. Even in its most mild form, AMS is an awful experience: headaches, nausea, dizziness, shortness of breath, swollen extremities, and irritability. Of these symptoms, it's worth noting that the last one—irritability—is one of the better indicators that a hiker is experiencing AMS versus normal mountain fatigue.

What is normal mountain fatigue? Hiking at a slower pace, having to catch your breath for longer than normal after exertion, a light dull headache, and a mild loss of appetite (or the inverse, a ravenous appetite) are common experiences. Part of knowing the difference between mild but anticipated discomfort and a legitimate medical emergency is one of the skills that comes with time and knowing your own body's typical responses to altitude. When in doubt, the best course of action is to head down to lower elevations.

For Colorado locals who live around 5,000 feet above sea level, sleeping at trailheads the night before is a good strategy to mitigate normal mountain fatigue on summit day. My personal experience from twenty years of mountain hiking is that sleeping between 9,000 and 9,500 feet the night before going to altitude is low enough for a restful night's sleep, but high enough to effect positive acclimatization. Of course, if you can spend extended time at high altitude, the effects of altitude will all but vanish as your body fully adapts. Summit days are a lot of fun when you've been camping over 10,000 feet for multiple days. That being said, most Coloradans that are reasonably fit can safely go from altitudes of around 5,000 feet to 13,000 feet without any major altitude effects, though headaches and slight dizzy spells are common. Ibuprofen liquid-gels are good at eliminating mild but irritating normal mountain fatigue symptoms.

Pushing up Clinton's steep slopes is a solid workout that may require traversing patches of snow. (hike 7)

Those coming from lower elevations would be wise to spend a few days at altitude before heading up to the mountains. A night's sleep at 5,000 to 8,000 feet, followed by a night at 8,500 to 10,000 feet works for most people. With this plan, hiking at altitude by day three is a reasonable expectation.

The caveat to all this advice is that altitude-related illnesses can strike seemingly well-acclimated hikers. While I wouldn't wish altitude sickness on anyone, if you do suffer from it there is a silver lining: You'll have a firsthand experience of how AMS differs from normal fatigue.

Hydration

Hydration is another element of hiking that can differ greatly from person to person. An efficient, experienced hiker can stay hydrated with a few sips every hour, while most casual hikers (who are physically working harder) will need more. The important thing is that you are taking in some water every hour of your hike—something a great many hikers neglect to do while descending. Dehydration can have serious effects: muscle cramps, nausea, and headaches. Overhydration is less common, but too much water can cause bloating and stomach upset.

The standard indicator of hydration is checking the color of your urine. Clear to light yellow is good, dark yellow means there is light dehydration, and brownish yellow means severe dehydration is already in effect.

Adding electrolytes to your water via tablets or flavorless powders is a winning strategy for maintaining energy levels and preventing cramps. On most hikes, I put electrolyte tablets in my main water source and bring along a 16- or 20-ounce water bottle filled with a sports drink.

Cold-weather hiking makes it easy to become dehydrated, especially when temperatures are likely to freeze the rubber straws of hydration systems. Keep a small water bottle in your insulated jacket and insulated hot drinks in your pack to make sure you always have a source of unfrozen water. It's helpful to schedule timed drink breaks, as it's very easy to simply not deal with the hassle of getting your water out.

Nutrition

Energy-filled foods that are easy to digest make the best fuel while hiking. Once again, personal experience varies greatly. Some hikers stay fully powered on blueberries, bananas, and water. Others need more significant sources of calories, though these should still be relatively easy to digest, such as peanut butter sandwiches, jerky, or salty crackers. Heavy foods dense with oils, butter, or excess sugar can be upsetting to your stomach and also provide very little in terms of usable nutrition.

My personal system consists primarily of gels and gummies, and I aim to take in 100 to 300 calories an hour—any more than that and your body can't do much with the excess. For longer days, I bring along a liquid endurance drink such as Hammer Perpetuem to keep easy-to-digest protein as "liquid food" when I'm on the mountain for 7-plus hours. I always have some kind of salty, palatable snack and my trustworthy "backup" peanut butter and jelly sandwich if I start to get hangry.

On mornings when I wake up at the trailhead, I'll skip breakfast or have a very light breakfast. This strategy helps the body access glycogen, a substance that stores glucose and provides a good kick of energy to start your day. I begin my normal habit of eating gels and gummies about 45 minutes into the hike. The caveat to this plan is that I do aim for a big meal the night before, usually pasta-based.

On days where I'm driving to the trailhead, I try to eat a hearty breakfast about 3 hours before beginning the hike to give my body time to digest. A bigger breakfast siphons glycogen resources to aid in digestion, so a big breakfast immediately before hiking can cause even fit hikers to drag.

Caffeine has long been speculated to aid in acclimatization, and there's no denying a good cup of coffee or the jolt of an energy drink can wake up a bleary-eyed hiker who gets up at 3 a.m. Caffeine will make you pee more on the trail, so be sure to keep up your hydration once you're on the move.

It's important to eat well after your hikes. Post-hike is the perfect time for a protein shake, followed by a satisfying meal. There's a good chance you'll be stuck in highway traffic after your hike, so plan for a few snacks in the car until you can take in a full meal.

First Aid

Every hiker should carry a first-aid kit in his or her pack, no exceptions. I'm a big fan of solo hiking and I still take along a well-stocked kit, not only for myself but for any other hikers I may be able to help along the trail. I also renew my wilderness first-aid certification every few years. It's a good idea for anyone spending time in the backcountry to take one of these classes.

Thankfully, most medical issues on mountains involve light headaches, minor scrapes and cuts, blisters, or upset stomachs. While these incidents aren't pleasant, they are not life-threatening. Being prepared for more serious medical events is important. On a hike written for this guide, my wife and I came across a hiker with a serious broken leg (tib-fib break) in a talus field. I was grateful we both had the medical training and experience to help until the hiker could be evacuated.

Along with a first-aid kit, I highly suggest investing in an emergency locator device. I use an inReach communicator, a handheld device that can reach out for help and pass along geo-coordinates from nearly anywhere in the world (and easily anywhere in Colorado).

Clothing and Hiking Gear

Outfitting yourself for a good day in the mountains means being prepared for whatever Mother Nature is going to throw at you. Here is a list of gear that will make your hiking experience the best it can be.

Most Important Items

There are three pieces of gear I consider the most valuable to hikers: footwear, sunglasses, and a good first-aid kit. All of these should be of the highest quality (high quality doesn't always mean the most expensive) and should be considered your most important investments. Skimp elsewhere!

- **Footwear**

    For summer, I like to wear light hikers with a waterproof liner and a sturdy Vibram sole. For over a decade, my choice has been the Lowa Renegade-Lo because of the features and fit. Any premium brand will offer a selection that may fit your foot better; just pay attention to the sole, the side material (too much stitching is bound to fail), and the feel of the shoe. I don't want anything too chunky for Class 3 or 4 scrambles.

    In colder months, when there is snow on the ground, or when the off-trail terrain is going to be rugged (boulder fields, off-trail forests), I prefer a full hiking boot with a waterproof liner and Vibram sole. Recently, I've used La Sportiva's

Trango Tech GTX boot as it has a nice balance of sturdy features and is relatively lightweight. As with day hikers, any premium brand will have a good selection of options, so find one that fits your specific foot.

- **Sunglasses**

    I've shifted to mostly wearing glacier goggles year-round in Colorado for most hikes. Dark lenses that protect from UVA/UVB light and have full peripheral coverage are vital to protecting your eyes. I still wear my lighter wraparound-style glasses for shorter days or in autumn when the sun is not as potent. Be certain, whatever you wear, that the lenses are quality enough that they don't distort your depth of field. I also leave older backup pairs in my truck, even if they are a bit scratched or beat up. I can improvise or do without certain pieces of gear, but no sunglasses means no hike for me!

- **First-Aid Kit**

    Buy a quality kit and be sure to update and refresh supplies on a regular basis. I add extra items like moleskin, ibuprofen, eye drops, quality forceps, and energy gels to my kit. I also have a cheap pair of sunglasses in my kit, a lighter, a small LED flashlight, fire starter cubes, and hand warmers.

Other Essential Hiking Gear

- **Day Pack**

    Normal-use day packs for Colorado should be between 1,500 to 2,500 cubic inches. Note that some day packs have slightly misleading names in relation to their storage space. For example, the REI Flash 22 has 1,343 cubic inches (the "22" refers to space as measured in liters). Be sure to check the specs so your pack is an acceptable size.

- **Hydration System**

    Hydration bladder systems are tops here, but in cold weather be sure to insulate the straw or go with water bottles.

- **Base Layers**

    Base layers worn against the skin should be non-cotton, wicking, and comfortable.

- **Jackets/Shells**

    Waterproof jackets and water-resistant wind shells will get a lot of use in Colorado. One feature worth checking out before buying is the fit of the hood.

- **Food/Snacks**

    Smash-proof containers are good for sandwiches and other smushable food.

- **Navigation Device (GPS, Compass) and Maps**

    I'm old school in the sense I believe every backcountry hiker should know how to use a map and compass, but I'm modern enough to realize that GPS devices are incredible for backcountry navigation. Most smartphones now have GPS receivers that are just as accurate or better than more-expensive handheld devices. If you're going this route, be sure to download any maps you need beforehand. GPS works without a data signal, but map info usually has to be downloaded first. (I used ViewRanger on an Android phone and a Garmin Oregon 600t for the tracks in this guide.)

I always bring a printed map along as well. If I'm going somewhere remote or completely new, I'll also invest in the USGS topographic quad for the area.

- **Hats**

  I bring two hats on most hikes (a visor and a winter hat), though in cold-weather months I'll use only my finest tuque paired with a neck gaiter/Buff.

- **Gloves**

  Lightweight for summer months, burly for cold weather.

- **Pants/Shorts**

  Zip-off pants that convert into shorts are a good choice for Colorado. It's amazing how much warmer it can be at the trailhead than on the windy summit.

- **Socks**

  Avoid cotton.

- **Sunblock**

  Be sure to apply a few times a day. Reapplying when you stop to pee is a good idea.

- **Bear Bell**

  Bear bells aren't just for bears. A jingle bell alerts animals that you are coming through. This warning is a preferred alternative to spooking a moose. I also put bear bells on my dogs' collars so I can keep tabs on them.

- **Emergency Locator Device**

  Remember that smartphone data signals are not reliable in the backcountry. Basic emergency locator devices can send signals in emergencies, while premium devices can send check-in texts, track GPS locations in real time, and come with topographic maps. I used the Garmin inReach, but there are several good brands to choose from.

Optional Items

- **Hiking Poles**

  I'm a big fan of hiking poles and recommend poles that have a snap-in locking mechanism vs. a twisting lock. They can also be used in other applications, such as creating a splint or shooing away bold marmots trying to chew through your pack. For the past fifteen years, I've used the Leki line of poles, most recently the Vario Carbon series.

- **Spare Key**

  It's always good to have an extra key for your vehicle, whether hidden on your vehicle or in your partner's day pack.

- **Gaiters**

  Knee-high gaiters are good for off-trail terrain, more so to keep debris and brush out of your boots than to keep your feet dry.

- **Arm Warmers**

  Arm warmers have become my favorite add-on for Colorado mountain hikes. When it's cool enough to warrant sleeves but you'll get too hot in a jacket, these are perfect. White arm warmers are good at keeping the sun off your arms.

- **Camera**

  Most folks will use their phone cameras these days, though there are still dedicated cameras out there. I listed a camera as optional because every once in a while, I think it's nice to take a hike without one.

- **Doggie Bags/Storage Bottle**

  It's good Leave No Trace ethics to pick up after your pups. Once you've bagged the poop, put it in a wide-mouthed container to pack it out.

- **Summit Pack**

  For days where you have a long approach or are setting up a base camp, a compact, foldable summit pack is perfect for a quick summit attempt with minimal gear.

- **Foam Pad**

  A 2-by-2-foot closed-cell foam pad is nice for breaks, especially if you'd otherwise be sitting on rocks or snow.

Hiking with Dogs

Sharing the mountains with dogs is one of life's great joys, but it comes with great responsibility. When hiking with dogs, be sure to bring supplies for them. Food, water, leash, collapsible bowls, and treats are a good start. Booties are great for cold-weather hikes if your dog will tolerate them; otherwise, paw wax for snow is a good option. During hunting season, reflective orange vests should be worn. Be certain you have updated tags on their collars/microchips.

Be sure that your dogs are under voice control, and don't let them antagonize wildlife (or other hikers). When the hike is done, make a safe, comfy spot for your dog in your vehicle—never put them in the open back of a pickup truck.

Beginning the modest traverse to Parry Peak from Mount Bancroft (hike 4)

How 13ers Are Different from 14ers

Colorado's most popular mountain hikes are unquestionably its 14,000-foot peaks. The 14ers offer a highly curated alpine experience due to their popularity and the passionate trail organizations that maintain the peaks. Every one of the standard summit routes on the accepted finisher list of fifty-eight is well documented in guidebooks and in hundreds of online personal trip reports. Because of this wealth of beta and established trails, a 14er finisher who ascends via the standard routes will have sampled only the larger skill set required to safely and efficiently travel in Colorado's deeper suite of mountains.

That's not to downplay the value of mountain time on 14ers. Hikers will learn a great deal on these peaks, with a relative margin of safety to make a few mistakes along the way. Some of the skills earned on 14ers include physical fitness, learning what nutrition works best for your body, how to read incoming weather, how to scramble on Class 3 and Class 4 rock, how to dress for the mountains, how your body reacts to altitude, basic route-finding skills, and navigation techniques—a great base to build on when you're ready to challenge the 13ers.

Here's a look at some of the major ways 13ers tend to differ from 14ers.

Fewer Established Trails

There are plenty of 13ers that follow the standard script for mountain trails, complete with signage, footbridges, and rock-hewn steps. More often, however, 13ers start on an established access trail and eventually get off the beaten path. This means a lot more off-trail navigation, something rarely found on the 14ers. On ridgelines and in open basins, this isn't all that difficult, but it's on the approaches and returns at tree line where strong navigation skills and good mountain instincts will come into play. A 10-mile day of off-trail navigation for a Gore Range 13er is a very different beast than a 10-mile day on-trail on a Sawatch Range 14er.

The hikes in this book intentionally avoid the especially gnarly and nasty stuff, but there are many off-trail adventures that will put your route-finding to the test.

Tougher Access Roads

It's not just the peaks themselves that offer a challenge. Many 13ers require driving on remote and unpredictable 4x4 roads to reach their trailheads (which may not be marked when you finally get there). There are definitely some tough standard access roads on the 14ers, but they have the advantage of regularly updated conditions and a certain degree of maintenance. Thirteener roads can be more of a wild card. Erosion, downed trees, flooded-out sections, deep mud, and rockfall are all part of the game—and here I'm talking about established 4x4 roads that should be passable by stock high-clearance SUVs. There are also plenty of rock-crawler-only roads that are suitable only for modified vehicles. Ranger stations are a good place to start for road condition updates, but sometimes you'll just have to see for yourself when you get there.

Less Documentation

As the 13ers gain popularity, there has been a modest rise in the amount of information available in the form of trips reports and online guides. However, there are still plenty of summits with sparse information or, worse still, bad beta. Several online sites are notorious for having heavily skewed trip reports, usually downplaying the danger or challenge of less-documented peaks. At the same time, there are also expertly written accounts by highly experienced hikers that rival the best guidebooks. When researching online, it's worth vetting the authors of 13er reports. In my own research for guidebooks, I've found certain trusted online authors (many of whom I've met over the years) whose work I highly respect and often compare against my own notes. In the end, a lot of 13ers will reveal themselves only in person. That's one of the charms of less-traveled mountains.

Greater Variety

With 584 ranked summits and over 200 more unranked or soft-ranked 13ers, there's a lot of ground to cover! Some of my favorite 13ers are often the oddball summits that seem out of place in relation to the reputation of the mountain range they call home. Technical scrambles hidden within the gentle domes of the Sawatch Range or humble walk-ups tucked in the jagged teeth of the Elks hold a special place in my mountainous heart. Thirteeners often have a great mix of terrain, such as UN 13,001 (see chapter 37), which begins with an easy, on-trail hike over Lost Man Pass to the serene, ink-dark water of Lost Man Lake. From there, it's an off-trail hill scramble to an exciting Class 3 ridge, wrapping up with a long descent down steep, flower-festooned slopes. Off-trail terrain can also include sections of swamp, ghostly burned-out forests, and fast-moving water crossings.

Less Upkeep

Even when there are trails on 13ers, there's no guarantee that those trails will be in prime hiking condition. This goes for trailheads and signage as well. UN 13,580 B lacks a formal name but is one of my favorite 13ers, in part because the trail to its summit materializes on a blank, grassy ridge whose approach lacks any formal trail. Other trails, such as the Bard Creek Trail, are slowly disappearing due to disuse. Knowing when a trail has temporarily dissolved into the weeds or when you are truly lost is a hard-earned 13er talent!

Tougher Route-Finding

Ever navigate a full mile through a dense pine forest? Even with a good map, GPS, and plenty of landmarks, it can be a challenging endeavor. Route-finding on 13ers isn't limited to approaches in the woods. Oftentimes, navigating a matrix of unmarked 4x4 roads can be just as hard (a lesson I learned by accidentally taking FR 248.1B instead of FR 248.1A en route to Argentine Peak). And then there is the mountain terrain itself. From dicey ridgelines to wobbly talus fields, from snow-choked basins to exposed summit blocks, reading the terrain encompasses challenges large and small.

Fewer Crowds

You won't hear avid 13er hikers complaining about the crowds—in fact, sometimes it's nice to have a little company on Colorado's more obscure mountains. In the summer hiking season, it's rare to have a 14er to yourself, even on the most challenging peaks in the middle of the week. Some 13ers have a nice balance of social interaction on approach trails but plenty of solitude en route to the summits. On many 13er hikes, you're much more likely to see wildlife than other people—which leads us to the final major difference from 14ers.

Emphasis on Self-Reliance

Thirteeners tend to offer a true backcountry experience. For many people, that is their great appeal. Perhaps the trait that separates mountain hiking experts from casual hikers is how well they know themselves. Knowing what technical terrain you can scramble safely, how comfortable you are with exposure, how to navigate challenging sections of the route, and how to anticipate weather are all part of the game. Some hikers know how to pack light 'n' fast, while others come prepared for anything. The freedom of the hills means that you will develop your own style in the mountains, and what works for you may not work for others. Knowing thyself also means having the awareness to turn around when things have gone pear-shaped, or simply because something in the ether is telling you today is not your day. Old-timers refer to this as listening to your mountain voice, but you don't have to be a grizzled alpine veteran to be a vigilant hiker.

The bottom line is that many 13ers have a wild side that demands more from those aiming to reach their summits. If you don't have a ton of mountain experience, never fear! This guidebook has a fine selection of good first-time 13ers, such as Mount Sniktau (chapter 11), that will help get your boots on the hill and help you acquaint yourself with the Rocky Mountains. And for experienced hikers who are up for a challenge, the 13ers in this book have been chosen to hit a sweet spot of "good challenge" without slipping into "miserable sufferfest" territory (to be clear, there *are* "miserable sufferfest" 13ers, but not in this book).

How to Use This Guide

The information in this book is made to be as straightforward as possible. As with any mountain climbing guidebook, it is implied that the act of ascending mountains brings with it a certain level of physical challenge. I am fond of saying there are no easy mountains in Colorado—weather, wind, ice, loose rock, and even wildlife represent semi-predictable elements that can change the most simple summit into an unintentional epic. Read on to understand the style and tone of this guidebook.

Class Systems

Class ratings for mountain hikes aren't perfect, but they do help establish the technical aspects of a given route. Note that class ratings generally don't account for exposure. For example, a 3-foot-wide catwalk with steep drops on either side would still be considered nontechnical Class 2. The class ratings for this book are relative to accepted grades for Colorado mountains, which are as follows:

Class 1

Easy, well-maintained trails and open tundra can be classified as Class 1. It can be argued that very few high peaks in Colorado qualify as true Class 1, as most contain some rocky portions or easy scrambles.

Class 2

This class represents a majority of mountain hiking trails: established paths with some rocky sections or off-trail terrain that doesn't have significant fall danger. Many boulder, scree, and talus fields fall into Class 2. The Class 2+ rating is used when there is light hands-on scrambling required.

Class 3

Classes 3 and 4 are highly debated ratings, partially because they invite subjectivity into the conversation. A brief downclimb may be considered Class 3 by a 6-foot climber, but Class 4 for a 5-foot, 5-inch climber—and they may both be correct assessments.

Class 3 refers to true hands-and-feet scrambling. Low-technical moves with relatively low fall consequences define this class, though be aware that doesn't imply there will be no consequence to a slip or fall.

Class 4

This class is scrambling on rock and isn't highly technical but has high consequences for failing to complete a move. Some climbers prefer to rope up for Class 4 terrain, especially on sustained sections with prolonged exposure. Class 4 terrain is basically the middle ground between scrambling and low-grade technical rock climbing.

Class 5

Class 5 is where technical rock climbing begins. Ropes, harnesses, anchors, and belay equipment are used. Class 5 uses the Yosemite Decimal System (YDS) to rank difficulty, from 5.0 to 5.15. There are no Class 5 routes in this book.

Difficulty Ratings

The difficulty ratings in this book are simplified into three designations: easy, medium, and difficult. "Easy" is relative to how hard it is to hike the average 13,000-foot mountain in Colorado. Or put another way: The difficulty is measured relative to the average *mountain hiker*, not the average person. An "easy" hike in this guide may be considered difficult in a guide that includes casual hikes or other less-strenuous outings.

Easy

Easy 13ers are half-day outings that have little to no scrambling, follow established trails or easy-to-follow off-trail terrain, and present minimal navigational challenges.

Medium

True to its rating, most 13ers fall in the medium difficulty category. These can be half-day or full-day treks, have off-trail sections that require good navigational skills, may have Class 2+ or Class 3 scrambling, and may include sections that demand solid route-finding.

Difficult

Difficult 13ers are usually a full-day affair, but not always. Difficult 13ers may feature long mileage, challenging off-trail navigation, tricky Class 3 or Class 4 moves, and advanced route-finding. The toughest 13ers in this guide are all nontechnical, meaning the routes don't require ropes for most climbers. The specific difficulties will be explained in each chapter.

Time

In the past, I used to estimate hours for each hike. The problem with this approach is that it doesn't account for stopping to smell the flowers, the fitness level of hikers, or the simple pleasure of lingering on the peaks when the weather is clear.

Taking in the length, difficulty, and route-finding challenges, the hikes in this guide fall into two categories that are good estimates for how long you can expect to be out.

Half Day

A hike that should take the average mountain hiker 3 to 5 hours.

Full Day

A hike that should take the average mountain hiker 5 to 10 hours (or more). I have intentionally avoided hikes that might take more than 10 hours, though there will be optional summits that could push a full-day outing into an all-day affair.

Overnight

Overnight hikes are best done by setting up a backcountry camp and making the adventure a two-day affair. Occasionally there is access to an established campground, but more often, hikers will be camping in dispersed sites.

When a hike is set up as a good overnight adventure (regardless of time), it will be mentioned.

Vehicle Access

There are four vehicle classifications used in this guide. They are:

1. **Passenger Car**—Your average low-clearance car. Trailheads for passenger cars are reachable by all vehicles in normal weather conditions and don't require four-wheel drive (4WD).
2. **Sport-Utility Cars (SUCs)**—SUCs have better clearance than passenger cars, and most have all-wheel drive (AWD), though some have true 4WD as well. SUCs can handle modest dirt roads and (very) light 4x4 terrain. Examples include Subaru Foresters, Honda CRVs, and Toyota RAV4s.
3. **Sport-Utility Vehicles (SUVs)/4x4 Trucks**—These are high-clearance vehicles with dedicated 4x4 drivetrains. Chapters mention if access roads are good for stock SUVs and when something a little beefier in terms of suspension or durability is advised. Whether stock or upgraded, it is highly recommended outfitting your vehicle with a premium 4x4 tire such as the BF Goodrich KO2. They can be expensive (a set of four ran about $1,000 in 2020), but you will be grateful in your investment when bashing through rutted rock gardens or crashing through a riverbed. It's always a plus to have a 4-low option as well.
4. **Dedicated Rock Crawlers**—These are highly modified Jeeps, buggies, and other crazy-cool vehicles purpose-made to roll over anything in their way. The toughest roads for stock SUVs are child's play for rock crawlers. There are several expert 4x4 roads in this guide that are written up as hikes, but if you happen to have a true backcountry vehicle, you can cut off some time by bashing up a portion of the hike in your crawler.

13er Playground

A special feature for this guidebook, the 13er playground designation signifies the potential to summit three or more 13ers from a single trailhead or access area (though not necessarily on the same day). If you're looking for a weekend of summit hikes or pushing a huge day to bag multiple peaks, 13er playgrounds have a lot to offer.

Map Legend

Transportation

≡(70)≡   Interstate Highway

≡(40)≡   US Highway

≡(7)≡   State Highway

≡[110]≡   County/Forest Road

= = = = ·   Unpaved Road

------   Featured Route

- - - - - -   Trail or Fire Road

Water Features

Body of Water

Glacier

River/Creek

Symbols

(1)   Trailhead

▲   Mountain/Peak

×   Spot Elevation

✕   Pass

🎿   Ski Area

■   Point of Interest

🗼   Tower

Land Management

National Park/Forest

Wilderness Area

1 Argentine Peak–Mount Edwards

This is a true 13ers playground. There are four 13ers within striking range here, and it's possible to get all of them in one big loop. This adventure starts at the ghost town of Waldorf, a boomtown that once boasted America's highest post office at 11,666 feet. The post office building is still there today, along with an assortment of mining ruins (and a few modern, privately owned cabins). Summit potential is big, including linking over to the ever-popular 14er Grays Peak—but come on, you're here for 13ers, right?

Primary route: Mount Edwards, 13,850 feet; Argentine Peak, 13,738 feet
Optional summits: McClellan Mountain, 13,587 feet; Mount Wilcox, 13,408 feet; Ruby Mountain, 13,277 feet (from the west side of Argentine Pass)

Difficulty rating: Medium–slight; moderate exposure along ridges
Class rating: Class 2
Round-trip distance: 6.2 miles out and back
Elevation gain: 2,320 feet
Round-trip time: 4–6 hours; half day for single-peak outings, full day for linkups

---

Finding the trailhead: The access road to the eastern side of the pass has taken a beating in the past five years. You'll now want a high-clearance SUV to get up to the Waldorf ruins—in the past, it was possible for a hardy sport-utility car (SUC) to muscle up. If you have an SUC, it is possible to access these hikes from the other side of the Argentine Pass.

From I-70 west of Denver, take exit 228 (Georgetown) and turn toward town (east) off the exit ramp. Reset your odometer here. Turn right onto Argentine Street and begin following the signs for Guanella Pass. Go 0.5 mile then turn left onto Sixth Street, then in a few blocks, right onto Rose Street. In 0.2 mile, go left and begin climbing Guanella Pass. At mile 3.5 in a sharp switchback, go right and leave the paved road.

Here's where the fun begins. Reset your odometer and get ready to rumble. The steep dirt road into the woods is the Leavenworth Creek Road, and it starts with a bang. The good news is that most of the hard-drivin' is in the first 1.1 miles. You may want to start in 4-low. It's important to stay on the "main" road, even when there are tempting turnoffs along the way.

Begin bashing up the rutted hill and take the first of several tight switchbacks. In 0.2 mile, pass a smooth-looking road on your left. There are some concrete buildings here. Stay right on the loose, rocky road as it climbs another hill. The steepness eases off a bit as you climb along the bumpy road. At mile 0.9, reach a juncture. In front of you is a flat, smooth, elegant road into the woods. To the right, a terribly loose, very steep hill. To quote the fishy Admiral Ackbar from Star Wars: "It's a trap!"

The correct way to go is up the steep road to the right. Even though the flat road (FR 248.1B) looks inviting, it quickly becomes a very rocky 4x4 adventure. (**Note:** If you happen to be driving a Jeep or an SUV with great tires and upgraded suspension, FR 248.1B is a fun road, but it will eat a stock SUV alive.) Stick with the easier option!

Push up the steep, punchy road to the right. At the top of the hill (mile 1.1) turn left onto . . . a nearly smooth dirt road? For the next 4.2 miles, enjoy the easygoing road all the way to the Waldorf parking area. Avoid any side roads—it will be obvious that they are not the main road. If you could teleport a Yugo up here, even it could handle the terrain. You'll pass a waterfall drainage under the road before reaching the vast, open basin below Argentine Pass. While Jeeps and even some SUVs can drive up to the top of the pass, it's better to park here.

Trailhead GPS: N39 38.262' / W105 45.912'

The Hike

This route gives you the option to get either Argentine Peak or Mount Edwards. Either summit as an out-and-back is a fine day hike, especially if you want to spend time checking out the ruins of Waldorf. These fantastic 13ers start above tree line, so you're in for incredible views all day. Navigation is straightforward and the terrain is nontechnical. Add in the historical elements of the ghost town, the mining ruins, the

Argentine Pass from the summit of Mount Wilcox. Mountains (left to right): Grays Peak, Torreys Peak, Mount Edwards.

Grays Peak (left), Torreys Peak (center), and Mount Edwards (right) from the west side of Argentine Pass

unbelievable relics of the railroad, and the engineering marvel of Argentine Pass for more intrigue. Linking up other peaks is a big draw—once you've gained the ridge-line, options to walk over to neighboring peaks are plentiful.

For linkups to other summits, read the Optional Routes section.

Miles and Directions

0.0   From the large parking area, simply follow Argentine Pass to its high point at 13,207 feet. Even though it's a 4x4 road, this is an enjoyable walk-up. Views of the old mining operations open up the higher you get.

2.1   At the top of Argentine Pass, you can finally see into Horseshoe Basin to the west. Your options here are simple: If you want to summit Mount Edwards, turn right (north) at the pass and follow the Class 2 ridge 1 mile to the summit. If Argentine Peak is your preference, go left (south) and hike 1 mile to the top. That's good symmetry!

3.1   From the top of your respective summit, simply reverse course to head back to the parking area. Chances are you may be tempted to add on some extra summits! Read the options below for more details. If you opt to tack on whichever summit you skipped when you made your decision from the pass, add 2 miles to your overall day.

6.2   Arrive back at the parking area. Driving back down is fairly tame, but make sure you don't miss the sharp right turn 4.3 miles in. Your brakes will get a workout on the last steep hills down to the paved road!

Argentine Peak–Mount Edwards

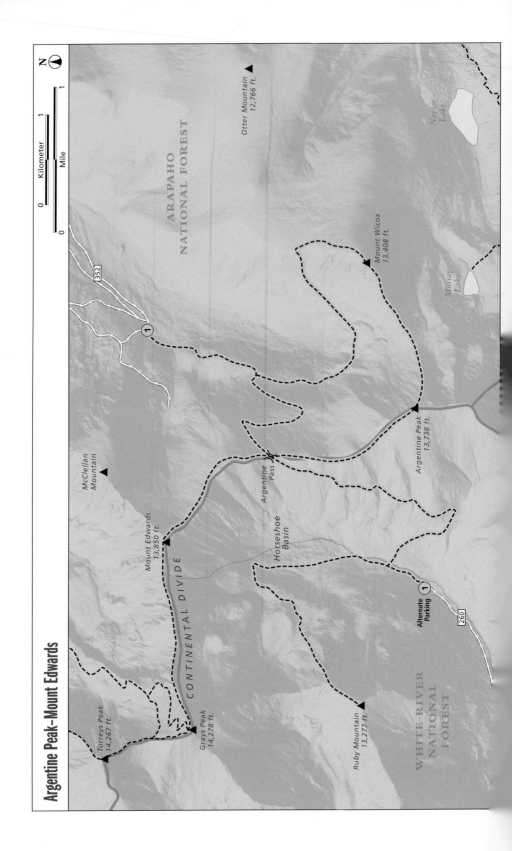

Optional Routes

So many options! Here are just a few:

McClellan–Edwards Loop: 6 miles / 2,400 feet of vertical gain

To score these two 13ers, follow the hodgepodge of mining roads north from Waldorf that go pretty close to the flat summit of McClellan Mountain. You may see a few daring Jeepers driving up these roads. From the high point on the ridge, walk southwest to the true summit. From McClellan it's an easy walk over to Mount Edwards, then back down Argentine Pass. This is a good option if you want to get a closer look at the mining ruins above the town.

Argentine–Wilcox Loop: 6.6 miles / 2,920 feet of vertical gain

This option continues from the summit of Argentine Peak and meanders over to 13,408-foot Mount Wilcox (Class 2). The toughest part of this outing is walking down the steep slopes of Mount Wilcox back into the basin. It's not technical but tough on the knees (bring hiking poles). Views of Argentine Pass from Wilcox's summit are the best around.

McClellan–Edwards–Argentine–Wilcox: 9.5 miles / 4,250 feet of vertical gain

Hoooo doggy! This loop combines all four 13ers. The up-and-down nature of the elevation gain is tough, but if you're fit and have a nice weather window, you can head for home with four 13ers under your belt . . . errr, boots. Start with McClellan and follow the ridges in a big circle.

Final Thoughts

The ruins of Waldorf are an area I visit again and again, much to my truck's chagrin. The lower Leavenworth Creek road seems to be getting more damaged every year, but stock SUVs should be able to fight their way up as long as they have good tires. The privately owned Tundra Hut is one of the private buildings just before the town of Waldorf and is a downright luxurious base camp if you and a few friends want to rent it out.

It staggers the imagination to picture Waldorf as a living, breathing city in the late 1800s. Even in 2020, access to the area is rough. Gold and silver was abundant in the area and that made all the difference.

The Argentine Central Railway used to chug up to the summit of McClellan Mountain. Edward Wilcox (namesake of the mountain) built the railroad from 1905 to 1906, but his timing was terrible. Silver prices plummeted, and this marvel of engineering operated only from 1906 to 1918. Had fortunes been better, Wilcox would have continued the tracks to the summit of Grays Peak. One thing you can say about turn-of-the-century Coloradans: They were ambitious.

2 Atlantic Peak

Atlantic Peak's incredible west ridge is a bona fide adventure. Don't let the low mileage fool you; this is an excellent day out. Linking up multiple peaks on a single day makes sense, especially pairing up Atlantic, Pacific, and Crystal Peaks.

Primary route: Atlantic Peak, 13,841 feet
Optional summits: Pacific Peak, 13,950 feet; Crystal Peak, 13,852 feet; Drift Peak, 13,900 feet; Fletcher Mountain, 13,951 feet; Father Dyer Peak, 13,615 feet; Peak 10, 13,633 feet
Difficulty rating: Medium; pick your way through a brief willow field en route to an exciting and accommodating ridge directly to the top of Atlantic Peak
Class rating: Class 2
Round-trip distance: 3.3 miles out and back
Elevation gain: 2,430 feet
Round-trip time: 4–6 hours; half day

Finding the trailhead: From I-70 west of Denver, take exit 195 (Copper Mountain) to CO 91S toward Fremont Pass. Steadily climb 5.9 miles until reaching the Mayflower Gulch parking area on the left (east) side of the road. If you're driving a passenger car (or snow is blocking the road), this is where you'll have to park. It's 1.5 miles to the start of the route, so you'll tack on 3 total miles and about 2 hours to your day if this is your option, which still puts the out-and-back hike for the primary route at only 6.3 miles—quite manageable as a day hike.

SUVs and high-clearance SUCs can continue on the dirt road up Mayflower Gulch 1.5 miles to a small parking area at the Boston Mine ruins. This road is fairly tame by 4x4 standards but does have some high, rolling ruts and a bit of steep terrain toward the end of the road. Even if you weren't here to hike the peaks, the beauty of this basin is undeniable. Park on the left side of the road as you enter the basin.

Trailhead GPS: N39 24.840' / W106 08.892'

The Hike

The primary route here (Atlantic Peak by itself) is a wonderful ridgewalk and can serve as the basis for a much bigger day. Other options include nearby 13ers Drift Peak and Fletcher Mountain, though neither is quite as aesthetic as Atlantic Peak.

Mayflower Creek Basin is incredibly photogenic—chances are photographers will be out and about near the trailhead as you return from the summit.

A bushwhack through the lower willow field is a scrappy but short-lived start to the day. Gaining the ridge takes a bit of time and muscle, but once attained, this is one of Colorado's premier ridgewalks. All the tough stuff is within the first mile of the adventure; after that it's hiking bliss. There is mild exposure as the ridge narrows near the summit, but the ridge never tightens so much that it becomes daunting. Overall, it's not a highly demanding route, and the two distinct vibes (the approach and the ridge) can amplify the sense of adventure. This is an excellent 13er for hikers making the leap from on-trail to off-trail navigation, thanks to the forgiving route-finding. Strong hikers can tack on Pacific and Crystal Peaks or jump in America's highest permanent lake, Pacific Tarn.

Miles and Directions

0.0   You can see Atlantic Peak's west ridge in all its glory from the parking area. There are quite a few mining ruins here as well. Your first goal is to bushwhack 0.5 mile northeast to the base of the ridge. Visually, this is a straight shot, but it's not quite as easy as it looks. Follow improvised trails into a willow thicket. Keep your eyes on your feet, as there are lots of sinkholes just waiting to suck your boots into the mud! Hop over a few streams before reaching a semi-forested hillside leading to the ridgeline.

0.5   Once you break tree line, you have a nice 1-mile ridgewalk to the top of Atlantic Peak. There is a slight bit of exposure the higher you go, but the terrain stays Class 2 all the way up. Toward the top will be a light patch of scrambling.

Nearing the summit of Atlantic Peak via the west ridge

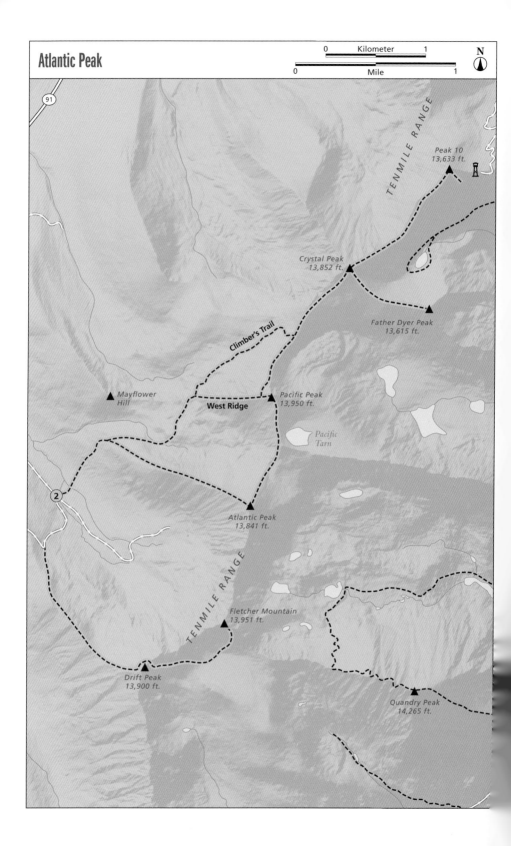

0   Kilometer   1

0   Mile   1

N

91

TENMILE RANGE

Peak 10
13,633 ft.

Crystal Peak
13,852 ft.

Father Dyer Peak
13,615 ft.

Climber's Trail

Mayflower
Hill

West Ridge

Pacific Peak
13,950 ft.

Pacific
Tarn

2

Atlantic Peak
13,841 ft.

TENMILE RANGE

Fletcher Mountain
13,951 ft.

Drift Peak
13,900 ft.

Quandry Peak
14,265 ft.

1.5 Boom! The summit of Atlantic Peak! Pacific Peak practically begs to be climbed to the north, but that's up to you (read the Optional Routes for details). Note that if you hike up Pacific (and beyond), the options for returning are either re-climbing Atlantic or navigating the basins below the summits. For now, let's settle on a fine day of hiking Atlantic Peak and return the way you came.

Descend the ridge and find the best line back to the parking area. It is possible to avoid the willows altogether by going high into the basin, though it tacks on a bit of extra mileage. However, this isn't a bad option if you want to explore some of the mining ruins in the area, plus the basin tends to explode with wildflowers in early summer.

3.3 Arrive back at to your car. Mileage may be slightly different depending on how directly you bushwhack to and from the ridge. The 3.3 miles listed here skirts the willows a bit to the east on the return.

Optional Routes

If you camp for the weekend, it's possible to go home with five (!) 13ers marked off your checklist—and possibly more! You'd have to be a fitness monster (and have a perfect weather day) to link them all together, but . . . this is Colorado. People are crazy about climbing mountains. Options for us mere mortals are below.

Atlantic–Pacific–Crystal Traverse: 6.1 miles / 3,560 feet of vertical gain

There may not be a better trio of 13ers to collect in a single outing (though other chapters in this guide make a case for a few others!). Start this route by heading up Atlantic, then following the obvious Class 2+ ridge north to Pacific Peak. The small lake off to your right is Pacific Tarn, the highest recognized permanent lake in America.

Pacific Peak's summit is incredible, but the adventure doesn't end here. The most technical part of the day is a downclimb (Class 3) into a small notch southwest of the summit, then scrambling back up to gain the north ridge between Pacific and Crystal. The Class 3 moves here are few, but there will be a bit of exposure though nothing crazy. Once you ascend the far side of the notch, the way down to Crystal will reveal itself via a climber's trail.

From the saddle between Pacific and Crystal, be sure to look back at Pacific Peak's majestic crack-top summit—it's one of the most distinct peaks in Colorado! The hike from here up to Crystal is easier than Atlantic or Pacific, and many hikers remark it goes much quicker than it looks.

Once you've summited Crystal, return south to the Pacific-Crystal saddle and follow a climber's trail west to lower ground. From here, you'll cross through two basins beneath Pacific and Atlantic Peaks as you head due south to return to the parking area. This walk back is tedious thanks to boulder fields blocking the best lines. Alternating grass fields and talus piles make for slow going until you've climbed back up to the start of Atlantic's west ridge. You're home free once you descend back into Mayflower Gulch. The mileage isn't big here, but the nature of the up-and-down elevation gain and off-trail hiking make this a very full day.

Looking back at Pacific Peak's distinctly cracked summit along the traverse to Crystal Peak

Some hikers like to reverse this route to get all the basin walking done early and scamper on the ridgeline back—Crystal to Pacific to Atlantic.

Pacific–Atlantic via Pacific Peak's West Ridge: 4 miles / 3,000 feet of vertical gain

If you're comfortable with exposed Class 3+ scrambling with some tricky route-finding, Pacific's west ridge is a lot of fun. For this route, start the same as Atlantic's west ridge but keep going north to Pacific's imposing west ridge. Scrambling here involves skirting around a trio of towers and possibly a touch of Class 4 climbing here and there. It's not long—the ridge itself is a little under a mile and the tough stuff is all in the first 0.3 mile. A little past halfway on the ridge, the hard work is over and you'll have a nice line to the summit. The fun Class 3 notch that splits Pacific Peak wraps up the final push to the top.

From here, the obvious return loop is south to Atlantic and down Atlantic's west ridge.

Father Dyer Peak Add-on from Crystal Peak: 1.1 miles / 630 feet of vertical gain

Once you find your way to Crystal Peak, Father Dyer Peak is a short Class 2 traverse to the southeast. It's 1.1 miles round-trip from the summit of Crystal and back, though you'll likely not revisit Crystal's summit if you do this option. Traverse below Crystal's summit slopes to save your legs and regain the Pacific-Crystal saddle.

Peak 10 Point-to-Point to Breckenridge from Crystal Peak: 4.4 miles/450 feet of vertical gain

If you have two vehicles and want a unique adventure, it's possible to link Crystal Peak to Peak 10. Peak 10 is a 13er within the boundary of the Breckenridge Ski Area. You'll leave car #2 at the base area and hike down the slopes/cat roads to make for an epic Class 2 point-to-point trip.

It's possible to go Atlantic–Pacific–Father Dyer–Crystal–Peak 10 in a single day of roughly 9 miles and about 4,200 feet of elevation gain. At least 3 miles of this hike will be walking down the Breckenridge ski slopes. One tip if you do this: Skirt over to Father Dyer before summiting Crystal so as not to add any extra elevation.

Drift Peak and Fletcher Mountain Options: 3 to 5 miles/2,900 feet of vertical gain

Drift Peak alone as an out-and-back climb is like the evil twin of Atlantic Peak. Instead of going north from the Boston Mine parking, go south along the 4x4 road

Hikers on the summit of Pacific Peak as seen from the prominent notch on the north ridge

up Gold Hill and take the northwest ridge to Drift's boulder-strewn summit. It's basically a mile of nonstop boulder-hopping, and it's steep in places. The saving grace is that the rock is mostly stable. It's 3 miles as an out-and-back hike.

If you want to add in Fletcher, my advice is . . . there is a better route. First, the direct ridge north between the two summits is a Class 4/5 disaster, riddled with loose rock, crazy exposure, and decomposing towers to work around. But . . . if you must, you can descend east off Drift's steep slopes and get to Fletcher's summit via a Class 2+ hike/scramble from the east. It's about a mile there and a mile back up to Drift. My two cents: Fletcher is better hiked as a pleasant Class 2 outing from the Blue Lakes parking area to the east. This option pairs nicely with the 14er Quandary Peak's tough-but-fair Class 3 ridge.

Final Thoughts

Options out of Mayflower Gulch are plentiful! One that I'll make only a passing mention of is a point-to-point hike that follows the route to Peak 10, then rolls all the way down to Peak 6 via the Colorado Trail. Park the second vehicle at the Copper Mountain Colorado Trail parking on the east side of the road (the overflow lot). That means it's possible to link Atlantic–Pacific–Father Dyer–Crystal–Peak 10–Peak 9–Peak 8–Peak 7–Peak 6 in a single day hike. And if you're an absolute maniac with the fitness of a mountain goat, it's possible to link all the way down to Peak 1 in Frisco. It's for super-strong hikers only, as fizzling out along the way would be a logistics nightmare.

In contrast, Mayflower Gulch proper is a fine place to simply wander around. There are quite a few mining ruins to explore, including old tram towers and exposed shaft openings. It's a nice winter snowshoe, too. Reduce avalanche danger by staying away from the base of the peaks.

For all the optional routes listed here, the simple out-and-back up Atlantic Peak is an excellent day hike that is worth the visit. For advanced hikers, the multitude of options offers an exciting array of adventure. (**Note:** Both Atlantic Peak and Drift Peak are local names—neither summit has an official USGS name.)

One final observation: It's interesting that the highest peak in this group, Fletcher Mountain, is visually bland in contrast to the others. From Mayflower Gulch, it doesn't even look like a summit, just a bump on the ridge between Drift and Atlantic. It's all of 1 foot higher than the much more photogenic Pacific Peak.

3 Bald Mountain A–Boreas Mountain

Bald and Boreas Mountains are a pair of easily accessed 13ers that nonetheless don't see a lot of human traffic. Bald is the more popular of the duo thanks to its northern views into the city of Breckenridge and to the Gore Range summits beyond.

Primary route: Bald Mountain, 13,684 feet; Boreas Mountain, 13,082 feet
Optional summits: Red Peak A, 13,215 feet; Hoosier Ridge, 13,352 feet; Red Mountain, 13,229 feet
Difficulty rating: Medium; an on-trail walk to straightforward off-trail summit hikes

Class rating: Class 2
Round-trip distance: 8.5 miles (both peaks) out and back
Elevation gain: 3,730 feet
Round-trip time: 4–6 hours; half day

Finding the trailhead: From Breckenridge: Take the signed Boreas Pass Road at the south end of town southeast 9 miles as it climbs to the summit of Boreas Pass. This is a maintained dirt road suitable for passenger cars, though it can be muddy/snowy in spring. The road is closed in the winter months after 3.5 miles. Parking is at the top of the pass where there is a large lot, two huts, and relics from mining ruins and the old train line.

From US 285: From the small town of Jefferson, follow US 285 South 7.2 miles to the right turn to Boreas Pass/town of Como. It's 11 miles from here to the parking area at the top of the pass at 11,480 feet. The road is passable to passenger cars during the warmer months.

Trailhead GPS: N39 24.616' / W105 58.101'

The Hike

Boreas Mountain is a great summit if you're short on time or looking for a tame half-day outing. Bald Mountain is just a smidge more challenging, and getting both in a single outing is very doable. This route begins at the top of Boreas Pass where two huts, Section House and Ken's Cabin, serve as base camps for winter adventures.

A smattering of pine forest fizzles out in the upper basin, giving way to a network of small creeks that keep the local wildflower population in bloom. At the top of the pass, it's time to go off-trail. Boreas has grassy, rock-infused slopes that get steep for about a half mile, while Bald is built on a solid boulder field crossed by social trails. These are just about the best summit views there are of the town of Breckenridge and the Tenmile Range to the west. Mysterious peaks in the far-off Gore Range ring the horizon to the north and the west.

Bald Mountain with Black Powder Pass to the right

Miles and Directions

0.0 The trail up to Black Powder Pass is signed on the northeast side of the road, north of the huts. The Black Powder Pass Trail is a popular day hike, but surprisingly few people continue on to the summits. Follow the Boreas Ditch No 2 as the trail enters a small patch of woods. Past this the trail spiders on the hillside, but as long as you are trending toward Black Powder Pass, you will be fine. Wildflowers here can be exceptionally vivid in late spring and early summer.

1.1 At Black Powder Pass, you have options. If you go right (south), it is 1.2 miles to the summit of Boreas Mountain. If you go left (north), it is 1.9 miles to the top of Bald Mountain. This route gets both peaks in one shot starting with Bald Mountain. Head left off-trail up the stable boulder field on the southern flank of Bald Mountain.

2.5 After a hearty push up the rocky slopes, you'll arrive on Bald's false summit at 13,679 feet—a mere 5 feet lower than the true summit. Unlike other false summits, this one won't take the wind out of your sails. It's a pleasant walk over to the true summit 0.5 mile north.

3.0 Bald Mountain summit. There is no better view of Breckenridge and its namesake ski area. The Tenmile Range towers above the town. Mount Guyot, at 13,370 feet, rises like a sliver above French Pass to the east. When you are ready, return to Black Powder Pass, 1,650 vertical feet below.

5.0 Back at Black Powder Pass, make sure you have the legs and the weather to continue on to Boreas Mountain. If you're ready, continue south on the north slopes of Boreas Mountain.

5.5 Boreas's false summit at 12,815 feet. Continue on to Boreas's true summit.

6.2 The 13,082-foot summit of Boreas Mountain has open views to the south. Mount Silverheels's enormous dome dominates this southern perspective. Return the way you came, one more time to Black Powder Pass.

7.4 Back at Black Powder Pass for the final time. Follow the trail roughly a mile back to the parking area. If you're unsure if you're on the correct trail, they all merge back at the Boreas Ditch.

8.5 Arrive back at the parking lot.

Bald Mountain A–Boreas Mountain

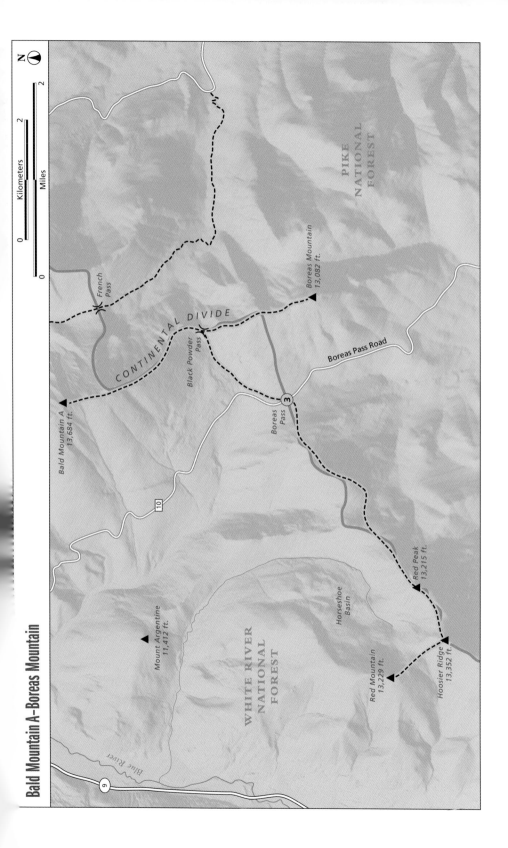

N

Kilometers
0   2

Miles
0   2

French
Pass

Bald Mountain A
13,684 ft.

CONTINENTAL DIVIDE

Black Powder
Pass

Boreas Mountain
13,082 ft.

Boreas Pass Road

Boreas Pass

PIKE
NATIONAL
FOREST

10

Red Peak
13,215 ft.

Mount Argentine
11,412 ft.

Horseshoe
Basin

WHITE RIVER
NATIONAL
FOREST

Red Mountain
13,229 ft.

Hoosier Ridge
13,352 ft.

Blue River

9

Optional Routes

It's 4.6 miles round-trip if you opt to hike only Boreas Mountain. Six miles is the distance for an out-and-back hike of only Bald Mountain. This duo is an isolated pair. On the map, it looks like nearby 13er Mount Guyot (13,370 feet) might link up, but there are much better routes from the north, south, and east.

It's worth noting that going southwest off Boreas Pass is an alternate way to get three other 13ers: Red Peak A (13,215 feet), Hoosier Ridge (a ranked 13er at 13,352 feet), and Red Mountain C (13,229 feet). The standard route is off Hoosier Pass. This Class 2 ridgewalk is a scrappy affair. After a short prelude trail to a minor summit at 12,029 feet, the rest of the adventure involves a surprisingly punishing pattern of steep ups-and-downs along the ridge. The drop down to the base of Red Peak and subsequent push up its west slopes are quite a bit of work. The mileage is roughly 8.2 miles out and back, with 4,300 feet of total elevation gain.

Another option is to do a point-to-point hike from Boreas Pass to Hoosier Pass along Hoosier Ridge. As a straight shot, this tour (Class 2) is about 7.6 miles but involves a lot of driving to make the car shuttles work out.

Boreas Mountain as seen from the upper slopes of Bald Mountain

The summit of Bald Mountain has excellent views of the Breckenridge ski area, as well as the full span of the Tenmile Range peaks.

Final Thoughts

This Bald Mountain is the tallest of the eighteen-plus mountains that are officially or informally known as "Bald Mountain." Many Breck locals call it "Baldy" or "Old Baldy," but the USGS name is Bald Mountain.

Boreas was the Greek god of the north wind, a harbinger of winter. According to mythology, he got into the same sort of hijinx as other minor gods and was especially revered in Athens.

Section House (the larger of the two cabins) was built in 1882 to house men working on the railroad. It fell into disrepair until the mid-1990s when it was restored. Ken's Cabin was likewise restored in the 1990s, and both buildings are part of the 10th Mountain Division Hut system. Ken's Cabin is even older than Section House, having been constructed in the 1860s when Boreas Pass was a wagon road, thus its original name, "Wagon Cabin." The cabin was renamed in the 1990s after Breckenridge local Ken Graff, who died in an avalanche in 1995.

4 Parry Peak–Mount Bancroft

This excellent Class 2 route follows Mount Bancroft's south slopes to its summit, then continues on to Parry Peak—the highest point in this pocket of 13ers. Unlike many other connecting ridges in Colorado, the traverse between these 13ers is along pleasant, rolling tundra with minimal exposure. This is Colorado hill walking at its very best.

Primary route: Parry Peak, 13,391 feet; Mount Bancroft, 13,250 feet

Optional summits: James Peak, 13,294 feet; Mount Eva, 13,130 feet

Difficulty rating: Medium; a great Class 2 traverse along solid, low-exposure ridges. A little light scrambling is required to summit Mount Bancroft, but it stays Class 2.

Class rating: Class 2

Round-trip distance: 5.3 miles out and back

Elevation gain: 2,760 feet

Round-trip time: 4–6 hours; half/full day

Finding the trailhead: The adventure begins at Loch Lomond. Note that the 4x4 road to the parking area has degraded in the past few years. As of 2020 I'd recommend a high-clearance SUV. Most of the trouble on the road comes in the form of deeply rutted rollers—in the worst possible places. A carefully driven SUC could still make the trailhead—if it has good ground clearance—but not without a few scrapes on the bottom. The road is also very rocky in places, so tough tires are a plus. There's a chance this road might be improved by the time you're reading this book, but roads like this are often low priority.

From I-70 west of Denver, take exit 238 to Fall River Road. Reset your odometer at the exit ramp. Go northwest on the paved Fall River Road 8 miles, then take a left onto Alice Road in the barely there town of Alice. This road quickly changes from pavement to dirt. Follow it up a steep hill to mile 8.9 and take a right at the signed turn for Steuart Road. (**Note:** The sign in town says "Stewart Road," while most maps use the "Steuart" spelling. It's the same road.)

You have 2.3 miles to go along this bumpy, washed-out, beat-down road. In 2020 there were big ruts carved into the few semi-steep hills along the way. There's nothing technical in terms of huge rocks, but high clearance is necessary to not bottom out on the ruts. The rest of the road alternates between smooth dirt and very rocky patches of baseball-sized stones. Stay on the main road to the trailhead, which has a large parking lot at the scenic Loch Lomond.

Trailhead GPS: N39 49.980' / W105 40.632'

The Hike

If you only have time for a half day out, an out-and-back hike on Bancroft is the way to go (about 4 miles round-trip). Adding on Parry is a tempting option thanks to it being a quick second summit for the day.

Loch Lomond is a fun jumping-off point. Most folks are up there to relax, fish, paddleboard, or just enjoy a picnic. Even on busy weekends, traffic to the upper lakes

Parry Peak–Mount Bancroft

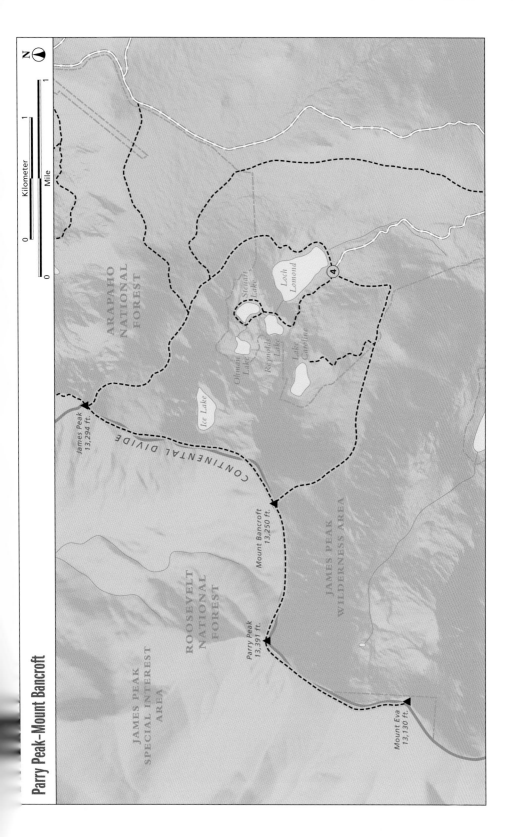

Views of Bancroft's east ridge from the lower slope along the primary hiking route

James Peak (center) and Mount Bancroft (right) from the summit of Parry Peak

and beyond is sparse. Bancroft's rolling slopes are rocky enough for boulder-hopping in places, though there are plenty of stretches of flower-festooned grass. The hike up is pleasant but persistent. Continuing on to Parry Peak offers up dazzling views into the Fall River Basin, which is largely blocked en route to Mount Bancroft. It's an easy traverse and makes for an awesome pairing. Detouring to Lake Caroline on the return is a fine option for soaking tired feet or letting your dogs cool off.

Miles and Directions

0.0   Loch Lomond is a popular fishing destination, so the parking lot may have quite a few cars. Thankfully, the parking area is huge, so you'll find a place to leave your car, no problem. Begin the hike by following the 4x4 road southwest up a hill and away from the lake. It's a nice start to the day. Don't worry, you won't be on the road all that long.

0.6   The upper basin above Loch Lomond reveals itself after your initial uphill hike. The direct line to the southeast ridge heads to a small saddle between Bancroft's ridge and Point 11,942. An optional trail goes north to Lake Caroline, which is an excellent detour on the way back. For now, work up to the ridge.

1.2   Once you have the ridge, the way up to Bancroft's summit will be obvious—aim for the highest point on the hill! There are very small boulder fields along the way, but they present no significant difficulties.

1.9   Bancroft has a welcoming summit. Better still, it has a gracious, nontechnical walk over to the summit of Parry Peak, 0.8 mile away. Go west off the summit to the sandy saddle between the two peaks. The final push up to Parry takes a little muscle, but it's on good footing. Deep views to the Fall River Reservoir open to the south the farther you go.

2.7   Parry's summit. Berthoud Pass twists its way down toward Winter Park to the west, while views north extend into the Indian Peaks. Return the way you came, which includes a re-summit of Mount Bancroft. It's only about 250 vertical feet from the saddle back to the top. From there, roll down the ridge. You can drop off the ridge to the slopes to the north to save a little time and track more directly down to Lake Caroline.

5.3   Arrive back at Loch Lomond. Even though this is a low-mileage day, give it 4 to 6 hours for both summits.

Optional Routes

Mount Eva sits 0.8 mile southwest of Parry Peak along a Class 2+ ridge. If you're doing this as an out-and-back hike, you'll have 3,500 feet of rolling elevation and about 7 miles total. An interesting variation is to do a point-to-point from Bancroft to Berthoud Pass, over Mount Flora (see chapter 21). This route is roughly 10 miles but has a whopping 4,700 feet of elevation gain and requires a lot of driving to set up your shuttle, but strong hikers can net four 13ers (Bancroft, Parry, Eva, and Mount Flora), all along gorgeous Class 2 ridge traverses.

Less of a grind is pairing up Mount Bancroft and James Peak to the north. This eschews Parry Peak but has the benefit of being a loop vs. an out-and-back. Summit Bancroft, then take the Class 2+ ridge north to James Peak's summit. To return, follow James Peak's southeast slopes along the James Peak Trail down to the broad flats below the peak. There is a fairly well-worn social trail from this tundra area to Loch Lomond. If you cross the 4x4 road, you've gone too far east—do *not* take the 4x4 road down, as it will put you all the way back in the town of Alice.

Final Thoughts

Parry Peak is named for botanist Christopher Parry, a bona fide Renaissance man who came to Colorado in the mid-1800s. He was a surveyor/surgeon/botanist/mountaineer who helped identify several new plant species in Colorado, including the Engelmann spruce and Torrey pine. If those names sound familiar, it's because several prominent Colorado peaks are named for Parry's flora-loving peers John Torrey, Asa Gray, and George Engelmann. That includes the 14ers Grays and Torreys Peaks, along with Engelmann Peak (an optional summit in chapter 5).

Bancroft, in particular, is a great 13er for those new to off-trail hiking. The ridge is very easy to follow thanks to the entire hike being more or less above tree line. That same lack of tree cover is why you should still get an early start on this outing, even with the low mileage.

Hopefully, the road to Loch Lomond will get patched up a bit in the future. Rangers I spoke to said it is due for work, but they couldn't say when. Finally, Loch Lomond is a nice alternative to James Peak for hikers who don't want to pay the private parking fee at the St. Marys Glacier trailhead.

5 Bard Peak

There's no quick way up Bard Peak, so why not fill a visit to this impressive mountain with adventure? Mining ruins, a gravesite, a quirky sub-summit, and wide-open tundra views await on this incredible Front Range adventure.

Primary route: Bard Peak, 13,641 feet
Optional summits: Mount Parnassus, 13,574 feet; Robeson Peak, 13,140 feet; Engelmann Peak, 13,362 feet
Difficulty rating: Hard; a long Class 2 day with brief off-trail forest navigation and a lot of adventure along the way

Class rating: Class 2+
Round-trip distance: 11.4 miles out and back (or 14.3 miles point-to-point to Herman Gulch)
Elevation gain: 5,010 feet
Round-trip time: 7–9 hours; full day

Finding the trailhead: From I-70 west of Denver, take exit 226 to Silver Plume. From the westbound exit, go right onto Woodward Street (dirt). Going left off the eastbound exit brings you to this same point. Go 300 feet on Woodward, then right onto Main Street (this is also dirt). In less than a quarter mile, turn left onto Silver Street. The trailhead is at the end of this road, about 400 feet beyond. Oddly, the last 150 feet is steep enough that having a 4x4 isn't a bad idea. The parking area only has space for about 4 vehicles. If you're driving a passenger car (or the lot is full), do not park on Silver Street. Instead, park on Main Street and walk up to the trailhead.

Trailhead GPS: N39 41.880' / W105 43.530'

The Hike

The opening section of this hike is along the 7:30 Mine Trail, a well-maintained Class 1 path that bypasses mine ruins and ends at the Clifford Griffin monument and burial site. From there, hop across a creek and wind through 0.5 mile of relatively easy off-trail trees to the open slopes of Silver Plume Mountain and on to Bard Peak.

Once you are into the open tundra, the high alpine plateau becomes your own private playground. Silver Plume Mountain is an out-of-place boulder outcrop that nonetheless is a worthy little summit. Bard Peak looks every bit the massive 13er it is from this vantage point, but fear not. The ridge that leads to its summit is bona fide Class 2. Beyond the summit are options to grab a couple more 13ers. In late summer, deep fields of crimson grass paint the ground a fantastic shade of maroon, especially on the traverse between Bard Peak and Robeson Peak.

Navigating back to the 7:30 Mine Trail means following Browns Creek back to the river crossing and one last leap across the swift creek at a long-abandoned mining boiler.

Miles and Directions

0.0 The first 1.8 miles of your hike is along the 7:30 Mine Trail, an excellent Class 1 path that tours the old mines of the area. The ruins are plentiful and the views west of I-70 are impressive. This portion of the trail goes by fairly quickly.

1.8 At the end of the formal trail at 10,400 feet is a gated mine on the right and the Griffin monument on the left. The concrete pillar is a memorial marker for Clifford Griffin, a nineteenth-century mine manager who would regale the town with his violin playing from that very spot. Continue west when the official trail ends toward Browns Creek on social trails.

1.9 It's time to cross Browns Creek. The best spot is near a large, rusted-out boiler. Even though it can be cleared with a strong leap, be extra careful if the creek is running high—especially if you have dogs with you. In mid- to late summer, the creek calms down quite a bit. Once you've crossed the creek, turn north (off-trail) and go 0.5 mile through the woods on the west side of Browns Creek. The bushwhacking here is relatively easy as you pass through spaced-out pines. There are some surprises waiting in the woods, including a few old mining cabins, more relics, and perhaps an errant ski or two!

2.4 The tundra begins to open up and the semi-challenging navigation is over.

Bard Peak's impressive profile from Silver Plume Mountain

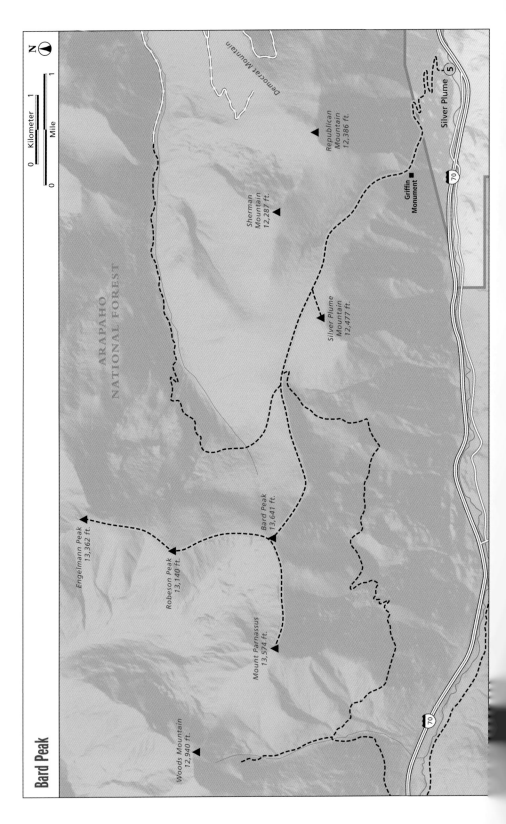

Bard Peak

2.5 Enjoy the incredible views as the high plateau reveals the hulking slopes of Bard Peak to the northwest. Make a note where you emerge from the trees into the low willows for the return (though simply staying close to Browns Creek works as well). Carry up the slopes on good terrain to the first summit of the day, 12,477-foot Silver Plume Mountain. Travel here is easy and the navigation is straightforward.

4.0 Reach Silver Plume Mountain's summit boulders. The highest one is about 10 feet tall and requires a mantle-style climbing move to top out. It's fun; just make sure you can get back down! When you are ready, set your sights on Bard Peak's summit along the east/southeast ridge. It's 1.7 miles from here and a hearty 1,650 vertical feet—so, in a way, your hike is just beginning. There is no trick to the navigation here. The most obvious line follows the flats over to a broad saddle, then gains Bard's southeast ridge. The terrain stays Class 2, with a little light scrambling just before the summit.

5.7 After the big push, enjoy the airy summit of Bard Peak. These may be some of the best 360-degree views in the entire Front Range. When you are ready, return the way you came. The most challenging part of the return hike will be pinpointing the way back down to the 7:30 Mine Trail. A GPS helps to retrace your tracks, but it's not necessary. Just keep Browns Creek nearby as you wind through the forest. The river crossing at the boiler will be fairly obvious. If you start to descend too far, you'll see Griffin's monument and the footing will become sandy and difficult. Once you have the 7:30 Mine Trail, it's an easy on-trail walk to wrap up the day.

11.4 Arrive back at the trailhead.

Optional Routes

There are a lot of options here!

Herman Gulch Point-to-Point

One of the better options is making the hike a point-to-point by parking vehicle #2 at Herman Gulch. Because both trailheads are easy to access by car, the driving between these two won't take long (compared to other point-to-point shuttles). The route here goes west off Bard Peak along the connecting ridge to Mount Parnassus (Class 2). Descend west of Parnassus into Watrous Gulch (see chapter 26, Mount Parnassus) and take the Watrous Gulch Trail to the Herman Gulch parking area. This route is about 14 miles and goes fairly quickly after topping out on Parnassus. Elevation gain is roughly 6,000 feet for the duo, so make sure you have the fitness chops before committing to this route.

Bard–Robeson–Engelmann

Strong hikers (and trail runners) may want to link up two more 13ers north of Bard Peak from the summit of Bard: Robeson and Engelmann. There is no quick way up either of these peaks, so traversing from Bard is one of the best ways to get to them. The tundra walk from Bard to Robeson then Engelmann is pure alpine bliss. I highly suggest waiting until early autumn, for two reasons: the likelihood of storm-free weather and the opportunity to walk among the incredible crimson grass and wildflower patches along the way. It's 1.8 miles one-way and 750 vertical feet from Bard

Silver Plume Mountain's summit block with Bard Peak in the background

to Engelmann, but about 1,600 vertical feet total when tacking on the elevation on the return (even skirting below Robeson and Bard's summits). So that's about 15 total miles and about 6,600 feet of vertical gain—a *huge* Class 2 outing! But for the super-fit, it's an epic day to remember. Despite the big numbers, the footing is excellent the entire way and should go quickly for strong hikers.

7:30 Mine Trail Hike

On the other end of the hiking spectrum, simply hiking out and back to the end of the 7:30 Mine Trail is a great year-round adventure and can make for a good family hike. The 8-mile out-and-back hike to Silver Plume Mountain (even though it's not a 13er) is a solid adventure in itself. There is also a smattering of 12ers near Silver Plume Mountain (Brown Mountain, Sherman Mountain, and Republican Mountain) that offer more peak-bagging options along rolling alpine tundra.

Final Thoughts

It's worth visiting the George Rowe Museum in Silver Plume to learn more about the incredible history in the area, including the sad tale of Clifford Griffin, the name-sake of the monument on the 7:30 Mine Trail. Griffin's brother owned the 7:30 Mine and recruited Clifford to manage it after the untimely death of Clifford's betrothed. Clifford gained a reputation for being an unusually caring leader of men and was beloved in Silver Plume for his kindness and hard work. Many nights, Clifford would walk to the mine (the site of the monument) and play his violin into the wee hours for everyone in town to enjoy.

One night, the serenade was broken with the shrill crack of a gunshot. Clifford Griffin, age 40, had shot himself after digging a grave at the site of the monument with a note to be buried in the place he loved most on earth. His heartbroken brother added the monument in 1887, the same monument you'll pass on the way to Bard Peak.

6 Bent Peak–Carson Peak–UN 13,580

There may not be a more spectacular area in Colorado for touring 13ers. The primary route here is a good one for mountain dogs. The terrain never exceeds Class 2, but there are some incredible surprises in store as the route traverses along the Continental Divide.

Primary route: Bent Peak, 13,393 feet; Carson Peak, 13,657 feet; UN 13,580
Optional summits: Tundra Top, 13,450 feet; Cataract Peak, 13,524 feet; Coney Benchmark, 13,334 feet; UN 13,581
Difficulty rating: Easy–medium; easy-to-navigate, off-trail ridgewalks combined with on-trail sections along the Colorado Trail. Bent Peak or Coney Benchmark as individual hikes are the rare routes in this guide that would warrant an "easy" rating.
Class rating: Class 2
Round-trip distance: 9.3-mile loop
Elevation gain: 3,030 feet
Round-trip time: 4–6 hours; half day

Finding the trailhead: High-clearance 4x4 required. Hoo boy, the access road to start this hike, Wager Gulch Road, is the roughest style of road that stock SUVs can handle. Be sure you have great tires on your vehicle and your brakes are solid. Don't try to push a sport-utility car like a Toyota Rav4 on this one; they don't have the clearance. If you don't have a 4x4, there are other options to get up the road. The peaks here are worth the effort, plus it gives you an excuse to rent an off-road vehicle. More on that in a moment.

From Lake City: (**Note:** from Lake City, it's roughly an hour's drive to the start of the hike even though it's only 15.8 miles.) From the intersection of CO 149 and Vine Street at the south end of Lake City, continue south on CO 149 toward Lake San Cristobal. In 1.8 miles, take a right onto the well-signed CO 30. Stay on CO 30 for 9.1 miles to the left-hand turn to Wager Gulch Road/Hinsdale County 36.

In a strange plot twist, the paved sections of CO 30 are in worse shape than the dirt portions (as of 2020). Stay on CO 30 as it skirts the western shore of Lake San Cristobal, mercifully transforming to a maintained dirt road at the lake's southern terminus. Most of the land along the road is private, though the USFS Williams Creek Campground is a great place to overnight if you've had a long drive to Lake City. The turnoff for Wager Gulch Road is about 2 miles past Williams Creek Campground. There will be signs for the ghost town of Carson, which is along the same road.

The left-hand turn to Wager Gulch Road is well signed, most notably by the blue Hinsdale County 36 and Wager Gulch Road/Carson Township signs. If you don't have a high-clearance 4x4, you can park here and hike up the 5 miles to the top of the road. Wager Gulch Road to the top of Carson Pass is a 5-mile road with an identity crisis. The start of the road is rutted, bumpy, and steep in sections. There are never any rock crawling obstacles, but the sustained road damage makes for slow going. At 0.7 mile you'll encounter the crux of the road. This is a very good time to shift into 4-low if your truck has it. This brief climb (about 200 feet long) is the steepest part of the road and also the most deeply rutted. For added fun, it's quite narrow too, with an exposed drop-off on the right side. Be bold pushing up this hill! After this the road mellows out considerably, to the point where passenger cars could drive up if they could be teleported past the rough stuff.

At 1.7 miles in, the road splits. Ignore the smooth, inviting road to the left and stay right. At 2 miles you reach the forest boundary. Beyond here, camping is legal. The first good campsites start about 2.3 miles up. Up to the restored ghost town of Carson at mile 4, the 4x4 road is in good shape. Carson is about 200 feet off the road to the left and can be easy to miss in the dark. It's worth a visit on your way back. Beyond Carson the road gets nasty again for the final mile to the top of Carson Pass. It's not as bad as the lower sections, but it's rutted from water erosion with plenty of loose rocks to dodge. The top of Carson Pass (12,360 feet) is flat and has ample parking for dozens of vehicles. Bent Peak appears to be a stone's throw away from here. Park here.

Trailhead GPS: N37 51.366' / W107 22.068'

Alternate Options for Getting to Carson Pass: If you don't have a high-clearance 4x4 or simply don't want to put the damage on your own vehicle, Lake City has several 4x4 rental companies. This is a fun alternative if you want to try something different. Rent a Jeep, a side-by-side, or a basic ATV, and make sure that you can start your hike no later than 6:30 a.m.

The Hike

Bent Peak is a friendly walk-up 13er that introduces a graceful ridge over to Carson Peak. A hidden legion of craggy towers guards the western slopes of Carson Peak, forcing a temporary retreat down to the Colorado Trail en route to an absolute gem of a summit in UN 13,580. Follow grassy slopes up to the broad shoulder of 13,580, where a perfect ribbon of trail etherealizes from the blank hillside. This magical path exposes a second, larger regiment of battered, craggy towers in the distance. Follow it to one of Colorado's premier viewpoints, where dozens of high peaks can be seen, none more commanding than Rio Grande Pyramid.

For fit hikers, tacking on two additional peaks, Tundra Top and Cataract Peak, adds only 2.8 more miles. That makes five 13ers in a pleasant, 12-mile circuit. From the same starting point, Coney Benchmark is an easy walk-up to the east. Determined peakbaggers also have a shot at UN 13,581, a peak best done as a single, dedicated outing.

Miles and Directions

0.0 Start your adventure by heading west up an "experts-only" 4x4 road toward Bent Peak. This is a nice, casual way to start your adventure. Leave the road roughly a half mile up and continue on easy slopes to the welcoming summit of Bent Peak. There are no trails beyond the 4x4 road, but the way up is obvious.

1.0 The first summit of the day was an easy one! From here the rolling, broad ridge to Carson is obvious as it traverses gentle terrain to the southwest. Rio Grande Pyramid surfaces on the southern horizon like a mystical beacon. Far west, the twin summits of Arrow and Vestal Peaks dominate the skyline.

1.8 Cruise over point 13,406 en route to Carson's summit. Near the top of Carson, there will be light scrambling.

The graceful slopes leading to Carson Peak, as seen from Bent Peak

2.3 Summit Carson Peak. If these views don't move you, you may want to check if you still have a pulse. Tundra Top is a neat-looking plateau directly west, but the bad news is that the ridge connecting it to Carson is blocked by crumbling towers. If you want to tag Tundra Top (see the Optional Routes section), it is best to skirt down to the Colorado Trail rather than press your luck on the loose ridge terrain.

Descend west off Carson where you will see a collection of what I'll call "distinct towers." Your goal here is to connect to the Colorado Trail roughly 1,000 vertical feet below. The easiest way to do this is to stay on the steep-but-stable, grassy slopes left of the "tower garden," though if you want to traverse through the towers, it's entirely possible—just know that the footing is loose and steep.

3.1 Connect with the Colorado Trail for a hot minute. UN 13,580 looks far away from here but is only about 1.3 miles from where its access slopes meet the Colorado Trail. Hop off the Colorado Trail to the left (south) and begin hoofing up the grassy slopes toward the high, broad shoulder of UN 13,580.

3.7 As the slopes ease into the broad shoulder around 13,330 feet, a well-worn Class 1 trail magically appears on the hillside. It's such an odd occurrence, it almost feels like a delusion. Follow this trail as it eases up to the summit dome, where a little light scrambling gets you on top of one of Colorado's most underappreciated summits.

4.5 The summit of UN 13,580. Just when it doesn't seem possible, the views here get even better than from Carson Peak! Another large "tower garden" juts out to the east from the

Bent Peak-Carson Peak-UN 13,580

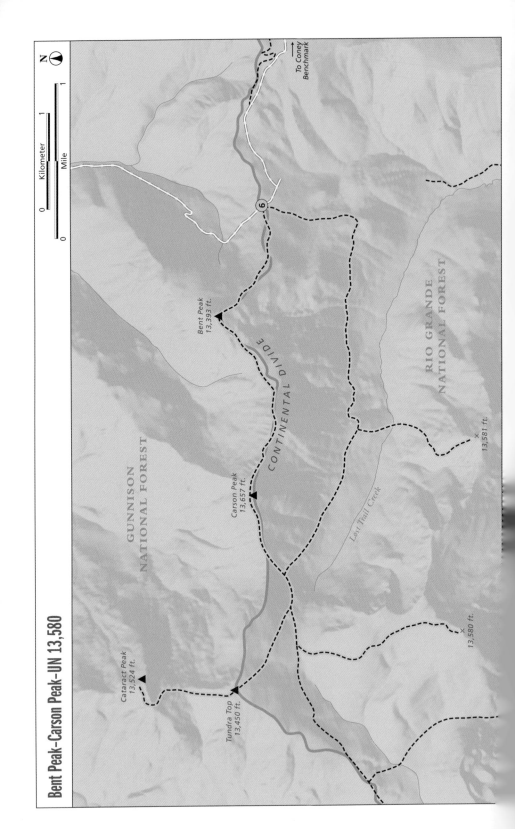

saddle between the ridgeline and UN 13,581—and just like the towers between Carson and Tundra Top, it makes for a frustrating barrier to another summit. Descend back to the Colorado Trail when you've had your fill of summit views.

6.0 Regain the Colorado Trail and head east back toward Carson Pass. Enjoy the views of the peaks you were on a few hours earlier. Moose are fairly common in the valley here. The Colorado Trail will take you all the way back to Carson Pass, so relax and enjoy the rest of the hike on-trail. The last portion of the Colorado Trail shares an old 4x4 mining road up to the parking lot.

9.3 Close the loop and finish the hike. Don't forget to visit the ghost town of Carson on the way back, and remember, the gnarly crux section of the road awaits (though it's easier to drive down than up).

Optional Routes

Tundra Top and Cataract Peak Add-on: 2.8 miles out and back

If you want to get these two summits, follow the primary route to mile 3.1 where you reconnect to the Colorado Trail. Instead of going left (south) toward UN 13,580, go right (north) up the low-angle natural ramp to the top of Tundra Top. The summit is marked by a cairn on an otherwise flat plateau.

Getting over to Cataract Peak from here is a little trickier than it looks. Stay to the right where the ridge from Carson continues north. The downclimb to the saddle between Tundra Top and Cataract is steep and the first part is riddled with loose dinner-plate-size rocks that can hold snow and ice. Closer to the exposed drop-off to the right is the best line. Be warned that if the wind is howling, this is a much more dangerous section than it initially appears. Once down to the saddle, the walk over to Cataract's summit is straightforward, taking you slightly left of the summit before topping out. Return the way you came and carry on to UN 13,580 or simply call it a day and take the Colorado Trail home.

Coney Benchmark: 2.6 miles out and back

This is a quick and easy 13er that goes east from the trailhead. Simply follow the mellow ridges along the Colorado Trail/Continental Divide Trail (they share a path here) 1.3 miles to the 13,334-foot high point.

UN 13,581: 4.8 miles out and back

For peakbaggers only. UN 13,581 is a ranked 13er, coming in at #196—so it's also a top-200 summit. It's the same elevation as another 13er, Mount Emma. The "standard" way up is to start by going south from Carson Pass along the Colorado Trail, then simply get off-trail at the point of least resistance and claw and scramble up Class 2 and 3 terrain to the top. It's a different kind of fun than the neighboring peaks, but if you like route-finding and chugging up steep slopes and gullies, the views at the top are just as good as from other local peaks.

A mysterious trail emerges near the summit of UN 13,580

Final Thoughts

UN 13,580 isn't just one of my favorite 13ers, it's one of my favorite peaks in the entire Rocky Mountains. It's hard to explain the grandeur of this area. The summits here are centralized altars surrounded by some of the most remote and majestic peaks in Colorado. The way Rio Grande Pyramid stands out in the distance seems to tap into the primal part of our brain that delights in mysterious contours and geometric cleanliness.

The paved road along Lake San Cristobal looks like it took heavy mortar damage—it was a mess in early 2020. Hopefully, it will be repaved sooner rather than later. The Alpine Loop along CO 30 is the access point to a few 14ers (Handies, Red Cloud, Sunshine) if you want to add them to your adventure.

7 Clinton Peak-McNamee Peak-Traver Peak

The ridgewalk connecting these three 13ers is an incredible experience. You can see the amazing shape of glacially carved valleys curling at the base of high peaks—as well as legions of tiny little hikers crowded on the summits of three nearby 14ers: Mount Lincoln, Mount Cameron, and Mount Democrat.

Primary route: Clinton Peak, 13,857 feet; McNamee Peak, 13,780 feet; Traver Peak, 13,852 feet
Difficulty rating: Medium; on- and off-trail hiking with a crux push up Clinton's rocky slopes, leading to an excellent 3-peak ridge traverse

Class rating: Class 2+
Round-trip distance: 10.6-mile lollipop loop
Elevation gain: 3,253 feet
Round-trip time: 6–8 hours; full day

Finding the trailhead: From Breckenridge, start mileage at the south end of town at CO 9 South and Boreas Pass Road. Continue on CO 9 South as it twists and climbs up the paved Hoosier Pass. After cresting the top of the pass at 9.6 miles, drive another mile downhill and take a sharp right onto CR 4 (dirt) at mile 10.6. Seemingly out of nowhere is a modern community on these roads.

Stay on CR 4 for 0.9 mile, then go straight onto the signed Montgomery Reservoir Road (listed as Pv32 on some maps). Continue on this road 1 mile as it passes the reservoir and a lower, larger parking area. Cars can make the upper trailhead, but there is a steep dirt hill near the finish. Go past the lower lot, over a bridge, and onto a slightly unnerving shelf road that climbs to the upper lot. A large parking area awaits at the top of the lot to the left. (**Note**: Overnight camping isn't allowed in the main upper parking lot, but there are a few legit car camping sites at the start of the flat portion.) On weekends this lot can fill up with casual hikers exploring the Magnolia Mine Ruins.

If you have an actual dedicated 4x4 vehicle like a modified Jeep or rock crawler, it's possible to drive 3.2 miles to Wheeler Lake along the Wheeler Lake Road. It's no place for stock SUVs. Case in point: I'll push my 4Runner down some pretty gnarly roads, but it has no business trying to attempt this one.

Trailhead GPS: N39 21.450' / W106 04.998'

The Hike

At the start of this hike, you'll pass the old Magnolia Mine complex. It's an impressive hulk of a building, even in decay. A doubletrack trail then leads to Wheeler Lake. It's a nice warm-up and yes, there are some Jeepers who drive the entire trail, but think of it as simply a wide hiking trail. Willows and other dense flora add a pop of color.

At the end of the road, Wheeler Lake transforms into a world of zippy waterfalls, trickling streams, beds of wildflowers, and rock gardens. Steep slopes beckon to the

A look at the full ridgewalk. McNamee Peak (left) and Clinton Peak (right) from the summit of Traver Peak.

high reaches of Clinton Peak, where the rim of the high cirque opens up exquisite views (including the cover shot for this guide). All the hard work to acquire the high ground rewards hikers with one of the best three-peak traverses in the Rocky Mountains.

Miles and Directions

0.0 The start of this hike can be a little confusing. From the main parking area (located near a concrete wall with a spillway building), go back up to the larger, flat area and follow the wide dirt road that heads northwest. The little matrix of roads here eventually combine in a couple hundred feet into a single road. The first 3.2 miles of this adventure is on a 4x4 road, but don't let that dampen your hiking spirits. Think of it more as a doubletrack hiking trail. About a quarter mile in, pass under a bridged walkway that is part of the larger Magnolia Mine ruins. Beyond this, the road continues at a comfortable pace and moderate grade through forests and willows. There may be a few detours around puddles. It's amazing that vehicles can drive up some of the boulders embedded in the road.

2.8 The road gets steeper as it makes the final approach to Wheeler Lake.

3.2 The scenic Wheeler Lake is the end of the road—but not the end of your hike! Find a social trail on the left (west) side of the lake that goes north for a short distance before fizzling out in a marshy field at the skeleton of . . . an old-timey car. Meep, meep! How the heck did that thing get up here?! The car is a good reference point. The goal here is to now hook southwest up a rocky slope to the upper basin. Waterfalls will likely be cascading to your left as you work up the hill (there is something of a use trail to follow, but don't count on it being all the way in).

4.1 The grade eases up at the top of the waterfall streams and there is a brief section of flat terrain. The hidden majesty of this basin begins to reveal itself, first with Traver Peak, then McNamee, and finally the imposing south slopes of Clinton Peak. Thus begins the "lollipop" portion of the hike. While you can make the loop in either direction, the north to south option offers better views, better footing, and gets the nasty stuff out of the way early. The first goal is to reach the base of Clinton's south slopes to the right of a small pond.

4.7 At 13,270 feet the burly, direct route up to Clinton's summit awaits. From here the top is 590 vertical feet and 0.3 mile away. The slopes are rocky and loose in places, but never desperate. Footing is on small-to-medium boulders and can get steep for short bursts. There also may be snow, especially in early spring—crampons and an ice axe should be

Clinton Peak–McNamee Peak–Traver Peak

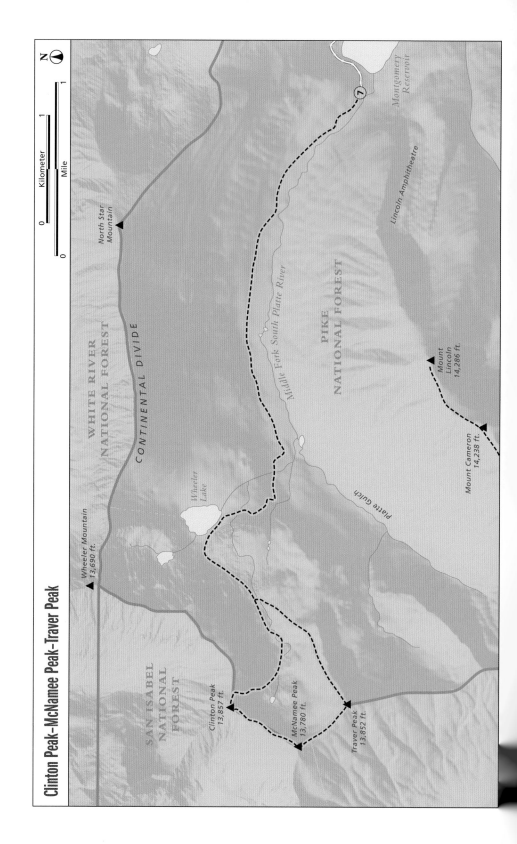

brought along for any climbs earlier than mid-July just for these sections. Keep pushing as you near Clinton's summit. One silver lining is that the highest point you can see (likely slightly to your left) is Clinton's actual summit, not a false one.

5.0 After the big grind, the fun begins at Clinton's summit. A shared ridge gracefully connects all three peaks to the south. Views of Mount Democrat and into the basin west of the ridge between Democrat and Mount Buckskin are impressive. For drivers familiar with Colorado's mountain roads, this basin is accessed at the big switchback on the east side of the top of Fremont Pass and the Climax Mine.

Speaking of the mine, it's hard to miss the decapitated remains of Bartlett Mountain and the large, open-pit known as the Glory Hole to the west. Chances are vehicles will be busy below, extracting ore while you're hiking. When you are ready, continue on to McNamee Peak.

5.5 McNamee's summit is a good place to look back at the route you took to get up Clinton. No wonder those slopes were so much work! Carry on southeast to Traver Peak, where a light bit of scrambling awaits before you top out.

5.9 The final summit of the day, Traver Peak, is an interesting one. Mining minutia such as wires, bottles, and what appears to be the base of an old tram tower in a rusted-out barrel are mixed in the rocks near the top. If you're climbing on a summer weekend, small figures will be visible on the ridgeline connecting the 14ers Democrat and Lincoln (and the sort-of 14er between them, Mount Cameron).

To descend Traver and get back to Wheeler Lake, follow the accommodating northeast ridge/slopes into the basin above the waterfalls and reconnect on the social trail somewhere on the east side of the upper basin. It's easy to visually track the way down. If you err too far to the right, you'll cliff out at the waterfalls, so simply continue north until you find the rocky slope back down to Wheeler Lake.

7.4 Back at Wheeler Lake (and possibly the old, rusted-out car), regain the social trail back to Wheeler Lake Road, and carry on to the end of the hike.

10.6 Arrive back at the upper parking area.

Final Thoughts

The rugged but photogenic mountain directly north of Wheeler Lake is 13,690-foot Wheeler Mountain. It does share a ridge with Clinton Peak, and the south ridge is the "standard" route (as much as there is one). It begins at Wheeler Lake. It is a difficult line on loose rock and requires demanding route-finding, constantly flirting with Class 3+/Class 4 terrain. Thus it isn't covered in this guide.

It's wild to watch Jeeps punch up the Wheeler Lake Road, though by off-roading standards, this is just an "average" 4x4 road.

One last note: When driving home, note that Montgomery Reservoir Road (Pv32) intersects with CR 4 in a switchback. If you plan on heading back toward Breckenridge, stay on the left fork of CR 4. The community up here, Placer Valley, has dozens of modern homes at 10,800 feet—quite a surprise if you aren't expecting to see them.

8 Conejos Peak

This pristine and remote 13er is a secluded pocket of paradise. Vibrant, grassy slopes offer a different look from the normal rugged, rocky peaks of the Rockies.

Primary route: Conejos Peak, 13,172 feet
Difficulty rating: Easy; a pleasant Class 1 walk-up on moderate grades
Class rating: Class 1

Round-trip distance: 6.8 miles out and back
Elevation gain: 1,860 feet
Round-trip time: 4–6 hours; half day

Finding the trailhead: It's a long drive from the Front Range to the trailhead for Conejos Peak–about 6.5 hours. The most efficient way to arrive there is to start at the small town of Antonito, south of Alamosa. (**Note:** From Antonito the trailhead is still close to a 2-hour drive.) From US 285 South, turn west onto CO 17 and follow it 22 miles to FR 250. Turn right (north) on FR 250 (marked with a sign for Platoro) and continue for 16.6 miles on this remote road.

At a sign for Lake Fork Ranch, turn left onto FR 105. This is a good place to reset your odometer. Stay straight on this road as it passes the junction for Lake Fork Ranch on your right. At 4.3 miles, stay left at a fork in the road (Google Maps lists this road as FDR-105). Continue on FDR-105, passing the trailhead for Trail 720 at a switchback in the road. At 7 miles, turn left on the signed Tobacco Lake Trailhead Road (Road 3A). Passenger cars will want to park at the bottom of this access road. SUVs/SUCs can continue another 0.5 mile on a rough road to the trailhead parking area at 11,600 feet.

Trailhead GPS: N37 18.360' / W106 32.220'

The Hike

Conejos Peak stands as the highest ground in an isolated mountain pocket in the San Juan Mountains. It is also one of the most beautiful and pristine Colorado summit hikes, both for the lush wildflowers en route to the top and the incredible, expansive views from the top. Along with Rio Grande Pyramid (see chapter 31), I consider this one of the very best "destination" 13ers in the state. For those in the Denver metro area, this makes for an awesome weekend overnight adventure. The hike itself is fantastic, and the journey to get there explores a section of Colorado that is often overlooked.

Miles and Directions

0.0 From the trailhead, take the signed Tobacco Lake Trail west. The first bit of this hike can be muddy in the spring, due to horse traffic and cattle grazing.

1.0 Pass a cattle gate and stay right on the trail to Tobacco Lake.

1.8 Much like another lake in this guide (Petroleum Lake), Tobacco Lake is much more beautiful than its gritty name suggests. You can pass the lake on the north or south. The grassy

Top: Looking out over the rolling terrain surrounding Conejos Peak. PHOTO CREDIT: PAUL PEREA
Bottom: Tobacco Lake with the modest slope to Conejos Peak in the background. PHOTO CREDIT:
PAUL PEREA

Conejos Peak

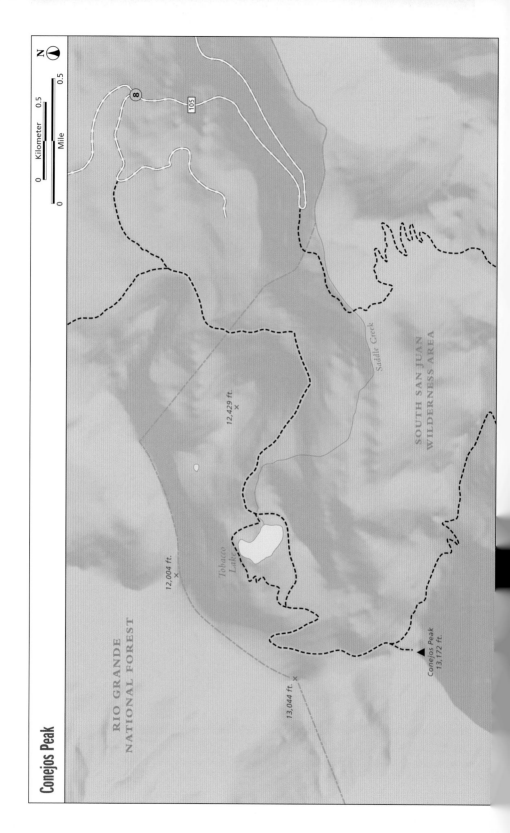

RIO GRANDE
NATIONAL FOREST

SOUTH SAN JUAN
WILDERNESS AREA

Tobacco Lake

Saddle Creek

12,004 ft.
×

13,044 ft.
×

12,429 ft.
×

Conejos Peak
13,172 ft. ▲

105

8

N

Kilometer   0   0.5

0   0.5

0   0.5
Mile

Green slopes en route to Conejos Peak from Tobacco Lake PHOTO CREDIT: PAUL PEREA

slopes and saddle you need to reach will be obvious to the west. Carry on up to the high ridge saddle. The trail occasionally disappears in rock and grass, only to reemerge, but the route is obvious. The cairns along the ridge seem to serve as beacons when there is snow on the ground.

3.1 At the high saddle at 12,890 feet, Conejos Peak is not far away to the south. Enjoy the tundra walk with exquisite views in all directions. One of the charms of stand-alone summits like Conejos is the fact there aren't neighboring peaks blocking the views.

3.4 Relax and enjoy the summit. This is a very different snapshot of Colorado than most other peaks in the Rocky Mountains can provide. Green, rolling hills give way to forests and low scrubland. When you have had your fill, return the way you came.

6.8 Arrive back at the trailhead.

Final Thoughts

Conejos Peak is an excellent dog/family hike. Paired with an overnight campout, it makes for a fine summer weekend adventure. It's also one of the more accessible summits in this region of the southeastern San Juan Mountains. This is a good adventure to pair with New Mexico's state high point, Wheeler Peak (13,159 feet), or simply a visit to Taos. It's also in the neighborhood of Great Sand Dunes National Park.

It's hard to put into words why certain mountains resonate with a different sense of epic adventure, but Conejos fits the bill—even though the hike itself is easy for a 13er. Perhaps it's the long roads in or the novelty of isolated mountains in a state where most high peaks are chained together.

One interesting note: One of the last confirmed grizzly bear sightings happened in this area in 1979. For the record, Colorado does not have a grizzly bear population, but chances are they do wander across the state borders from time to time.

9 Gold Dust Peak

Gold Dust Peak is a semi-isolated summit that stands tall in a deep section of the Holy Cross Wilderness. Unlike many other mountains, the biggest challenge (and a lot of the fun) is the scrambly off-trail approach to get to the base of the peak. After breaking tree line in the basin, a Class 2 ramp is the standard route to the summit. An interesting Class 3 variation can be climbed by going directly up the south face.

Primary route: Gold Dust Peak, 13,365 feet
Optional summit: Pika Peak, 13,126 feet
Difficulty rating: Hard; the challenge in hiking Gold Dust Peak isn't so much the peak itself, but rather the off-trail approach needed to reach the elusive lakes of Negro Basin. The face of Gold Dust Peak offers fun Class 3 options for those inclined to scramble.
Class rating: Class 2+
Round-trip distance: 9.8-mile lollipop loop
Elevation gain: 3,930 feet
Round-trip time: 7–9 hours; full day

Finding the trailhead: West of Vail, take exit 147 (Eagle) off I-70, then head south on Eby Creek Road. Stay on Eby Creek Road through two roundabouts. At the third roundabout, go right (west) onto US 6/Grand Avenue. Quickly turn left onto Capitol Street and go 0.8 mile through town to Brush Creek Road. Take a left onto East Brush Creek Road and follow it 17 miles to its terminus at the Fulford Campground/Fulford Trailhead. Along the way, the road turns to dirt but is passable by passenger cars. The last mile or so past the Yeoman Park Campground is the roughest.

At the campground area, there is a roundabout of 8 first-come, first-served camping spots. The trailhead for the Lake Charles Trail is on the east end of the road, on the north side of the round-about. There is a large parking lot here. Be certain to start on the Lake Charles Trail to the east, not the Fulford Cave Trail to the north (there are signs for both trails).

Trailhead GPS: N39 29.532' / W106 39.486'

The Hike

Gold Dust Peak is a big day! The route is organically skewed toward strong hikers with solid navigation skills. The off-trail portion of the hike leading to the peak is particularly challenging and is not a good place for novice navigators. After a moderate warm-up on the well-established Lake Charles Trail, hop off-trail into a steep basin riddled with rounded cliffs and islands of flat rock outcrops. Breaking tree line opens up a spectacular basin of small ponds and white stone shelves—and the weather-worn face of Gold Dust Peak.

The path of least resistance is along a ramp of rock that pushes up to a boulder-strewn ridge, culminating at the summit, which, disappointingly, seems to be absent of any significant gold dust.

Breaking through tree line on the way to Gold Dust Peak's challenging summit

Miles and Directions

0.0 Enjoy a long on-trail warm-up to start your day along the Lake Charles Trail. Follow this well-maintained trail 3 miles as it gradually climbs through a dense pine forest with the occasional outcrop of polished rock.

3.0 A small pond to the south (your right) is a clue that you've found your way into the start of the Negro Basin drainage. There is a stream that cuts through the basin, which will serve as a reference point as you ascend. This is the beginning of a challenging section of off-trail hiking. Leave the trail to your left and stay on the right (east) side of the creek. There are several improvised social trails here, but no established trail into the basin.

It's important to stay on the right (east) side of the creek as you ascend northeast into the basin. The left side does have an old access trail, but in about a half mile it's heavily blocked by dozens of very large downed trees, slabby cliffs, and lots of loose rock. Staying right offers its own set of challenges. Several optional slabs of rock can be climbed (Class 3) or skirted to the right. It's roughly a mile into the basin, but the going is tough at times. The higher you get, the more rounded the rock slabs become. It's no use staying close to the creek due to cliffy terrain, so stay on the high shoulder until the trees open up into the basin proper.

4.0 Several ponds and streams await in Negro Basin. Tasteful rock slabs add prehistoric flavor to the grassy meadows. Gold Dust Peak looms large to the north, and its chunky neighbor Pika Peak sits to the east. The easiest way up Gold Dust is via a rocky ramp on the Class 2

Gold Dust Peak

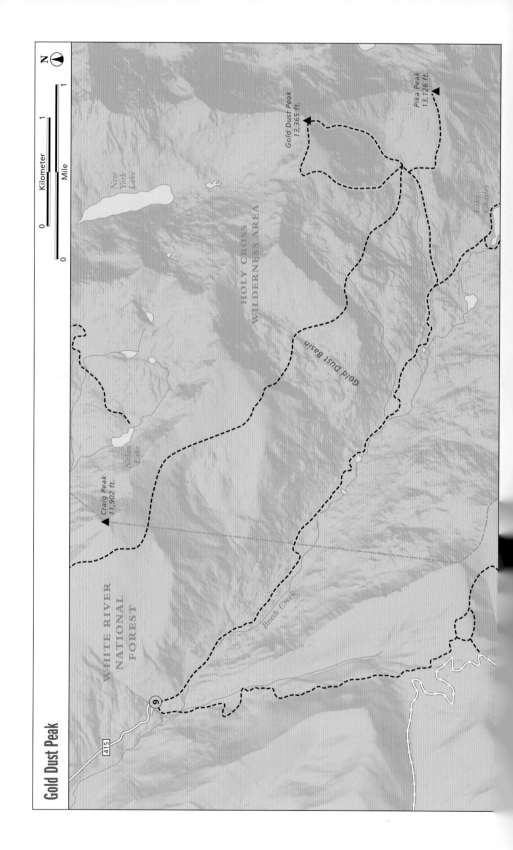

Gold Dust Peak's summit from the optional, airy false summit

southwest slopes. Cross the basin west to the base of the ramp. *(Note:* It's also possible to hit a fun Class 3 scramble directly up the face; see the Optional Routes section.)

4.2 Arrive at the base of the ramp. Begin the push up on alternating rocky and grassy slopes. The footing is mostly good, but watch out for loose boulders here and there. It's a 0.7 grind to the top of Gold Dust. The ramp leads nearly to the top, which is just right of the point where the slope meets the ridge proper.

4.9 The summit of Gold Dust Peak is dazzling. Fools Peak sits to the south while Mount Jackson dominates views to the east. Gold Dust also has a small "eastern" summit that is just a touch lower than the true western summit (see Optional Routes). When you are ready to descend, head back down the way you came via the ramp into Negro Basin. Traverse back to the east side before heading down. As you descend, the west side of the creek repeatedly gets cliffed out so stay on the east side (the same way you came up).

6.0 If you thought your work was done for the day . . . it's not. Here you'll leave the open meadows of the basin and drop back into the forest. Navigation down is tricky. Going too far right cliffs you out time and time again. Stay central and slightly left as you make your way down. Some light scrambling may be required. If you start to feel lost, don't panic—keep moving south downhill. Eventually you'll reconnect with the Lake Charles Trail, as long as you keep a southerly bearing.

6.8 Regain the Lake Charles Trail and take it west back to the trailhead.

9.8 Arrive back at the trailhead.

Optional Routes

The Class 3 options on Gold Dust Peak's face are fun and the rock is mostly solid until the highest reaches. Avoid going up the wide, sandy gully that splits the face. Going left offers Class 3 chutes that end up on the summit plateau. Going right has more solid rock but puts you on Gold Dust's "east summit." For daredevils, there is a brief, 75-foot Class 4 catwalk with big exposure to reach the true summit. Take the Class 2 ramp down, being sure to stick a bit closer to the left of the cliffed face for the most direct line.

Pika Peak can be climbed on its own or tacked on to your adventure to Gold Dust. The ridge between the two looks tempting, but it's a horribly loose, not-much-fun Class 3 and 4 mess. Avoid it.

The "standard" way up Pika is to simply bully your way up the west ridge/slope from Negro Basin. Start by chugging up to a small saddle from the southern part of the open basin. Once you gain the ridge, hammer your way up Class 2+ boulder fields and talus-strewn slopes. Pika's west ridge is a knee-punishing 0.6 mile (one-way), and the rock can be very loose in places. If you're a peakbagger, knock yourself out (not literally). The lousy terrain does eventually lead to pretty sweet summit views.

Final Thoughts

Don't be surprised if the off-trail access to Negro Basin takes a good hour to navigate. Even though it can be tricky finding the best route, the rock slabs along the way can be a lot of fun to scramble on. Try to use the creek as a reference point, and don't stray too far east or you'll end up below Pika Peak's miserably loose and cliffed-out south slopes.

It's possible to go west off Gold Dust Peak and stay high on the ridge connecting it to UN 12,911, but I don't recommend descending via UN 12,911's southwest ridge. If you follow this deceptive line, by the time you get into the forest, there are a lot of steep cliffed-out sections with lots of blowdown to boot.

Maps show the old Gold Dust Trail here, but there's not a whole lot left of it, at least in the area near Negro Basin.

10 Golden Bear Peak–Hagar Mountain

Golden Bear Peak is pure hiking goodness. Starting on a Class 1 trail, many familiar sights await as you ascend to the ridgeline and cross into Loveland's area of ski operations. From high atop the Continental Divide, I-70 winds back into the civilized world. Hagar Mountain brings your senses back to the backcountry. Traverse across the skyline to Hagar's fun summit scramble. This is an excellent day hike for casual and experienced mountain trekkers alike.

Primary Route: Golden Bear Peak, 13,010 feet; Hagar Mountain, 13,195 feet
Difficulty rating: Medium; a Class 1 trail leads up to a Class 2 ridgewalk to Golden Bear Peak. Light Class 3 climbing awaits on the summit block of Hagar Mountain.

Class rating: Class 2
Round-trip distance: 7.8 miles out and back
Elevation gain: 2,870 feet
Round-trip time: 5–7 hours; full day

Finding the trailhead: *Note:* The parking area here can now be accessed only from westbound I-70. In the past, it was possible to use an access road to drive over to eastbound I-70, but the Colorado Department of Transportation (CDOT) asks hikers not to use this emergency access road. This means that when your hike is done, you'll have to exit back onto westbound I-70 and drive down to Silverthorne to regain I-70 eastbound. Hey, it's a good excuse to get a bite in town before heading back home!

From Denver, take I-70 westbound to the Eisenhower/Johnson Memorial Tunnel, which literally goes through the Loveland Ski Area. As you enter the tunnel, stay in the right lane. Slow down a bit as you near the western exit of the tunnel. A few hundred feet after coming out of the tunnel, take the exit marked "Truck Brake Check" on the right. This large parking lot is the base of operations for CDOT, so please park on the western side of the lot.

Trailhead GPS: N39 40.722' / W105 56.256'

The Hike

Golden Bear is a gem of a 13er. Driving access is easy, yet the area still doesn't see many hikers. Perhaps it's because the adventure begins with the roar of traffic on a brief section of paved road. After a few hundred feet, the auto din begins to die down as a surprisingly lush basin introduces a well-established Class 1 trail up to Golden Bear's south ridge, terminating inbound of the Loveland Ski Area. Walking among ski terrain signs out of season is a hoot. Easy off-trail slopes lead to the summit of Golden Bear. It's one of the better 13ers for a casual summit day or a group hike with friends of varying fitness.

Traversing over to Hagar Mountain escapes the boundaries of Loveland and mixes in light scrambling to the hike. The ridge between the two is broad, grassy, and pocked

The accommodating switchbacked trail to Golden Bear Peak (left of center) cut into the western slopes

with prospecting dents from old mining exploration. Approaching the final push to the summit of Hagar Mountain introduces a fun, solid, and short-lived scramble up to its tiny summit pyramid.

Miles and Directions

0.0   Start by walking east along a service road. Stay left as the road heads toward a surprisingly lush basin (Straight Creek Basin). Early summer wildflower blooms often color the valley with waves of red, yellow, and blue. You will see your trail switchbacking up to the ridge on your right (east).

0.3   At the end of the paved service road, a well-worn trail heads into the willows. As of 2019 the old, battered sign that stood at the start of the trail was knocked over. No worries—the walk up to the ridge is very straightforward. Head north on the trail as it steadily climbs into the valley.

1.9   Take the large switchback that swings south. It is the more worn of the two trails (the other just heads into the basin and fizzles out). Continue up on the trail.

2.4 This is a good time to break off the trail and head north onto the broad ridge. If you stay on the trail, you'll simply end up in a saddle where the trail ends. The inert lifts of Loveland Ski Area are to the south, and Golden Bear Peak waits to the north. Go north about a mile to the summit of Golden Bear. Light Class 2 scrambling guards the last few steps to the summit.

3.3 Golden Bear Peak's summit. Technically this is an unnamed summit, so it will be marked on the map as 13,010 feet. If Golden Bear was your only summit of the day (a fine outing), once you've had your fill, return the way you came for a 6.6-mile out-and-back hike. (**Note:** If you'd like to continue to Hagar Mountain, you'll save time by descending the ridge between Hagar and Coon Hill, which will bring you to the trail you ignored at the big switchback at mile 1.9.) Descend north and downhill off Golden Bear Peak. A little easy scrambling gets you off the summit and over to Point 12,808. Hagar's ridge can look tough from here, but it's not as bad as it looks.

4.5 After rolling up and down along the ridge, you'll reach the final saddle at 12,880 feet at the foot of Hagar. It's only 0.4 mile to the summit, but there's a steep stretch of scrambling to gain the high ridge. Footing is good and the exposure is relatively low.

4.7 Top out on Hagar's airy south ridge. It's going to be an exciting finish! Walk along the ridge to a notch blocking access to the summit pyramid. Downclimb this notch (Class 3) into the sandy notch and have fun climbing up the solid blocks (Class 3) to Hagar's highest point. (**Note:** If you have pups on the hike, I'd suggest not taking them farther than the west summit before the notch. When I hiked here with my dogs, my wife and I took turns getting to the top while the other person waited on the west summit with the dogs. Plus, hero summit shots look great when the photographer stays on the west summit!)

Hagar Mountain from the saddle between it and Golden Bear Peak

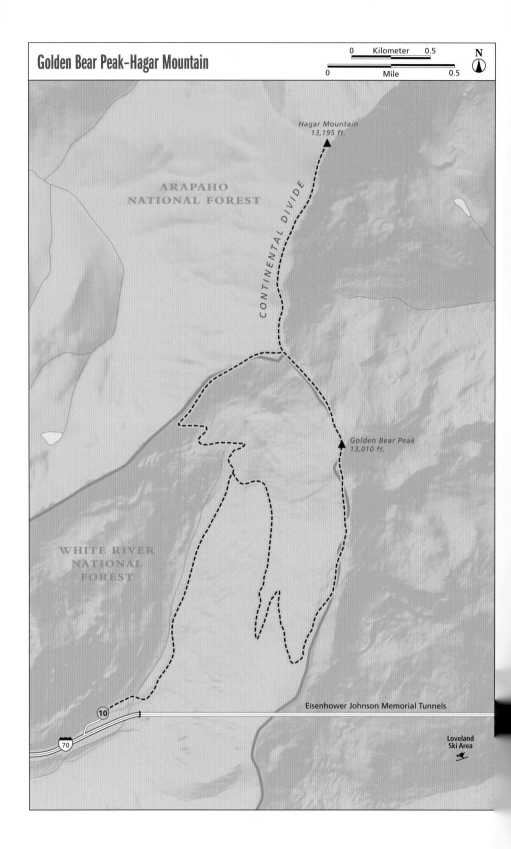

Golden Bear Peak-Hagar Mountain

0   Kilometer   0.5

0   Mile   0.5

N

Hagar Mountain
13,195 ft.

ARAPAHO
NATIONAL FOREST

CONTINENTAL DIVIDE

Golden Bear Peak
13,010 ft.

WHITE RIVER
NATIONAL
FOREST

Eisenhower Johnson Memorial Tunnels

10

70

Loveland
Ski Area

4.9 There is not a lot of room on Hagar's summit—space for three or four hikers. When you're ready to descend, take your time regaining the west summit and scrambling back down to the ridge connecting over to Coon Hill to the west. You can shortcut a little by going right (west) off the ridge and following broad slopes over to the ridge. There are pockets of mining prospecting holes along the way.

6.0 Eventually gain the ridge proper that heads west to Coon Hill. Views here are phenomenal, especially considering how close you are to I-70. Continue west and downhill toward Straight Creek Basin. A faint climber's trail will get more pronounced the closer you get to a flat section at 12,210 feet.

6.2 From the flat area, begin to head south and down into the basin. The trail here disappears in a section of muddy willows, but the navigation is easy. Aim for the big switchback from earlier in the day—chances are you'll regain the climber's trail without even trying.

6.8 Regain the main trail at the big switchback. It's a nice mile walk back through the flowers, streams, and willows. After such a thrilling day in the mountains, the sight of I-70's perpetual traffic may bum you out a little.

7.8 Arrive back at the large parking lot. Remember that you'll need to exit onto I-70 West and drive to exit 205, about 7 miles down the pass. Regain I-70 East here. It's worth contacting CDOT (http://codot.gov) to see if the road (West Loop Road) is open to the public. It has been in the past and is a much quicker way to get back on I-70 East. As of 2020 the contact number for the Denver regional section of CDOT is (303) 759-2368.

Final Thoughts

These two 13ers are about an hour's drive from the Denver metro area. They have a very easy-to-access trailhead yet don't see a lot of visitors. The peaks along the Continental Divide never fail to deliver exceptional views, and Golden Bear and Hagar are no exception. The primary route here is perfect for groups of different abilities—in the time it takes slower hikers to do an out-and-back on Golden Bear, faster hikers can tag Hagar and get back to Straight Creek Basin at around the same time.

Golden Bear on its own is a great half-day outing. I've hiked it in the morning while en route to points west as a way to break up the drive. Golden Bear is also popular with trail runners, though they are a different breed when it comes to "enjoying" running in the thin air at 13,000 feet!

11 Grizzly Peak D

Grizzly Peak features a long approach along a high ridgeline, culminating with a fun, low-exposure scramble to the top. The highlight of this adventure is the extended time spent on the broad skyline traverse. Easy access from the top of paved Loveland Pass makes this a great Front Range hike.

Primary route: Grizzly Peak D, 13,427 feet; Cupid Peak, 13,117 feet

Optional summits: Mount Sniktau, 13,284 feet; Lenawee Mountain, 13,204 feet

Difficulty rating: Medium; a Class 1/2 walk-up with light Class 2+ scrambling near the summit of Grizzly Peak

Class rating: Class 2+

Round-trip distance: 5.5 miles out and back

Elevation gain: 2,850 feet

Round-trip time: 3–5 hours; half day

Finding the trailhead: From Denver, take exit 216 off I-70 to US 6 (Loveland Pass). Simply follow Loveland Pass as it climbs 4.3 miles to the top of the pass at 11,990 feet. There are about a dozen parking spots and they go fast—try to get to the mountain early on summer weekends. If the main parking area is full, you'll have to continue south down the pass a few hundred feet to overflow parking areas. The trail begins on the east side of the mountain from the main parking area. The road up is paved and maintained year-round, making it passable by passenger cars. If you're planning on going up in the winter months, snow tires and AWD/4WD are vital.

Trailhead GPS: N39 39.828' / W105 52.734'

The Hike

There are five (!) "Grizzly Peaks" among the 13ers, including the highest of all the 13ers, Grizzly Peak A. Of the quintet of Grizzly Peaks, Griz D is the most accessible and my personal favorite. It is the rare 13er that is accessible and (mostly) safe to hike year-round. The entire hike is done on ridges and the lion's share of the work will be done in the first three-quarters of a mile. Nearby Mount Sniktau is one of the very best 13ers for beginners—or anyone who wants a quick workout in the mountains. Views from this area showcase both the high peaks of the Front Range and the deep cut of I-70 as it snakes through the valleys below.

Prolonged time on the high ridges equals excellent photo opportunities and, oftentimes, robust winds. The scramble to the top of Grizzly Peak is a nice change of pace after an enjoyable approach.

The ribbon-like trail that leads to Grizzly Peak's summit

Miles and Directions

0.0   This hike wastes no time in gaining altitude. Head east and uphill up the well-worn trail to a bump on the ridge at 12,915 feet. Note that you don't have to actually top out on this humble point. At about 0.6 mile up, a spur trail cuts off to the right (south), where you can gain the ridge without gaining and losing elevation by going up too high. Taking the spur saves about 200 feet of elevation gain and loss. No matter which you choose, gain the ridge and continue southeast. This is tundra walking at its finest. The ridgelines are broad, with little to no exposure, and navigation is simple.

1.5   Arrive at Cupid Peak (13,117 feet), a ranked 13er. Cupid's flat summit offers good views southeast to Grizzly Peak and the challenges that await. Dominating the views farther east are two of the most popular 14ers in Colorado: Grays and Torreys Peaks. Continue toward Grizzly Peak.

2.2   Arrive at Point 12,936. The walk up to this point has mostly been a casual ridgewalk; now you have work to do. Scramble down on Class 2+ terrain to the saddle between Point 12,936 and Grizzly Peak at 12,700 feet. From here it's only 0.3 mile to the top, but you'll have to scramble 690 vertical feet to get it! The difficulty never surpasses Class 2+. There are a few different social trails, so pick one and grind up to the summit.

2.7   Grizzly Peak's summit! The long Class 2+ ridge from Grizzly to Torreys Peak is impossible to miss (and is an interesting way to ascend the trendy 14er). Return the way you came. The toughest part of the return hike is the descent off Grizzly back to Point 12,936. Enjoy the walk back!

5.5   Arrive back at the trailhead.

Optional Routes

Grizzly Peak Winter Ascent

Grizzly is an excellent choice for a winter 13er. Avalanche danger is very low (though not completely gone), and Loveland Pass is plowed year-round. It's also a very popular

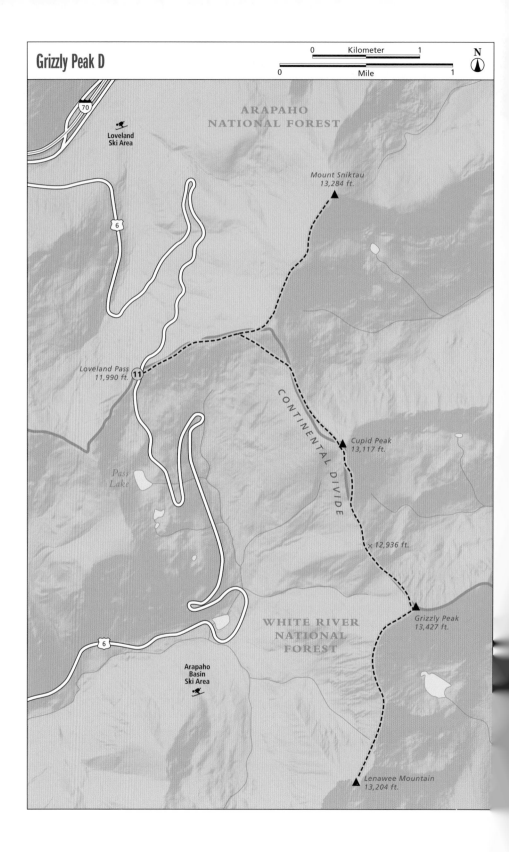

Kilometer

Mile

N

ARAPAHO
NATIONAL FOREST

Loveland
Ski Area

70

6

Mount Sniktau
13,284 ft.

Loveland Pass
11,990 ft.

11

CONTINENTAL DIVIDE

Cupid Peak
13,117 ft.

Pass
Lake

× 12,936 ft.

Grizzly Peak
13,427 ft.

6

WHITE RIVER
NATIONAL
FOREST

Arapaho
Basin
Ski Area

Lenawee Mountain
13,204 ft.

Grizzly Peak (center) with Torrey's Peak (left) and Grays Peak "peeking" out in the distance

area for backcountry skiers and snowboarders. One of the reasons the ridge is relatively safe is the fierce wind that blasts snow off the mountain. Any winter ascent should account for strong winds and very cold temps. The wind may not become apparent until you get to the high ridges. Avoiding the spur trail and taking the time to go directly to the ridge further mitigates avalanche risk. Crampons and ice axe are required.

Mount Sniktau

The round-trip for a solo outing to Mount Sniktau is just over 3 miles, making it one of the easiest 13ers to hike. From Point 12,915 where the starting east ridge tops out, it is only 0.8 mile north to Sniktau's summit. For 1.6 miles, you can add it to your Grizzly Peak day to give you three ranked 13ers in a single hike.

Grizzly–Lenawee Traverse

This interesting point-to-point traverse starts at Loveland Pass and ends at the main parking lot for Arapahoe Basin Ski Area. Follow the primary route to Grizzly, then continue southwest along an exciting Class 3 ridge to Lenawee's highest summit point. A few places may require a move or two of Class 4 scrambling. The rock is relatively solid. After scaling and descending Lenawee, you'll arrive at the A-Basin ski area, where you can follow access roads down to the base and your waiting vehicle. The traverse adds roughly 1,100 feet of vertical gain due to lots of ups and downs. Total mileage is roughly 7.3 miles.

Note: The scrambling on the ridges past Grizzly can be quite exposed in places.

Final Thoughts

Grizzly is a Front Range classic and one that many people return to year after year. Going out to Cupid Peak as an out-and-back hike is a great dog-friendly adventure (Grizzly itself isn't good for pups, as the scramble up the summit block has a lot of loose rock).

Besides the five "Grizzly Peaks," there is also a "Grizzly Mountain" among ranked 13ers. At 13,708 feet it falls between Grizzly Peaks B and C. It is the 142nd tallest peak in Colorado and the 89th highest 13er. Interestingly, all six officially named Colorado mountains with "Grizzly" in the title are 13ers.

Finally, the optional Grizzly–Lenawee traverse is best done in the summer. Get an early start because the entire day will be above tree line.

12 Hesperus Mountain

Hesperus Mountain is a remote, magnificent summit that waits deep in the lonely La Plata Mountains. It sports a striking, striped profile that would likely be a photographer's darling if it wasn't so isolated. The hike up follows a rock-plated ridge to the heart of this largely overlooked mountain range.

Primary route: Hesperus Mountain, 13,232 feet

Optional summits: Centennial Peak, 13,062 feet

Difficulty rating: Medium; reaching Hesperus's west ridge requires some off-trail navigation savvy. Though the route stays Class 2+, accessing the ridge is done along loose talus fields.

These solidify as you climb higher on the peak, though the footing is always a bit suspect.

Class rating: Class 2+

Round-trip distance: 5.3 miles out and back

Elevation gain: 2,840 feet

Round-trip time: 5–7 hours; full day

Finding the trailhead: The Sharkstooth Trailhead is reached via a rough, rutted dirt road. A carefully driven passenger car can get within 0.7 mile of the main lot. SUVs and SUCs can make the parking area without too much trouble, though the more clearance, the better.

From the town of Mancos, start at the intersection of US 160 and CO 184. Turn north onto CO 184 for 0.3 mile, then turn right onto CR 42 (FR 561). You will see signs here for Mancos State Park/West Mancos Road/Jackson Lake. This is a good place to reset your odometer. This road starts as pavement then turns to dirt 1.2 miles in. Past the Transfer Campground, 12 miles up the road, go right onto FR 350 (Spruce Mill Road). It is 7.5 miles to the trailhead from here (there are signs for Sharkstooth Trailhead at the turnoff). Follow this road 6 miles, then go right and downhill on FR 346, which is signed as Aspen Loop ATV Trail and Mancos 17. A short way in, a reassuring sign for Twin Lakes/Sharkstooth Trailhead is posted. Cars can go about a mile in here before the rutted road gets too rough. They should park at or near the Twin Lakes parking area. Along FR 346 are plenty of good dispersed camping spots. High-clearance vehicles can drive the full 0.7-mile length to the main trailhead, battling ruts and deep, muddy puddles along the way.

Trailhead GPS: N37 27.798' / W108 05.796'

The Hike

The La Plata Mountains are an overlooked sub-range of the San Juans. Because of their isolated location—and perhaps because the range doesn't sport a 14er—they don't see a lot of visitors. There are six named 13ers in the range: three ranked (Hesperus Mountain, Lavender Peak, and Babcock Peak), two soft-ranked (Centennial Peak and Mount Moss), and unranked Spiller Peak. Hesperus is the most striking of these mountains, thanks to its banded red-and-white rock stripes. The skin of the peak is rich in obsidian, a resource that made it a valuable mountain to the ancient

Storms gather around Mount Hesperus.

Navajo people who lived in the area. Hesperus Mountain was known as Dibé Nit-saa (meaning "big mountain sheep") to the Navajo, and it is one of the four sacred mountains in their culture.

The hike up Hesperus is an interesting one. It starts out at the Sharkstooth Trailhead, following an established trail for a short distance before heading off-trail. Track through a forest section and gain the rocky west ridge. From there the route is straightforward on semi-stable rock fields, leading to a semi-exposed, thrilling summit block. Despite the low mileage, this is a good, tough 13er that is worth the visit. A GPS is highly recommended, specifically for backtracking your route after reaching the summit.

Miles and Directions

0.0 This route starts from the Twin Lakes parking area. Simply hoof it up the road to the Sharkstooth Trailhead to start your day.

0.7 Here's the trailhead. If you parked here, congrats! You saved yourself 1.4 miles of hiking. Even subtracting that total from the adventure, this is still a challenging hike. Start on the West Mancos Trail 621. The trail is threadbare at the beginning, but it's as good as it's going to get for trails on this outing. Follow the path downhill, past a sign for North Fork of the West Mancos, and across a river.

1.3 Another 0.6 mile from the trailhead is a good time to get off the trail. The goal from here is to find the path of least resistance to Hesperus's west ridge to the south. Aim for a grassy slope right of a talus gully splitting the ridge and left of a line of pine trees. Willows and

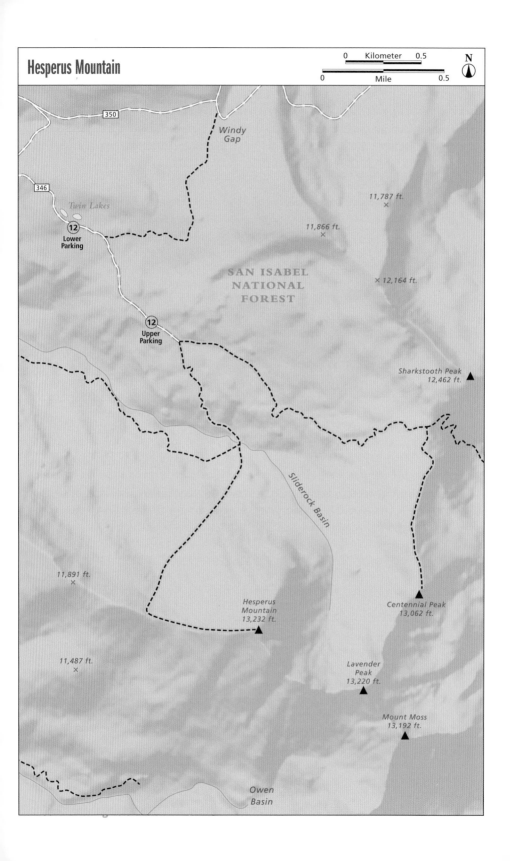

Hesperus Mountain

0   Kilometer   0.5

0   Mile   0.5

N

350

Windy
Gap

346

Twin Lakes

11,787 ft.
×

12
Lower
Parking

11,866 ft.
×

SAN ISABEL
NATIONAL
FOREST

× 12,164 ft.

12
Upper
Parking

Sharkstooth Peak
12,462 ft. ▲

Sliderock Basin

11,891 ft.
×

11,487 ft.
×

Hesperus
Mountain
13,232 ft. ▲

Centennial Peak
13,062 ft. ▲

Lavender
Peak
13,220 ft. ▲

Mount Moss
13,192 ft. ▲

Owen
Basin

pine trees make staying on track tricky. A GPS and/or a solid bearing with a compass will help. It's only about 0.6 mile through the woods. When in doubt, trend right. Eventually, you'll gain sight of the ridge proper. Don't be tempted to shortcut up a series of cracked rock faces left of the talus gully—the rock is rotten throughout.

1.9 At roughly 11,650 feet, locate a gully with a moderate grade. This is the second prominent gully west of the summit along the ridge. It's the first reasonable place to gain the ridge, though if it looks too dicey, continue right (west) down the ridge to more amenable slopes.

2.2 Once you top out on the west ridge, the navigation to the top is easy—simply ascend the ridge east to the summit. Most of the best footing is along the ridge, which may invite an easy Class 3 move here or there. There are always Class 2 walk-around options to the south (right of the ridge), though the semi-stable talus "plates" of rock might be more trouble than a few scrambling moves.

Rock colors are interesting on the ridge; red, white, black, and gray mix along the surface of the mountain. As you near the summit, there is a brief flat section of about 60 feet that leads to the true top.

2.6 There is some wicked exposure from the cliffs on the north side of the peak! The summit itself is mostly white rock. A dangerous-looking ridge connects Hesperus to Lavender Peak to the southeast. Before heading off the summit, take in the great views of the amazing La Plata Range. When you are ready to return, simply retrace your route back. The descent goes fairly quickly, especially if you can navigate back to the West Mancos Trail without trouble. The low mileage leaves open a realistic shot of grabbing Centennial Peak, assuming the weather is good.

4.6 Reach the Sharkstooth Trailhead.

5.3 Arrive back at the Twin Lakes parking area.

Optional Routes

Centennial Peak, formerly known as Banded Peak, was renamed to celebrate Colorado's one hundredth birthday in 1976. It is not, however, in the group of high 13ers known as the Centennials (the 13ers that are part of Colorado's one hundred highest peaks). At 13,062 feet, it's almost not even a 13er! To hike it, return to the Sharkstooth Trailhead and take the Sharkstooth Trail to the saddle between Sharkstooth and Centennial. Hop off the trail at the saddle and follow the north ridge along blocks and blocks of rocks (Class 2+) to the summit. Round-trip from the parking area is only 3.4 miles with 2,200 feet of vertical gain.

The other intriguing 13er in the area is 13,220-foot Lavender Peak, connected via a frightening-looking ridge to Hesperus Mountain. On my second visit to Hesperus, I connected the two along this ridge, which is mostly sustained Class 3+, with a few moves that I'd call Class 4. The route-finding is also quite tricky and the rock is bad in places. Because this guide aims to stay on nontechnical, Class 3-and-below terrain, I mention this option for advanced mountain hikers and climbers. Descent from Lavender is along steep gullies/slopes into Sliderock Basin. With that in mind, if your goal is to climb Lavender Peak, I'd suggest the route from the west via Tomahawk Basin (Class 3), which is considered the standard.

Sharkstooth is an accurate name for this pointed peak. Photo is taken from the summit of Mount Hesperus.

Final Thoughts

Hesperus Mountain is named after the Hesperus Mine that operated in the area. Lavender Peak is named after Dwight Lavender, an incredibly talented young climber born in Telluride in 1911. He was responsible for many first ascents in Colorado in the 1920s, including one of the most difficult 13ers, Jagged Peak. Along with his elite climbing ability, he was a gifted writer, chronicling his adventures in the *American Alpine Journal* and *Trail and Timberline*. Sadly, he died at age 23 from polio.

Hesperus means "evening star" (referring to the planet Venus). There was a Greek god of the same name, who was the embodiment of the evening star and is connected to a confusing set of minor Greek gods.

13 Horseshoe Mountain

This aptly named summit is popular for both its aesthetic appeal and its enjoyable hiking access. Mining ruins at the foot of Horseshoe Mountain and its neighbors reflect the hardscrabble history of the area—including a still-standing cabin just off the summit proper!

Primary route: Horseshoe Mountain, 13,898 feet
Optional summits: Peerless Mountain, 13,348 feet; Finback Knob, 13,409 feet; Mount Sheridan, 13,748 feet
Difficulty rating: Easy–medium; a straight shot to Horseshoe Mountain is mostly Class 1 with a touch of Class 2 terrain near the top. The

optional summits add more challenge to the day but never surpass Class 2.
Class rating: Class 2
Round-trip distance: 4.4 miles out and back
Elevation gain: 2,260 feet
Round-trip time: 4–6 hours; half day (with lots of options to make it longer)

Finding the trailhead: Passenger cars can navigate the bumpy road to the lower parking area—which is only 0.2 mile below the upper parking lot and serves as a better starting point for a direct summit of Horseshoe Mountain.

From the town of Fairplay, go south on US 285 for 1 mile past the intersection of US 285 and CO 9 and turn west (right) onto Park CR 18. Reset your odometer here. It is 12 miles to the parking areas. The road starts out paved and turns to dirt at a four-way intersection. Small rocks and washboards make for a rumbling ride; 10.5 miles in, you'll pass the large ruins of the old Leavick Mill. Continue on up the road another 1.5 miles to the car parking lot in the open basin. If you have a high-clearance SUC or SUV, you can drive another 0.2 mile to the upper lot. The only thing preventing passenger cars from reaching this upper lot is a single large, natural, dirt speed bump that requires a bit of clearance to roll over.

Trailhead GPS: N39 12.484' / W106 10.137'

The Hike

Come for the mining history, stay for the summits! Horseshoe Mountain isn't the tallest peak in the area, but its unique, broad summit makes it perfect for a half-day hike. Did I mention there's a ghost cabin on top of the mountain? Below the mountain are the ruins of the old Leavick township, founded in 1873. Leavick once boasted a population of over 1,000 people and stuck around until the 1920s when a last-ditch effort to mine zinc proved to be unprofitable. A brief resurrection in 1948 was the last gasp for the town (and the aptly named Last Chance Mine).

The hiking trail isn't marked well but is easy to follow. The higher you ascend above the basin, the more mining history emerges in the pockets and shadows of the valley. Nearing the highest point, the mountain becomes nearly flat. The red-and-orange

Hikers nearing the summit of Horseshoe Mountain

rocks on the summit plateau are punctuated with growths of tiny, defiant wildflowers. Broad slopes connect summits along the ridge, opening the possibility to tag additional peaks without a lot of added effort.

Note: The majority of hikers at the trailhead will be here to hike the very popular 14er Mount Sherman. Since this is a guidebook for 13ers, I'll focus on the 13ers, but take note that linking the 14er Sherman with the 13ers Sheridan, Peerless, and Horseshoe is a great four-pack of summits that isn't terribly difficult, especially for fit hikers.

Miles and Directions

Note: From the parking area, Mount Sheridan is the big peak directly west of the access road. To the south (left) of Sheridan in a low saddle is a small bump on the ridge. This is Peerless Mountain, your first objective.

0.0 Starting from the lower parking area, wander a combination of tundra and mining roads to the saddle west of Peerless Mountain. While there are no formal trails here, there are old roads everywhere and many social trails. You can peruse various ruins along the way.

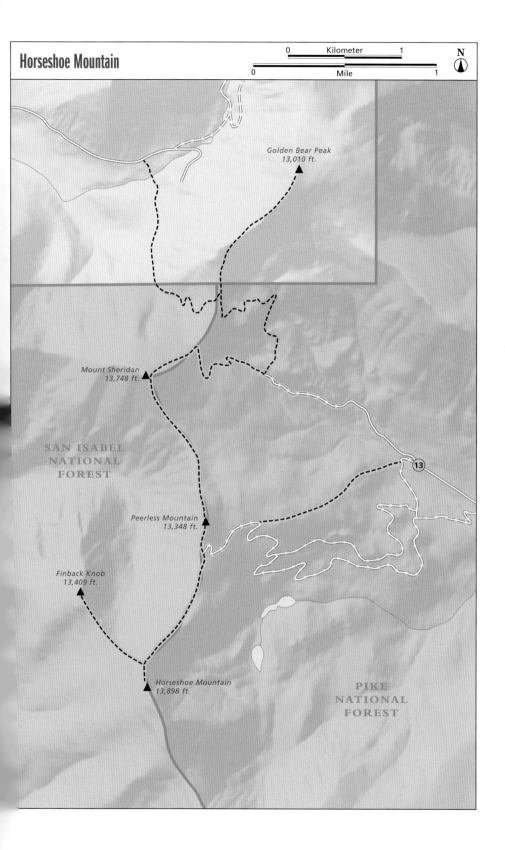

Golden Bear Peak
13,010 ft.

Mount Sheridan
13,748 ft.

SAN ISABEL
NATIONAL
FOREST

13

Peerless Mountain
13,348 ft.

Finback Knob
13,409 ft.

Horseshoe Mountain
13,898 ft.

PIKE
NATIONAL
FOREST

There is a road that practically goes up to the summit of Horseshoe Mountain. You have the option of following those roads/trails to the saddle between Sheridan and Peerless to the north, or Peerless and Horseshoe to the south. The key is to hike up the low ridge that separates the basins between Mount Sheridan and Horseshoe Mountain. Peerless Mountain (the little peak with the overstated name) is a very easy add-on to your day. However you get there, the path to Horseshoe Peak begins south of Peerless Mountain.

1.3 Just south of the summit of Peerless, the way up to Horseshoe Mountain to the south will be obvious. There is something of an old doubletrack road up the slopes (as well as other roads cutting down into the valley to the left). The grade is pleasingly accommodating (at least compared to many other 13ers), making this a very enjoyable walk-up.

2.2 The summit of Horseshoe Mountain looks like it was deliberately coated in crushed rock. It's very flat and the panoramic views are wonderful in all directions. Mount Sheridan clearly stands out to the north. Mount Elbert, Mount Massive, and many other Sawatch Range giants loom to the west.

On the southern side of the summit plateau is an old mining cabin. It's a testament to the builders that a structure at 13,890-plus feet is not only still standing but also seems to have aged fairly well. Be extra careful if you explore the cabin interior (especially if you have off-leash dogs). There is an open mineshaft (!) in the building.

Return the way you came. Feel free to mix up the descent route to see other ruins and artifacts, but just remember there is a low ridge between you and the parking area (north of Peerless Mountain) that must be crossed. Even though the way back is easy to navigate, you don't want to drop too low and have to make up ground walking back up the road to your vehicle.

4.4 Arrive back at the parking area.

Optional Routes

There's a lot of history in this area—simply walking around and checking out the historic structures is a great "optional route." However, if you're looking for 13ers, the obvious line is to follow the masses up the well-worn path to the saddle between Sherman and Sheridan, then cut south and ascend Mount Sheridan. The hike up Sheridan is Class 2 and there is something of a social trail, but the footing is a bit of a pain. Sheridan's skin is composed of loose rocks that feel like ceramic plates underfoot. They aren't too bad on the ascent (via the north ridge). On the south ridge connecting to Peerless Mountain, they are more numerous and looser, and the slope is steeper. Eventually, they give way to better terrain. After crossing Peerless Mountain, continue up to Horseshoe. This route is still only about 5.5 miles and 2,700 feet of elevation gain (though the up and down off Sheridan is more work than the raw numbers imply).

Peerless Mountain is one of those summits that has an official USGS name but isn't a ranked peak. For hard-core 13er fans, there is a second named, unranked 13er within striking distance: Finback Knob. It can be reached by walking northwest from the summit of Horseshoe down a steepish slope 0.5 mile to the 13,409-foot peak. In the full mile for the out-and-back trek to Finback Knob's summit, you'll tack on a taxing 700 feet of vertical elevation on semi-stable rock.

Final Thoughts

Mount Sherman and Mount Sheridan are named for the famous Civil War Union generals William Sherman and Philip Sheridan. Both men continued their military careers after the Civil War in the western plains, a distinction that has garnered scrutiny in modern times. Lt. George Armstrong Custer was following orders from General Sheridan when the lieutenant was killed at the Battle of the Little Bighorn.

The mines in the area produced a great amount of silver and zinc in the late 1800s. It is a coincidence that the Sherman Silver Purchase Act, passed in 1890, caused the bust of the silver-rich mines of Leavick at the foot of Mount Sherman. The Sherman associated with this legislation was not the fabled general but rather Senator John Sherman.

Despite Mount Sherman being the highest peak in the area, many early accounts reveal that it was Horseshoe Mountain's distinct cirque (when viewed from the east) that caught people's attention.

Early morning sunlight illuminates the traverse between Mount Sherman and Mount Sheridan. In the center is the broad, flat profile of Horseshoe Mountain.

14 Huerfano Peak-Iron Nipple

This duo of high 13ers makes for an excellent hike/scramble combo and can be paired with the 14er Mount Lindsey. Both peaks are representative of the Sangre de Cristo Range, a place where craggy summits rise from the surrounding flat farmland and semi-desert sand dunes.

Primary route: Huerfano Peak, 13,828 feet; Iron Nipple, 13,500 feet
Optional summits: California Peak, 13,849 feet
Difficulty rating: Medium; this Class 2 adventure shares a start with the popular standard northwest gully route on the 14er Mount

Lindsey—Huerfano and Iron Nipple are often paired with Lindsey for a big day out.
Class rating: Class 2+
Round-trip distance: 7.7 miles out and back
Elevation gain: 3,680 feet
Round-trip time: 6-8 hours; full day

Finding the trailhead: This hike starts at the Upper Huerfano Trailhead, which requires a decent-clearance vehicle. SUVs will be fine and I've seen sport-utility cars at the upper trailhead as well (Subaru Outbacks, Honda CRVs). The main challenge comes in the form of steep hills with ruts that require at least 8 inches of ground clearance. Two-wheel-drive and low-clearance cars can park at the lower trailhead, which adds about 2 easy miles each way to the hike.

These directions start from the town of Gardner on CO 69. For most people, this means coming down I-25 South, but it's the same exit in either direction off I-25. Take exit 56 toward Red Rock Road, then take a right onto Red Rock Road. Follow it 2.5 miles, then turn right onto CO 69 North and proceed 19.8 miles to Gardner.

From Gardner continue 0.5 mile and go left (west) into CO 550 (Mosca Pass). You'll see signs for "Upper Huerfano—21.5" and "Lily Lake Trailhead 22.5." At 7.1 miles the road turns from pavement to dirt. At mile 11.9, stay left at the junction onto FR 580. At 15.8 miles, stay left as you pass the Singing River Ranch's driveway. At mile 19.9 you'll pass out of the private property zone and into San Isabel National Forest. Just past a landslide zone is the 2WD parking and the Lower Huerfano Trailhead—there are only a few spots here, but more parking is about 200 feet farther up the road. High-clearance vehicles can carry on 2 miles to the Upper Huerfano/Lily Lake Trailhead. Another good reason for a summer/early autumn date is to let the steep hills that lead to the trailhead dry of their slick mud. There are good dispersed camping sites in a meadow near the end of the road.

Trailhead GPS: N37 37.350' / W105 28.368'

The Hike

UN 13,828 (better known by its non-USGS name, Huerfano Peak) is Colorado's 93rd highest ranked peak. It's an excellent Class 2 adventure with a bit of boulder-hopping, a touch of light scrambling, and an inevitable trip up the cheeky Iron Nipple (which, interestingly, is an official USGS name). The Huerfano River basin is an

Iron Nipple (left) and Huerfano Peak (right)

exceptional late summer/early autumn destination. As the seasons change, the flora explodes into vibrant colors, fed by the lakes and streams that are plentiful in the area. So plentiful, in fact, that early season adventures can make for soggy river crossings. (**Note:** There is a river crossing early in this hike, so consider bringing along sandals to keep your boots dry.)

Nearby California Peak is a nice Class 1 summit that can round out a two-day hiking adventure to the area (and is the 84th highest ranked peak in Colorado). Pairing Huerfano and California in a single outing, however, doesn't make a lot of sense as the two are split by the Huerfano River drainage.

Miles and Directions

0.0 This mileage starts from the Upper Huerfano/Lily Lake Trailhead. Take the Lily Lake Trail to start. The dominant summit from this vantage is the hulking, stony east face of Blanca Peak. This is a very smooth trail with little elevation gain at the start.

1.0 At the Lily Lake Trail junction, stay left on the main trail (do not go toward Lily Lake). About 300 feet after this junction is the river crossing. By late summer it should be low. Cross it and continue along the well-defined trail.

1.3 The trail starts climbing through the forest. You'll be following this trail past tree line and to the saddle between Mount Lindsey and the Iron Nipple. The elevation gain here designates the start of the real work!

2.9 At 13,150 feet, reach the saddle. The more worn path heads right (southeast) up Lindsey, whose standard route looks intimidatingly vertical from here (it's only Class 3). Leave the trail and instead go northeast toward the Iron Nipple along rocky Class 2 terrain.

3.1 Shortly after starting the ascent, the terrain diverts you into a (cool) slot on the northwest side of the ridge. If you are aiming to summit the Iron Nipple, the Class 2 scrambling will be dead ahead—and this is the best time to get it, as it is only a 0.1-mile detour. After summiting, return to the flattish, grassy patch just beyond the slot. Contour east and descend about 70 vertical feet to bypass the Nipple on the east side. As you bypass the Nipple, the route to Huerfano will be obvious.

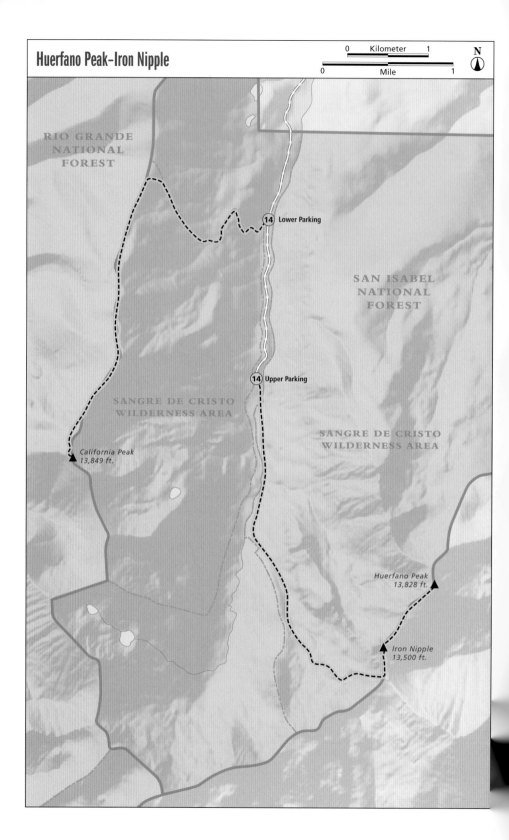

Huerfano Peak-Iron Nipple

0   Kilometer   1

0   Mile   1

N

RIO GRANDE
NATIONAL
FOREST

SAN ISABEL
NATIONAL
FOREST

14 Lower Parking

14 Upper Parking

SANGRE DE CRISTO
WILDERNESS AREA

SANGRE DE CRISTO
WILDERNESS AREA

California Peak
13,849 ft.

Huerfano Peak
13,828 ft.

Iron Nipple
13,500 ft.

3.2 Endure a chunky, semi-loose talus field before reaching the solid south slopes of Huerfano Peak. After you get through the rocks, the rest of the hike is on accommodating alpine slopes.

3.8 Welcome to the summit of Huerfano Peak! The 14ers Mount Lindsey and Blanca Peak look like absolute monsters from here. The elongated ridges culminating in California Peak stand out to the northwest. If you happen to catch the foliage at peak autumn, the yellow, green, and gold hues of the forests to the east will be spectacular. When you are ready, return the way you came, once again passing the Iron Nipple's summit block to the east.

4.5 Back at the saddle, the main trail returns and will guide you back to the parking area.

7.7 Arrive back at the Lily Lake Trailhead.

Optional Routes

The obvious add-on for your day is the 14er Mount Lindsey. If you opt for this, start with Lindsey then backtrack to the Nipple and Huerfano.

California Peak is in the area and is worth a mention, as it is in the one hundred highest Colorado summits. It's a pleasant—if long—Class 1 walk-up that is 8.3 miles out and back and features a burly 4,100 feet of elevation gain. Start from the Lower

Mount Lindsey dominates the skyline from the notch just below the summit of Iron Nipple.

Huerfano Trailhead mentioned in the driving directions (about 2 miles below Lily Lake Trailhead). A small sign denotes the Zapata Trail to the west. Some maps call this the "Raspberry Trail." Take this trail 1.7 miles to a saddle at 11,860 feet and the start of California's north ridge. Note that this trail phases out in some of the lower, grassy sections (keep an eye out for cairns).

Once you hit the north ridge, it's 2.5 more miles and a little over 2,000 feet to the top. There is no official trail, but the route is obvious. There's nothing technical, but don't underestimate the work in pushing up 4,000 feet in a little over 4 miles on the ascent.

Final Thoughts

Mount Lindsey is named for Malcolm Lindsey, a leader in the Colorado Mountain Club in the 1940s. When the mountain was renamed in 1954, it was changed from the all-too-common, boring name "Old Baldy." There are over thirty-five mountains in Colorado with "Baldy" in their official names (and several more with informal Baldy names).

"Huerfano" means orphan in Spanish. As for the Iron Nipple, it is the tallest of the nine (!) mountains with "Nipple" in their official names in Colorado. Some of the others include a pair of Nipple Mountains, two separate Maggies Nipple peaks, the seldom-visited Grannys Nipple, and, of course, simply "The Nipple."

15 James Peak

James Peak is the perfect moderate 13er. The hike up is work, for sure, but it breaks up the effort by mixing in one of Colorado's remaining year-round snowfields, St. Marys Glacier (which is now classified as a semipermanent snowfield but retains the "glacier" name).

Primary route: James Peak, 13,294 feet
Difficulty rating: Medium; a Class 2 walk-up with a few rocky trail sections
Class rating: Class 2

Round-trip distance: 7.3 miles out and back
Elevation gain: 2,950 feet
Round-trip time: 5-7 hours; half day

Finding the trailhead: West of Denver, take exit 238 (Fall River Road) off I-70 (both eastbound and westbound exits funnel to the same place). From the highway, follow the twisting, paved Fall River Road 8.6 miles as it ascends and switchbacks toward the small town of Alice. At 8.6 miles, pass the entrance to the St. Marys Glacier Trail on your left. The parking area is a few hundred feet past this on the left side of the road.

As of 2020 the parking lot here is still privately owned and there is a minimal parking fee (parking was previously free for many years). Only the parking area and a very small portion of the land is private. About 100 feet into the wilderness you'll be back on public land.

If you really don't want to pay to park, it's possible to hike James Peak from Loch Lomond (see chapter 4, Parry Peak-Mount Bancroft), but you'll need a good-clearance 4x4 vehicle to get there—and you'll miss the glacier unless you hike down to it.

Trailhead GPS: N39 49.680' / W105 38.544'

The Hike

The first mile of James Peak's standard route leads to St. Marys Lake at the foot of St. Marys Glacier. As of 2020 the semipermanent snowfield is no longer classified as a glacier due to the fact it isn't moving. The entire snowfield is expected to melt out in the next twenty-five to fifty years, so enjoy the novelty of hiking on summer snow while you can!

Above the glacier, the hike is a classic Rocky Mountain ramble—open tundra leading to a trail that ascends a broad shoulder, topping out on a wide summit with stunning views in all directions. Hikers have the option to follow the main trail or enjoy a Class 2 scramble up the southeast ridge.

Miles and Directions

0.0 This hike begins a few hundred feet south up the road from where you parked—you passed it on your way in. Turn right onto a signed, rocky dirt road that marks the start of the trail.

0.2 At the top of the first little hill, go left. Going straight quickly dead-ends. Continue on the path (which is more like a trail than a 4x4 road from here).

1.0 The trail more or less ends at St. Marys Lake at the foot of the glacier. Continue past the lake, over a bridge, to the foot of the glacier itself. From here, hike up the glacier. It's only a little over a half mile to the top and it's not terribly steep—at least by mountaineering standards. It's a good idea to bring poles. In summer months, you likely won't need micro-spikes, but if you are not used to hiking on hard-packed snow, they can be helpful.

1.2 At the top of the glacier, stay straight as the last remnants of the snowfield trickle off to your left. A trail emerges from the ice and heads up toward the flats below James Peak (which you'll see in its entirety from this vantage). Continue toward the peak, using a large rock outcrop as a good halfway point between the glacier top and the start of the summit slopes.

1.7 At the rock outcrop, known informally as Lunch Rock, it's worth taking a glance back to see where you came up. Because of the open tundra, it's possible to mistakenly drop into the basin to the south of the glacier . . . which makes for a *long* day! Carry on toward the base of James Peak, crossing a 4x4 road.

2.7 At the base of the slopes, a cairned trail will emerge slightly south of your approach. This is the easiest way up to the summit. (**Note:** If there is snow or you want a more direct route, the east slopes work just as well—they just have a lot more boulders to navigate and there is no formal trail.)

2.9 At the saddle between James Peak and Mount Bancroft, turn north and get ready for the final push to the top. The trail fades out a little in places, but the way up is obvious from here.

3.8 James Peak's summit. Enjoy the amazing views, including the abrupt drop to the northeast to James Peak Lake. When you are ready, head down the way you came. If there is enough snow on the east slopes, they can offer a speedy shortcut back down to the flats.

James Peak

James Peak

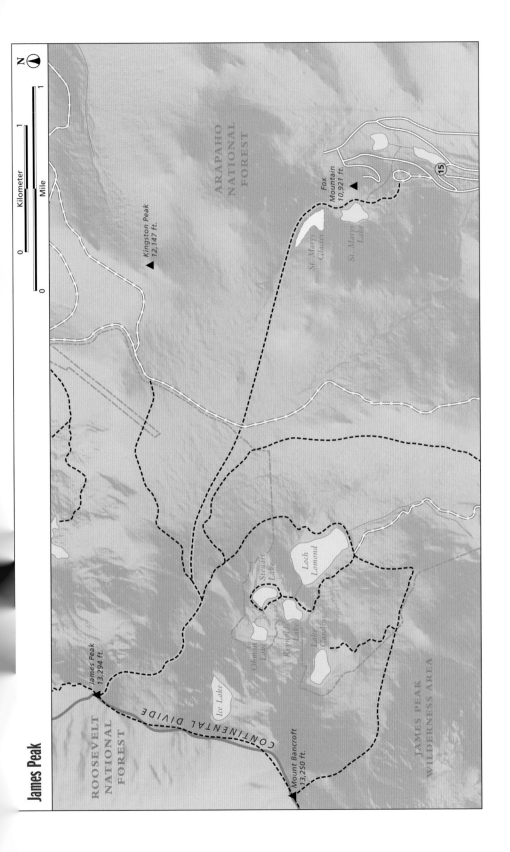

N

Kilometer
0   1

Mile
0   1

Kingston Peak
12,147 ft.

ARAPAHO
NATIONAL
FOREST

Fox
Mountain
10,921 ft.

St. Marys
Glacier

St. Marys
Lake

15

James Peak
13,294 ft.

ROOSEVELT
NATIONAL
FOREST

CONTINENTAL DIVIDE

Ice Lake

Ohman
Lake

Stewart
Lake

Reynold
Lake

Lake
Caroline

Loch
Lomond

Mount Bancroft
13,250 ft.

JAMES PEAK
WILDERNESS AREA

5.9 On your way back, pass Lunch Rock once more and trend toward the top of the glacier—slightly left.

6.4 Back at the top of the glacier, follow it down back to the formal trail and head to the parking area. Please do not shortcut down to the parking area from the trail.

7.3 Arrive back at the parking area.

Optional Routes

It's possible to link up with the 13er Mount Bancroft, but that route is better done starting from Loch Lomond and getting Bancroft first (see chapter 4), as it makes a better loop. From this route, the quickest way back is the out-and-back hike on the connecting ridge between the two (1.1 miles summit to summit).

Final Thoughts

St. Marys Glacier isn't long for this world. As Colorado gets warmer, the snowfield is expected to disappear in the next twenty-five to fifty years. Enjoy it while you can.

James Peak is named for Edwin James, a botanist who was part of the first recorded ascent of Pikes Peak in 1820. For many years Pikes Peak was known as James Peak, until the current name was formalized in the mid-1800s. The current James Peak was recognized in 1866.

Finally, James Peak is a great summer hike, but it is also a good option late into the autumn or even early winter. Wind tends to blow off a lot of the snow, minimizing (but not eliminating) avalanche danger. If you go off-season, keep a sharp eye for the many ptarmigan that roost in the flats between the glacier and the south and east slopes.

St. Marys Glacier—see it while it's still there!

16 Landslide Peak–Geneva Peak

The ridge running north from Webster Pass to Santa Fe Peak contains four 13ers, two ranked (Geneva Peak and Santa Fe Peak) and two unranked (Sullivan Mountain and Landslide Peak). All are connected by the "sort of there" Continental Divide Trail, making for an excellent ridgewalk in the clouds.

Primary route: Landslide Peak, 13,238 feet; Geneva Peak, 13,266 feet
Optional summits: Sullivan Mountain, 13,134 feet; Santa Fe Peak, 13,180 feet
Difficulty rating: Easy–medium; most of the terrain here is Class 1, whether it is on trail or tundra. Extending the hike to grab the bonus peaks gets into easy Class 2 terrain for short sections.
Class rating: Class 2
Round-trip distance: 5.6 miles out and back
Elevation gain: 1,740 feet
Round-trip time: 4–6 hours; half day

Finding the trailhead: Webster Pass is a fun 4x4 road that requires good clearance. Stock SUVs with good tires will be fine, but I suggest waiting until mid- to late summer to let the inevitable snowdrifts thaw out. The main parking area is along a switchback just below the pass.

Reach the start from the quirky town of Montezuma, southeast of Keystone Ski Resort. From the intersection of Main Street (Montezuma Road) and St. John Road, go south out of town on Montezuma Road. In 0.5 mile turn left onto Webster Pass Road. In 2020 this sign was small, but it was marked. From here it is 3.3 miles to the parking area along a switchback just below Webster Pass. The first 2 miles of the road are standard "stock SUV" 4x4 fare—rocky and rutted but nothing intense. About 3 miles in, a very slow-going section at roughly 11,220 feet beside a marshy section is deeply rutted and narrow. High clearance is a must! Beyond this are a series of steep switchbacks. If you're nervous about the steepness, you can park near the bottom—it's only about a half mile up to the upper parking area. Upper parking is at the last switchback before the top of the pass, where there is room for 3 or 4 vehicles. (**Note:** If you have made it that far, going a short way up to the top of the pass and parking there is possible, though the Continental Divide Trail that accesses the peaks starts between the last switchback and the top, so you'll have to hike down to start the hike.)

Trailhead GPS: N39 31.968' / W105 50.370'

The Hike

The standard route here covers Landslide and Geneva, but it's not a big push to add in the other two. You'll need a 4x4 with good clearance to make it to the main parking area below Webster Pass, but there are options for sport-utility cars and even 2WD vehicles listed in the Optional Routes section (these start from the north end of the ridge rather than the south).

Closing in on the summit of Geneva Peak

Wandering along the Continental Divide Trail is a real treat, especially in this particular region. Connecting ridges tend to be flat and wide open, meaning views will remain spacious along the entire hike. This is one of the better dog hikes in Colorado, too, but keep an eye out for local mountain goats!

Miles and Directions

0.0 Starting from the last switchback, hike up the road a few hundred feet toward Webster Pass. (**Note:** Check out the crazy steep 4x4 road up Red Cone in front of you, which is for experienced 4x4 drivers only—do not take your SUV up there!) On your left is a turnoff for the Continental Divide Trail. It's not signed, but it has a ramshackle cairn and the trail itself is clearly defined. Head up on the trail to save a little effort getting up to the tundra en route to Landslide Peak.

1.4 Reach Point 13,214. The trail more or less fades away (as the Continental Divide Trail has a habit of doing), but the way to Geneva Peak is clear—just walk ridge tundra north.

Before getting to Geneva, there's the matter of Landslide Peak. Landslide is really just a high point on the very broad shoulder of Geneva Peak. It's so flat, it's not entirely clear where the highest point is. The trail reappears here and there, skirting the high point to the west. Aim for the highest part of the flat hump; there is a summit cairn there.

2.4 Landslide's flat summit lines up nicely with the remaining walk over to Geneva Peak. Follow the ridge northwest 0.4 mile to reach it.

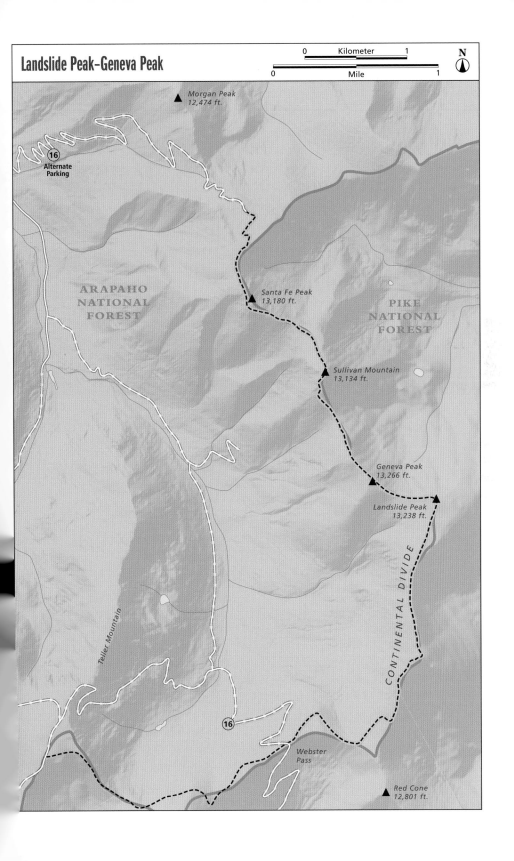

0   Kilometer   1

0   Mile   1

N

▲ Morgan Peak
12,474 ft.

⑯
Alternate
Parking

ARAPAHO
NATIONAL
FOREST

▲ Santa Fe Peak
13,180 ft.

PIKE
NATIONAL
FOREST

▲ Sullivan Mountain
13,134 ft.

▲ Geneva Peak
13,266 ft.

▲ Landslide Peak
13,238 ft.

Teller Mountain

CONTINENTAL DIVIDE

⑯

Webster
Pass

▲ Red Cone
12,801 ft.

Enjoying a pleasant walk to Landslide Peak's flat summit

2.8 Geneva Peak's top feels more like a proper summit than Landslide! Mountain goats frequent these peaks—keep an eye out for them if you have dogs in your hiking party. Sullivan Mountain and Santa Fe Peak are not far away from here. It's only 1.4 miles between Geneva and Santa Fe Peak, with Sullivan Mountain between them. If you're up for extra credit, check out the Optional Routes below. Otherwise, head back home the way you came. You can opt to stay on the ridge and pop out at Webster Pass if you like. Or take the Continental Divide Trail back down.

5.6 Arrive back at the parking at the switchback below Webster Pass.

Optional Routes

Adding on Sullivan Mountain and Santa Fe Peak as an out-and-back makes this an 8.4-mile day with a little under 3,000 vertical feet of gain—fairly reasonable by 13er standards. There's no technical terrain nor is there much exposure (Class 2). Local mountain goats are bold, so give them space if you come across them.

There are two interesting 12ers off Webster Pass: Red Cone (12,801 feet) and Handcart Peak (12,518 feet). Both are relatively easy extra-credit summits. Red Cone has a dang road right up to the summit!

If you have a sport-utility car with good clearance (Honda CRV), you may want to start this hike from the north. When you enter Montezuma, take the second left onto Third Street (FR 264). This road actually goes nearly to the summit of Santa Fe Peak, but good parking is about 1.7 miles up at 11,270 feet. Near the bottom, pass the somewhat strange water tank/basketball court park and several residences that seem out of place, then claw up seven switchbacks along a bumpy 4x4 road. There are parking pullouts along the way. I prefer to park at the aforementioned spot, which is still at tree line, though you can go higher if you choose—the road doesn't get that much more difficult.

If you hike from the north, you may opt to summit a pair of endearing 12ers: Morgan Peak (12,474 feet) and Tiptoe Peak (12,053 feet), both Class 2 and a lot of fun.

Hiking from the north may offend aesthetic mountain hikers, as you basically summit Santa Fe by walking up a 4x4 road (albeit a cool, scenic 4x4 road).

Final Thoughts

Even though Webster Pass is relatively close as the crow flies to Whale Peak (see chapter 40), the two trailheads are hours apart by vehicle and don't make for a logical linkup.

The old mining road that heads up the mountain northwest of Webster Pass ends at the Cashier Mine on Teller Mountain. The mine produced copper, lead, silver, zinc, and gold and is an interesting side hike.

The town of Montezuma that you pass en route to Webster Pass was established in 1865. Unlike many other boomtowns, it survived into the modern day, thanks in part to the presence of the Keystone ski mountain. Once boasting a population of over 10,000 around 1890, its recent census data pins its full-time residents as 68 in 2020, though there are many second homes as well.

Want to tack on a 12er? At 12,518' Handcart Peak is an easy walk up that is just under a mile (one-way) southwest off Webster Pass along the Continental Divide Trail.

17 | Mosquito Peak–Treasurevault Mountain

Colorado hikes with pristine lakes, vibrant meadows of wildflowers, and dazzling summit views are tough secrets to keep. Those that also have good access roads and fun, nontechnical trails (great for dogs) are even more popular. And two summits in a single day? It sounds like the recipe for the best hike in the Rocky Mountains, yet these peaks are seldom visited! Maybe it's the "mosquito" moniker that keeps people away?

Primary route: Mosquito Peak, 13,781 feet; Treasurevault Mountain, 13,701 feet
Optional summits: Kuss Peak, 13,548 feet; London Mountain, 13,194 feet
Difficulty rating: Medium; a thoroughly enjoyable Class 1/easy Class 2 outing

Class rating: Class 2
Round-trip distance: 5.7-mile lollipop loop
Elevation gain: 2,400 feet
Round-trip time: 4–6 hours; half day

Finding the trailhead: Take CO 9 south from Breckenridge over Hoosier Pass to the small town of Alma. (It's also possible to reach Alma from the Boulder/Denver metro area by taking US 285 to CO 9 and heading north.) About a mile south of Alma off CO 9 is Park CR 12, also known as Mosquito Pass. To reach the parking area involves driving on a bumpy 4x4 road with lots of rounded, embedded stones. SUVs and Subaru Outback–type vehicles will be fine, but low-clearance passenger cars might be challenged by a few ruts.

From the start of the road at the junction with CO 9, follow CR 12 past the small community of Park City, staying on the main road (Mosquito Pass) for 6.9 miles. At a bend in the road is a small parking area at 11,400 feet, just past the ruins of the North London Mill on your left. Most vehicles, stock SUVs included, should park here. Beyond this, Mosquito Pass transforms into a more legit 4x4 road that Jeeps and tougher SUVs can handle. This route doesn't ascend via Mosquito Pass, so driving farther than the parking area isn't really worth much—it saves only a couple of hundred feet of hiking and could really punish a stock SUV.

Trailhead GPS: N39 17.970' / W106 09.420'

The Hike

These two incredible summits don't see a lot of visitors but feature gorgeous alpine meadows, glistening lakes, spectacular views, and, as a bonus, a few interesting mining relics An early summer visit to these peaks promises to be a spectacle of color, thanks to the variety of flora that lights up the lower flanks of the mountains. The terrain is a mix of old mining roads, easy grassy slopes, and bare-bones Class 2 tundra walking with no significant exposure. A few interesting mining vehicles have been abandoned in the saddle between the peaks—they look like they'd fire right up if you had the key!

Cooling off below Mosquito Peak

Views to the west look out on the highest points of the Rocky Mountains in the Sawatch Range. In a state that is rich in gorgeous mountain vistas, these peaks stand out for their incredible perspective in all directions. There is no doubt that if these mountains were 14ers instead of 13ers, they would be among the most popular hikes.

Miles and Directions

0.0 The parking area at a switchback in the road has plenty of room for a dozen or so cars. Start the hike by continuing up the road (Mosquito Pass). It becomes immediately apparent that the nature of the pass morphs into a legit 4x4 road, but it's quite nice for hiking. As you ascend, check out the ruins of the old North London Mill to the south. There are several buildings, tram towers, and other relics to be seen.

0.6 Get off the main road (Mosquito Pass) and head right (north) on a less-traveled 4x4 road toward Cooney Lake. This road is more like a double-wide hiking path. If it has been a big snow year, water may stream down sections of the road like a river. Thankfully, there are detours through the willows. (**Note:** If you have dogs, it's best to keep them on-leash for this section—it is prime porcupine territory.)

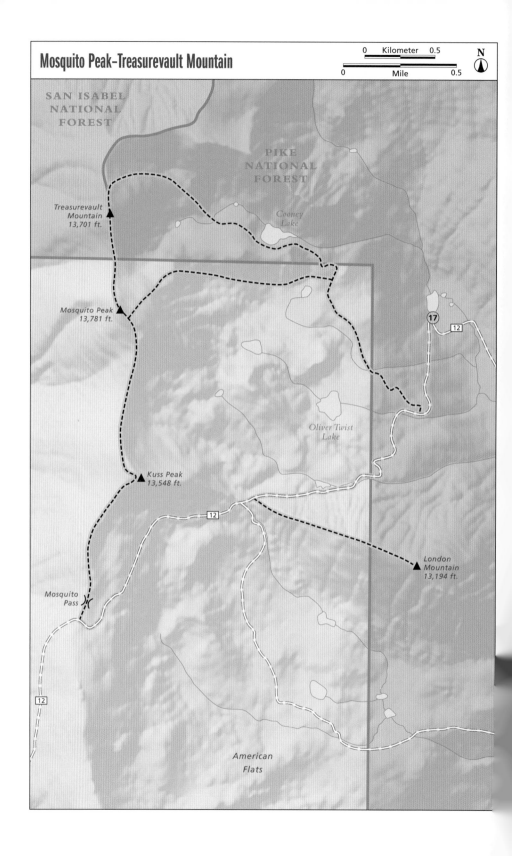

Mosquito Peak-Treasurevault Mountain

SAN ISABEL
NATIONAL
FOREST

PIKE
NATIONAL
FOREST

Treasurevault
Mountain
13,701 ft.

Cooney
Lake

Mosquito Peak
13,781 ft.

17
12

Oliver Twist
Lake

Kuss Peak
13,548 ft.

12

London
Mountain
13,194 ft.

Mosquito
Pass

12

American
Flats

0.9 Continue on the main road north/northwest as it passes a split on the left to the Dickensian body of water known as Oliver Twist Lake.

1.7 The 4x4 road ends on the shores of Cooney Lake at 12,582 feet. Mosquito Peak and Treasurevault Mountain are the obvious big peaks to the west. Even though the way up is off-trail, it is along very easy-to-follow grass slopes. Head to the northeast slopes of Treasurevault Mountain, aiming for the broad north ridge to the right of its summit. The footing is solid all the way up.

2.6 There's no reason to hit the low point in the saddle. As you ascend, veer left, toward the summit of Treasurevault Mountain. When you hit the ridge, it's an easy walk up to the summit.

2.7 Welcome to the first summit of the day, Treasurevault Mountain! To the west are commanding views of Colorado's highest peaks: 14,433-foot Mount Elbert (#1) and 14,420-foot Mount Massive (#2). When you are ready, head south along the slopes to the saddle with Mosquito Peak.

2.9 At the saddle, an old mining road twists up the western side of the slopes. As of 2019, there were still two large, yellow mining vehicles sitting in the saddle. They look more modern than most abandoned vehicles. From the saddle, carry on south along the ridge (not the road) via a social trail to the summit of Mosquito Peak. The slopes here are rocky but not terribly steep—easy Class 2 terrain.

3.1 The summit of Mosquito Peak. To the south, you can see the rest of the Mosquito Pass 4x4 road dropping west along with an array of communication towers. The bump between Mosquito Peak and Mosquito Pass is Kuss Peak, a 13,548-foot soft-ranked 13er (see the Optional Routes section for more info).

For this route, descend the gradual, grassy northeast slopes of Mosquito Peak. At the start of the hike down, this way looks rocky and steep, but walking over to the "edge" will reveal its true accommodating nature. Rather than heading back to Cooney Lake, trend right (southeast) down a modest hillside to an unnamed lake southeast of Cooney Lake. This will line you up nicely for the 4x4 road for the rest of the way down.

4.3 Reconnect with the 4x4 road. Follow it back to the junction with Mosquito Pass/CR 12 and return the way you came.

5.7 Arrive back at the parking area.

Optional Routes

For a longer day, you can hike up and over Kuss Peak to the pass, and descend Mosquito Pass east back to the parking area. This adds only 340 vertical feet and makes for a 7.1-mile round-trip.

It also makes it possible to snag 13,194-foot London Mountain (a ranked 13er) along with the trio you already will have hiked. From Mosquito Pass the obvious northwest ridge starts at the low saddle between Kuss Peak and London Mountain at 12,644 feet. The out-and-back hike is only 1.6 miles on Class 2 terrain from this point and is well worth the visit. Getting all four summits (Treasurevault, Mosquito, Kuss, London) is a great 13er four-pack that isn't overly strenuous in terms of terrain or relative difficulty.

Finishing up the traverse to Mosquito Peak with Treasurevault Mountain in the background

Final Thoughts

Of the four summits, only Mosquito Peak and London Mountain are ranked 13ers, Both Treasurevault Mountain and Kuss Peak are soft-ranked. Compared to the nearby 14er circuit of Mount Democrat, Mount Cameron, Mount Lincoln, and Mount Bross, the 13er option is much more enjoyable and far less busy.

The North London Mine started prospecting in 1870 and hit one of the biggest motherlodes in Colorado. It is connected via tunnels to the South London Mine and was operated by the London Mine Company. Gold ore was extracted for an incredibly long time by mining standards: sixty-one years (from 1870 to 1931). The mine yielded over $9 million worth of ore—and that was in early 1900s money!

I mention all this because this area was the only place in all my thousands of miles of mountain hiking in Colorado that I found a small piece of gold out in the open. It's probably not worth all that much (it's a 3-ounce stone that has other rock intrusions), but for all the mines I've hiked near, this is the only one where I "struck gold."

18 Mount Adams

An extended adventure that involves steep slopes and Class 3 scrambling, Mount Adams is made for gutsy scramblers who appreciate a well-earned summit. Beautiful ridgelines pass both north and south from the summit. This route takes the south ridge from Willow Lake.

Primary route: Mount Adams, 13,931 feet
Optional summits: UN 13,546; UN 13,580 A
Difficulty rating: Hard; a long warm-up on a Class 1 trail, off-trail into a high alpine basin, and a daring ridge connecting UN 13,546 and Mount Adams. The mostly Class 2 ridge concludes with a thrilling Class 3 summit scramble on classic Crestone conglomerate rock.

Class rating: Class 3
Round-trip distance: 11.2 miles out and back
Elevation gain: 4,970 feet
Round-trip time: 6–9 hours; full day or overnight

Finding the trailhead: Starting from the intersection of US 50 and US 285 in Poncha Springs, take US 285 south 26 miles and then take a left onto CO 17 toward the town of Moffat. In 13.5 miles, just south of Moffat, is the signed turnoff to the left (east) for the weird little town of Crestone along CO Road-T. At 11.4 miles Road-T ends and turns into Birch Street at a left bend in the road. This is the main road through Crestone. Follow it to another bend (Golden Avenue), then a second bend (Alder Street) into town. After a few hundred feet, take a right onto Galena Street. It is 2.3 miles to the trailhead from here. The road eventually turns to dirt and has a few sandy ruts, but 2WD cars can make the trailhead if driven carefully. The road ends with ample parking at the Willow Creek Trailhead.

Trailhead GPS: N37 59.334' / W105 39.756'

The Hike

The 13ers Mount Adams and UN 13,546 share a common ridge, but it's a tall order to knock out both in a day (most folks go one at a time). The primary route here is Mount Adams, but the two peaks are so similar in character that either will make for a great mountain day. They share a common saddle and both start with easy ridgewalks that lead to exciting scrambling on fantastic Crestone conglomerate rock.

Navigating to Mount Adams's airy summit block takes you into Class 3 territory with a bit of route-finding at the very top. The aforementioned Crestone conglomerate rock is characterized by sturdy slabs firmly embedded with rounded stones—quite unlike most of the other alpine rock in Colorado.

The approach hike shares a well-worn trail to Willow Lake, better known as the jumping-off point for two popular 14ers: Challenger Point and Kit Carson Peak. You'll quickly break from the pack when you detour up to the 13ers instead of the

Checking out Mount Adams's distinct summit block from Willow Lake

14ers. Because of its long-ish approach to Willow Lake (4.25 miles), this is a good one to consider as an overnight. With nearly 5,000 feet of vertical gain, breaking up the adventure into two days is a wise choice.

Miles and Directions

0.0 From the Willow Creek Trailhead, you have a long 4.25-mile Class 1 hike to Willow Lake. The trail is very well defined and gains elevation quickly—2,680 vertical feet just to get to the lake. There are plenty of dispersed campsites around the lake, making this a prime candidate for an overnight adventure. If trying the climb as a single-day hike, be certain you have a safe forecast and start very early (3 or 4 a.m. would be prudent). Either way, your first goal is to reach Willow Lake.

4.25 Arrive at Willow Lake. Stay on the trail to the north side of the lake. The route is about to get off-trail to the north, but you want to avoid the worst parts of a large boulder field that skirts the bottom of the basin. Where the forest thins along the established trail is a good place to get off-trail and begin to ascend north. There are some social trails heading up into the basin but no single established trail. The slopes into the basin are strewn with rock and a few patches of trees. Continue to gain elevation as you head into the main basin. Stay on target for the saddle between Adams and 13,546, making sure not to trend into the gully on your left or the rocky slopes to your right. Eventually, the trees and flora give way to open views.

Mount Adams

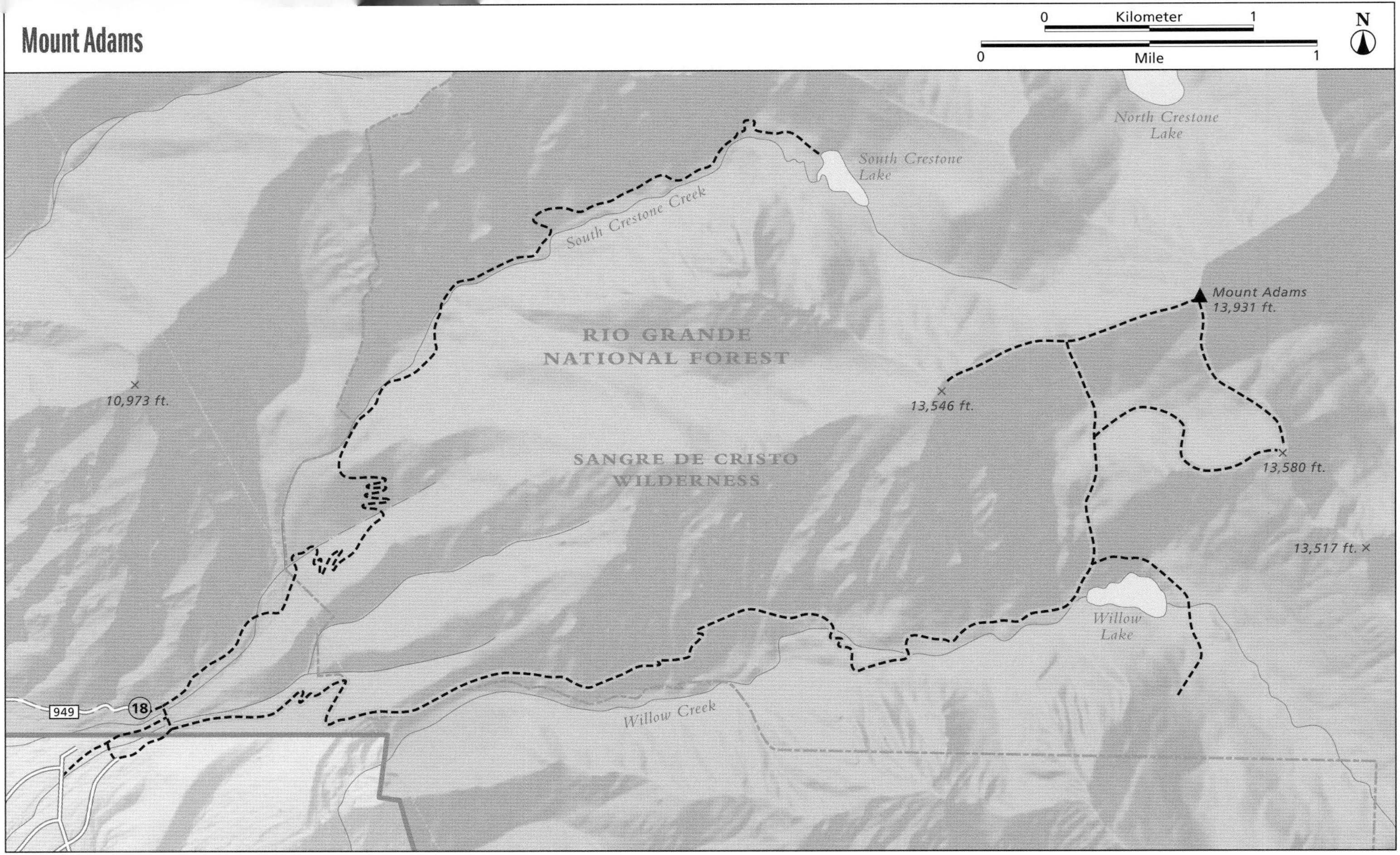

North Crestone Lake

South Crestone Lake

South Crestone Creek

Mount Adams
13,931 ft.

13,580 ft. ×

13,517 ft. ×

Willow Lake

Willow Creek

RIO GRANDE
NATIONAL FOREST

SANGRE DE CRISTO
WILDERNESS

13,546 ft. ×

10,973 ft. ×

18

949

N

Kilometer

Mile

0   1

0   1

4.7 Arriving at the flattish upper basin north of Willow Lake, the saddle appears dead north with UN 13,546 to the left, Mount Adams to the right. Grunt your way up the saddle along grassy slopes. If your goal is Adams, stay just right of the sandy gully that splits the slopes as the grassy footing will be better. For 13,546, you can start angling left of the saddle as the slopes offer a nice bypass of the low point of the saddle.

5.0 At 12,940 feet, reach the saddle. The summit of Adams is only about 0.6 mile away, but there are still close to 1,000 vertical feet to go. Go right (east) along social trails along easy Class 2 terrain to start. These trails stay right and below the ridge and offer the best footing, though the ridge proper is still fairly tame at this point—either works for now. As the ridge climbs and gets steeper, conglomerate slabs start to appear. Staying right of the ridge is still the best way to go once you've reached the halfway point. If sticking to the ridge, you will eventually have to drop down to skirt a rock wall barring the way to the summit. Staying below the ridge saves you this minor detour.

5.5 The closer you get to the summit, the more intimidating the finish looks. As you approach the last 100 vertical feet, you'll have to drop right (south) below the ridge when faced with a rock outcrop guarding the finish. Traverse this rock feature below it on the south (right) side. Skirt low enough to go around the tower and find a hidden notch of Class 3 rock that offers a ramp to the summit block. After about 30 feet of climbing, you'll meet what is likely the crux of the climb (for most people). Atop the Class 3 gully, turn right onto exposed rock (Class 3) for a brief scramble before the last steps to the summit ease up into Class 2 terrain. Take note of where you came up so you can scramble back down!

Mount Adams (right) and UN 13,546 (left)

5.6 The sparse summit of Mount Adams has great views in all directions, including the twisting, shadowy northeast ridge. Getting off the summit block and back onto the south side of the ridge requires a bit of brave downclimbing to regain the notch below the rock outcrop. Once beyond the crux scramble, the walk down resumes its less-intense demeanor.

6.1 Descending into the basin is relatively easy on a clear day. Go directly south until reconnecting with the Willow Lake Trail, and return along the Class 1 path to the parking area.

11.2 Arrive back at the Willow Creek Trailhead.

Optional Routes

UN 13,546

From the saddle between Adams and UN 13,546, take a left (west) and follow this ridge 0.4 mile to the summit. The terrain along the ridge has a bit of tricky Class 2+/3 routefinding, and the better terrain is going to be along the left (south) side of the steep slopes. It's about 590 feet from the saddle (depending on where you can gain the ridge).

UN 13,580 A

This scrappy 13er might not be for everyone, but it's possible to get it as an add-on from Adams's summit (Class 2+/3), then descend into the basin along its western slopes north of its stubby western ridge.

Another option is to climb it as its own adventure, getting into the high basin below Mount Adams and going east (right) up the western slopes (Class 2+). The rock is loose in places and there are a lot of boulders, but it does have its own charm.

Combo

Knocking out all three in a single outing (best done from a base camp at Willow Lake) is the semi-famous "Adams Family Tour." Most Adams Family Tourists go up the saddle to UN 13,546 to Mount Adams to UN 13,580 A, then descend its creepy and kooky western slopes.

Final Thoughts

Mount Adams has an equally thrilling northeast ridge, accessed from the Horn Lakes. You'll get a great look at it from the summit. The west ridge is a more enjoyable route thanks to better rock and avoiding the 1,000-foot grassy slopes used to access the northeast ridge.

Summit-crazy climbers can make a *huge* weekend out of Willow Lake by grabbing the 14ers Challenger Point and Kit Carson one day, then whatever Adams Family peaks they like the next.

UN 13,580 A is one of five (!) ranked 13ers with an official elevation of 13,580 feet! UN 13,580 B is also in this guide (see chapter 6, Bent Peak–Carson Peak–UN 13,580) and is my favorite of all of them (Mount Powell is the "highest" of the group). These five make up the 198th to 202nd highest ranked 13ers.

19 Mount Alice–Chiefs Head Peak

While Longs Peak is the undisputed king of Rocky Mountain National Park, Mount Alice makes for a very fitting queen. This noble 13er follows a similar blueprint to Longs: a lengthy approach followed by robust, late-in-the-game scrambling.

Primary route: Mount Alice, 13,310 feet; Chiefs Head Peak, 13,579 feet
Difficulty rating: Hard; solid Class 3 scrambling on good rock with several interesting descent options. Big mileage, but the approach will go quickly for fit hikers. Good overnight potential.
Class rating: Class 3

Round-trip distance: Mount Alice only, 16.0 miles out and back; Chiefs Head Peak only, 16.8 miles out and back; combo, 18.4-mile lollipop loop
Elevation gain: Mount Alice, 4,825 feet; Chiefs Head, 5,050 feet; combo, 5,800 feet
Round-trip time: 9–12 hours; very long full day or overnight

Finding the trailhead: This adventure begins at Wild Basin in Rocky Mountain National Park. All cars can make the trailhead via a well-maintained dirt road. The turnoff to Wild Basin is off CO 7. Coming from the south, the turn is 6.5 miles north of CO 7 and CO 72 (past Allenspark). Coming from the north, the turnoff is 13 miles from the intersection of US 36 and CO 7. The road is well signed. From the turnoff, go 2.6 miles to the Wild Basin Ranger Station and the parking beyond. If you plan on doing either of the summits or the combo as a single-day outing, I highly advise the alpine start—being on the trail no later than 3 a.m. For overnight camping options, read below.

Trailhead GPS: N40 12.486' / W105 33.906'

Fees, Regulations, and Overnight Camping: Standard National Park Service entrance fees apply. If you'd like to overnight in the park, you'll need to secure a backcountry permit (fee per trip, not per person) from Rocky Mountain National Park. Please visit www.nps.gov/romo/planyourvisit/wild_guide.htm or call (970) 586-1206 for more information.

The ideal backcountry sites for this adventure are North St. Vrain, which is 3.5 miles from the trailhead and sits at 9,500 feet (a good elevation for acclimatization), or the Siskin site just past North St. Vrain, at 3.7 miles and 9,600 feet. There is also camping at Thunder Lake, which can be part of a large lollipop loop (more on this in the Optional Routes section).

The Hike

Mount Alice features a beautiful approach and excellent scrambling. The Class 3 terrain here isn't terribly exposed or perilous, meaning you'll get to enjoy good hands-on movement without big fall potential.

Chiefs Head doesn't offer the excitement of Mount Alice's enjoyable scramble, but its summit ridge does get whittled down to about 15 feet wide for a thrilling finish.

Mount Alice's Class 3 ridge is a fun, exciting scramble.

For a single day out, Mount Alice is the better option. Despite the monster mileage, the approach from Wild Basin to Lion Lakes (roughly 6 miles) will go quickly for fit hikers. Many hikers choose to knock these peaks off one at a time, and that's a reasonable approach. Uber-fit hikers with a perfect weather window can get both in a single outing. Thankfully, there are some nice overnight camping options available that can break up the effort into two or three days.

It is highly advised to save this hike for midsummer through early autumn. Snow tends to linger in the basin, and it is a miserable experience to post-hole through miles of alpine meadows. This route assumes an out-and-back hike of Mount Alice but will also provide beta for Chiefs Head.

Miles and Directions

0.0   Start at Wild Basin's main trailhead along the Thunder Lake/Ouzel Falls Trail. Continue on the Thunder Lake Trail as it passes the split to Copeland Falls.

1.4   A marked sign splits the trail. Go right onto the Campground Trail rather than left toward Ouzel Falls. This is a more direct path to the Lion Lakes area and will save you about 2 total miles on your day (though you will miss the falls). If you're absolutely crazy about waterfalls and don't want to miss them, visit on the return hike.

2.8 The Campground Trail ends and connects back into the Thunder Lake Trail at a bridge. Stay on the Thunder Lake Trail for another mile.

3.8 At another marked junction, leave the Thunder Lake Trail and head toward Lion Lakes on what is now the Lion Lakes Trail. (If you're curious why the mileage back to the ranger station is listed as 4.8 on this sign, it is because it is measuring the extra mile along the Thunder Lake Trail that you bypassed by taking the Campground Trail.) Stay on the Lion Lakes Trail for another 2 miles until it fades out at the namesake lakes. This is one of the most beautiful wilderness areas in all of Colorado.

5.8 The formal trail fades out into meadows of grass and rock as you enter the basin. Mount Alice's distinct pyramid comes into full view. If you catch this area when wildflowers are in full bloom (midsummer most years), you will traverse along a spectacular carpet of color as you ascend. This is the end of the formal trail. Continue into the basin, passing the first Lion Lake and scrambling up to the "shelves" that guide your way up. There are some faint social trails and cairns in the area.

6.0 Reach Trio Falls, a nifty waterfall area that may have one, two, or all three cascades streaming down when you arrive. Above these falls is Lion Lake 2. Stay on the left side of this lake (southwest) and aim for the spur that connects to Hourglass Ridge, which is the high ground that connects Alice and Chiefs Head.

6.2 Stay high and left (south) of Snowbank Lake, the last of the large lakes in the basin. Most years, ice and snow cause this 11,526-foot lake to glow ghostly blue. The spur is easy to follow, with a little Class 2 scrambling along the way.

7.2 At 12,540 feet you'll finally hit Hourglass Ridge—the very long warm-up is over! Mount Alice's tough-looking north ridge awaits to the south. If Mount Alice is your only goal, skip the next paragraph.

    If you're aiming for Chiefs Head (or the combo), follow the broad plateau north, then head east along Chiefs Head's Class 2 west/northwest slopes. It is roughly 1.2 miles and 1,050 feet of vertical gain from the spur to the summit. Most of this is done along easy tundra, though the last 0.25 mile introduces a boulder field into the fray. The summit approach narrows down to about 15 feet in width, making for an exciting finish! Return the way you came to the spur and head for home or continue to Mount Alice.

    To reach the summit of Mount Alice, go south and a little bit downhill to a distinct notch.

7.5 At the notch, you are only 0.5 mile to the top, and the route looks tricky. However, the rock here is better than it looks from a distance. The Class 3 scrambling is a lot of fun, and staying slightly right (west) can minimize exposure. After all your hard work to get here, you've earned one of the best scrambles in the Rocky Mountains. Follow it to the top.

8.0 Alice's impressive summit offers some of the very best views in Rocky Mountain National Park—and that's saying something! The quickest and most efficient way back is to return the way you came—though it's not my favorite way down (read the Optional Routes for details on the Boulder-Grand Pass descent). Navigating back through the Lion Lakes area is fairly easy in good weather—just follow the trickling streams to the main lakes and regain the trail. Remember, you'll have the option to take the Campground Trail or Ouzel Falls Trail on the return. If you have the legs and the time for it, Ouzel Falls is worth the visit.

16.0 Arrive back at Wild Basin's main parking area.

Mount Alice–Chiefs Head Peak

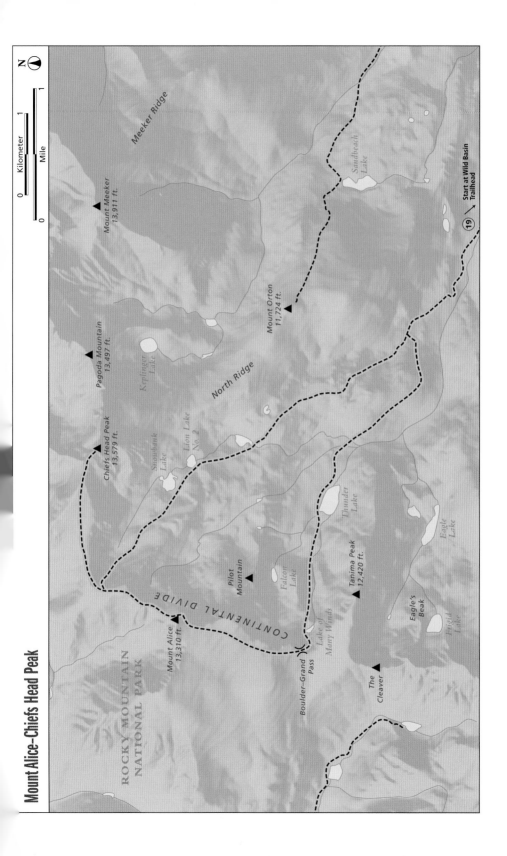

ROCKY MOUNTAIN
NATIONAL PARK

Mount Alice
13,310 ft.

Chiefs Head Peak
13,579 ft.

Pagoda Mountain
13,497 ft.

Mount Meeker
13,911 ft.

Meeker Ridge

Keplinger Lake

North Ridge

Snowbank Lake

Lion Lake No. 2

Mount Orton
11,724 ft.

Sandbeach Lake

CONTINENTAL DIVIDE

Pilot Mountain

Falcon Lake

Thunder Lake

Boulder–Grand Pass

Lake of Many Winds

Tanima Peak
12,420 ft.

The Cleaver

Eagle's Beak

Eagle Lake

Pool Lake

19 → Start at Wild Basin Trailhead

N

0   1   Kilometer
0   1   Mile

Boulder–Grand Pass Descent

Note: This adds only about 0.2 mile (about 16.2 miles total) to your total day versus the out-and-back but requires a bit of bushwhacking to reach Thunder Lake. It's 4.3 miles back to the Thunder Lake/Lion Lakes Trail junction.

This is my preferred full route for Mount Alice. It's roughly the same mileage as descending Hourglass Ridge and traversing down through the Lion Lakes basin. It is best done in late summer due to the fact that Boulder–Grand Pass can hold on to bulletproof ice and snow late into the year. If you are aiming to do this route at any time before August, you'll want to have crampons (not microspikes) and an ice axe. It's a good idea to call Rocky Mountain National Park about conditions before you go.

This option descends south off Mount Alice along a dreamy, Class 1 tundra walk to Boulder–Grand Pass. From there it drops down the pass to the accurately named Lake of Many Winds, then down a drainage that requires a short (but easy) bit of bushwhacking before reaching Thunder Lake and the Thunder Lake Trail.

Before descending Boulder–Grand Pass, there is an optional easy Class 1 walkup to nearby 12,420-foot Tanima Peak. It's 0.5 mile from the top of Boulder–Grand Pass and gains only 340 feet. It's worth the extra mile of work just for the views of Isolation Peak to the southwest and the elusive Moomaw Glacier/Frigid Lake to the south.

Boulder–Grand Pass does have something of a climber's trail that thaws out in warmer years. But chances are you'll be skittering down the Class 2 dirt off-trail to the Lake of Many Winds before the terrain eases up to the clearly visible Thunder Lake.

From Thunder Lake, it's a welcome 1.4 miles on an easy, established path (the Thunder Lake Trail) back to the junction with the Lion Lakes Trail, then 3.8 miles back to the parking area via the Thunder Lake Trail (assuming you again take the Campground Trail option).

Thunder Lake Camping Option

Thunder Lake has a designated campground and a patrol cabin, so it is possible to overnight and day hike Mount Alice by going up and down Boulder–Grand Pass. While this is an efficient way to grab the summit, it completely misses the Lion Lakes area. Of course, it is possible to make a loop by descending Hourglass Ridge to the Lion Lakes area and taking the trails back up to Thunder Lake.

If you're going big—Chiefs Head and Alice in a day—and want the best overnight location, camp at the Siskin site. Get up nice and early, then ascend via Lion Lakes to Chiefs Head, over to Alice, and then, ideally, down via Boulder–Grand Pass.

Final Thoughts

Mount Alice is one of my top ten 13ers—heck, it's one of my top ten summit hikes in the entire state of Colorado. It's hard to put into words just how stunning the Lion Lakes area is. Amazingly, the tundra walk south off Mount Alice is equally moving, especially if you are touring the area in early autumn when the flora is holding on to its last flecks of color and the low sun casts long shadows across the plateau.

Chiefs Head is by no means a "bad" 13er, but it is a lot more straightforward than Mount Alice and lacks the excitement of a good scramble. One bonus exclusive to Chiefs Head is the view to the north of the craggy, spiky ridge to The Spearhead (12,575 feet).

Nearing the summit of Mount Alice with Lion Lakes in the background

20 Mount Audubon–Paiute Peak

Mount Audubon's familiar dome dominates the western skyline from Boulder's high mesas. It's also one of the most enjoyable day hikes on any 13er, thanks to its mix of terrain and stunning views. Pushing on to Paiute Peak makes for a big day and requires good route-finding along a Class 3 ridge that has sections of exposure.

Primary route: Mount Audubon, 13,223 feet; Paiute Peak, 13,088 feet
Difficulty rating: Medium (Audubon); hard (Paiute). Mount Audubon follows a Class 2 trail to a high saddle, where a brief section of light scrambling opens the way to the summit. Strong hikers have the option to link up with Paiute Peak via an exciting Class 3 out-and-back ridgewalk.

Class rating: Class 2 (Audubon); Class 3 (Paiute)
Round-trip distance: Mount Audubon only, 7.7 miles out and back; combo, 9.5 miles out and back
Elevation gain: Mount Audubon only, 2,700 feet; combo, 3,300 feet
Round-trip time: 6–9 hours; full day

Finding the trailhead: This hike begins at the Mitchell Lake Trailhead at the popular (and busy) Brainard Lake Recreation Area. It's no exaggeration that trailhead parking here tends to fill up by 6 a.m. most summer weekends. Brainard Lake can be reached by taking CO 72 (Peak-to-Peak Highway) 11.8 miles from the town of Nederland and turning left (west) onto Brainard Lake Road. It's also possible to go up Left Hand Canyon from US 36 in Boulder, through the town of Ward, and top out on CO 72. Take a right here and a quick left to go up the Brainard Lake Road. Follow the paved road 2.5 miles to the pay station, then 2.8 miles more to the signed Mitchell Lake Trailhead.

An entrance fee, which covers a 3-day pass, is required. Access to the area is free when the gate closes for the season (usually October to May), but you have to walk/bike from the winter parking lot at the pay station to the trailhead. If you get there too late, you'll have to park at one of the alternative lots.

Note: The Pawnee Campground is a nice place to stay the night before your hike. It does fill up quickly, so check the website at www.recreation.gov/camping/campgrounds/232282 for reservations.

Trailhead GPS: N40 04.974' / W105 34.896'

The Hike

Mount Audubon is a classic 13er, thanks to its well-traveled Class 2 trail that leads to a final Class 2+ scramble to its broad, open summit. Paiute Peak kicks up the adventure, offering a daring Class 3 ridge whose summit block requires scrambling up grippy rock slabs. Paired up, they make for a big day.

This is a very popular area thanks to its proximity to Boulder and Denver, but traffic on the mountain disperses nicely—most people at the Brainard Lake Recreation

Descending the summit of Mount Audubon

Area are there to hike to the lower-elevation lakes. Both summits are good respective representatives of the kinds of mountains found in the Indian Peaks Wilderness: either rounded domes encrusted with rocky summits (Audubon) or jagged, dramatic spires (Paiute).

Miles and Directions

0.0 Begin on the signed Mount Audubon Trail on the north side of the parking area. This trailhead is often crowded because it shares a starting point with the very popular Mitchell Lake/Blue Lake Trail. Thankfully, the Mount Audubon Trail is the less busy of the trails. The first mile is through a shaded forest with slight elevation gain, making for a nice warm-up.

1.0 Views briefly open to the west as you begin a series of switchbacks that climb to tree line. As you ascend, trees give way to alpine shrubs and the on-trail footing gets rocky in places.

1.7 At the junction with the Beaver Creek Trail, stay west on the obvious trajectory toward Mount Audubon on the Mount Audubon Trail. The walk up to the saddle between Mount Audubon and its neighbor UN 12,706 (aka "Mount Notabon") is subject to fierce winds, so don't be surprised if gusts get pushy.

3.4 If it's windy, the gale will reach its maximum fury at the saddle at 12,690 feet. Oftentimes the wind at the summit is less intense than at the saddle—hopefully, you're up

The snowy approach to Mount Audubon's summit

Mount Audubon–Paiute Peak

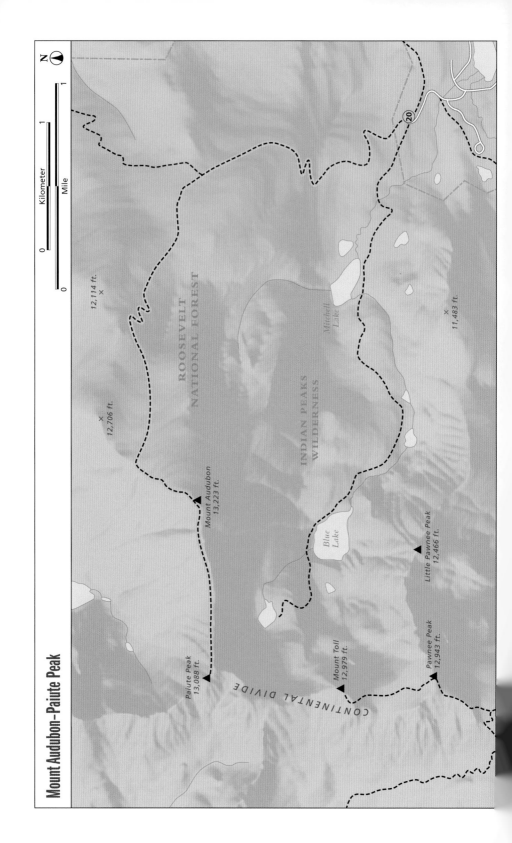

N

0 Kilometer 1

0 Mile 1

20

12,114 ft.
×

ROOSEVELT
NATIONAL FOREST

12,706 ft.
×

Mitchell
Lake

INDIAN PEAKS
WILDERNESS

11,483 ft.
×

Mount Audubon
13,223 ft.

Blue
Lake

Little Pawnee Peak
12,466 ft.

Paiute Peak
13,088 ft.

Mount Toll
12,979 ft.

CONTINENTAL DIVIDE

Pawnee Peak
12,943 ft.

there on a calm day. From here a patchwork of trails goes southwest up to the summit of Mount Audubon. There is no single established trail, but the scrambling here is relatively straightforward—even if it takes your breath away in places! It's less than a half mile to the top from here, but this last push is work. At 13,200 feet the hill levels off and it's a short walk to the summit. Not surprisingly, hikers have built several wind shelters on the summit plateau.

3.8 From the summit of Audubon, the ridge to Paiute heads dead west. The ridge is 0.8 mile one-way and gains 390 feet. (If Audubon alone was your goal, pick your way back down to the Mount Audubon Trail and head for home.) Paiute's out-and-back hike from Audubon's summit will take most hikers between 90 minutes to 2 hours. It's better done in late summer/early autumn when the rocks tend to be free of ice and snow. Most of this ridge is Class 2+ with some exposure. The Class 3 route-finding comes into play near the summit of Paiute Peak. A series of slabs on the south side of the ridge offers the best terrain. Don't underestimate the challenge to finish Paiute; it's the toughest scrambling you'll have all day.

4.6 The summit of Paiute Peak. This route returns the way you came, back to Mount Audubon. Carefully descend the summit of Paiute Peak and carry on back to the summit of Mount Audubon.

5.4 Back on the summit of Audubon, follow the route back down to the Mount Audubon Trail and to the parking area.

9.5 Arrive back at the Mitchell Lake Trailhead.

Optional Routes

Experienced climbers can continue south to 12,979-foot Mount Toll, but this involves some very tricky route-finding on the west side of the ridge between the two with sustained Class 3/4 terrain—even a few Class 5 moves if your route-finding isn't precise. From Mount Toll, hikers can drop down to Blue Lake on its eastern slopes or carry all the way over Pawnee Peak (12,943 feet) and Pawnee Pass.

If the winds are howling, you may want to hold off on making the traverse to Paiute. That said, Mount Audubon on its own is a fantastic summit and the scramble over to Paiute Peak is a lot of fun when conditions cooperate.

Final Thoughts

I mention the presence of the wind because Mount Audubon is my "backyard 13er." At the time of this writing, I've been to the summit twenty-six times, including winter ascents, midnight climbs, and ascents via five different routes (Mount Audubon Trail, SE Ridge, Crooked Couloir, North Couloirs, and South Slopes). Rarely have I had a day where the wind wasn't blowing with authority. The wind gauge I carry has gotten pinned at 65 mph (its max reading) more than once.

"Mount Notabon" (UN 12,706) is a nice add-on summit on the way back down off Audubon. Views north to Longs Peak are spectacular, as are the views in all directions. You can see the shimmering office buildings of Denver to the east on a clear day from Audubon's summit.

21 Mount Flora

Mount Flora is an excellent introduction to 13ers. It's a fine day hike that grants efficient access to the Continental Divide. Tour the defunct Berthoud Pass Ski Area en route to this ranked 13er. Views west make the heart soar as they gaze out to the rugged kingdom of the Gore Range. This may be the best, most accessible tundra walk within about an hour of Denver.

Primary route: Mount Flora, 13,132 feet
Difficulty rating: Easy; a Class 1/2 trail to the scenic summit high on the Continental Divide
Class rating: Class 2

Round-trip distance: 6.4 miles out and back
Elevation gain: 1,830 feet
Round-trip time: 4–6 hours; half day

Finding the trailhead: West of Denver, take exit 232 off I-70 onto US 40 toward the small town of Empire. Follow the paved road up Berthoud Pass 14.8 miles to a large parking lot at the former Berthoud Pass Ski Area. There is an abundance of parking as well as a warming hut and restrooms at the base. The ski area closed in 2003 but is still very popular with backcountry enthusiasts.

Trailhead GPS: N39 47.886' / W105 46.620'

The Hike

The standard route up Mount Flora begins on the grounds of the defunct Berthoud Pass Ski Area. Many hikers also choose to make a quick and relatively easy detour to the summit of the 12er Colorado Mines Peak, where an array of concrete buildings and communication towers decorate the former ski area's summit.

Mount Flora's trail is easy to follow as it rolls along rounded ridgelines and slopes, culminating in a flat summit field. From here, gaze east upon the Colorado plains all the way to Denver, or take in the western views of the foreboding Gore Range. Wildflowers coat the tundra in late spring. Seeing the wild contours of Berthoud Pass may give you a new appreciation for the engineering involved in creating paved mountain passes!

Miles and Directions

0.0   Start by walking over to the access road on the southeast side of the parking lot. This is the old snowcat access road from the Berthoud Pass Ski Area. The bottom part of the road provides a nice bit of shade and is a good warm-up for the hike ahead. Stay on the road as it switchbacks up to the Mount Flora Trail junction.

0.8   The Mount Flora Trail is signed at a switchback along the road. Take the singletrack trail as it side-cuts Colorado Mines Peak en route to the saddle between Colorado Mines Peak and Mount Flora's southwest shoulder. Views begin to open up to the west and south.

Enjoying a shoulder season traverse to Mount Flora with Colorado Mines Peak in the background

Vehicles on Berthoud Pass look like toy cars as you ascend. Stay on the trail as it gains the ridge and continues to climb northeast.

2.3 At 12,805 feet arrive at Flora's "false summit." It's not really a false summit because the hulking dome of Mount Flora has been visible for most of the hike, but it's easy to mistake this point as Mount Flora's summit if you weren't sure where on the ridge it was. The next push up steep slopes follows a rocky Class 2 trail. This will be the toughest part of the day if you're doing Mount Flora as an out-and-back hike. The ridge eventually flattens out the closer it gets to Flora's broad summit plateau.

3.2 Mount Flora's summit is marked with a large cairn. Views here are spectacular in all directions. To the north, Mount Eva (only 2 feet lower than Flora) stands tall along the Continental Divide and behind it is the highest peak in the area, 13,391-foot Parry Peak. To the southeast is an off-trail ridge that connects to 12,889-foot Breckenridge Peak in 1.2 miles one-way. When you're ready to head home, simply go back the way you came.

6.4 Arrive back at the old ski area parking lot.

Optional Routes

Mount Flora is the only 13er that is easily won from Berthoud Pass, though hardcore hikers can do a point-to-point hike along the Divide that connects the 13ers Flora, Eva, Parry, Mount Bancroft, and even James Peak (park the second car at the James Peak/St. Marys Glacier parking area).

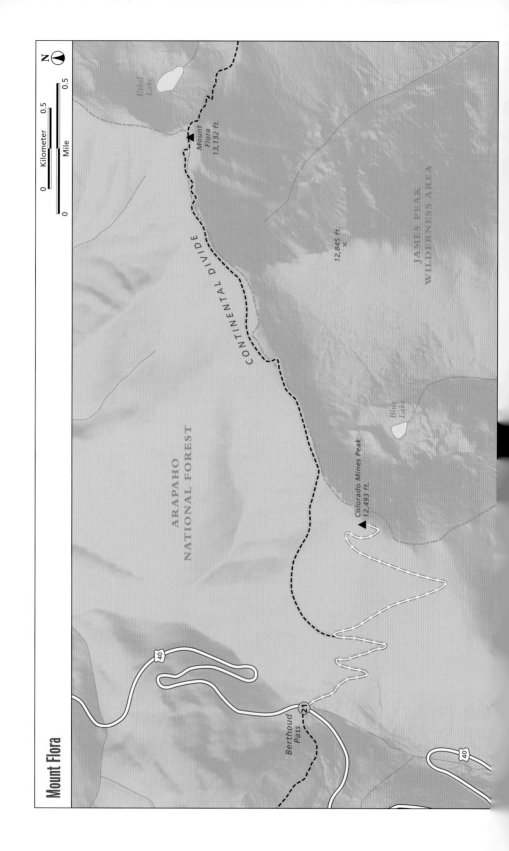

Mount Flora

A snowy wonderland seen during a spring descent of Mount Flora

Less burly would be the obvious detour up to Colorado Mines Peak (12,493 feet). It makes sense to get this one before Flora if you want to add it on. Simply follow the snowcat road to the top to get a closer look at the communication buildings on the summit. Walk off the summit north and reconnect with the Mount Flora Trail in the saddle.

Two named 12ers spur southeast off the Divide here: the aforementioned Breckenridge Peak and 12,244-foot Cone Mountain. Both are rugged, Class 2, off-trail walks.

Final Thoughts

South of Mount Flora, one can see an impressive collection of 13ers: Engelmann Peak, Robeson Peak, Bard Peak, and Mount Parnassus. This quartet can be climbed in a single outing, though this guide takes two different routes to explore them (Mount Parnassus, chapter 26, and Bard Peak via the 7:30 Mine Trail, chapter 5).

Mount Flora is rare in that it is a 13er with an established trail all the way to its summit. In that sense it's a very good "normal" hike that doesn't demand navigational savvy. Because you are above tree line most of the day, the amazing views are well worth the visit. This is also a nice hike for pups—just watch out for the steep drops and cornices of snow off the east ridge.

22 Mount Hope

Mount Hope pushes up Hope Pass, then takes the express route along a ridge that is mostly Class 2+ scrambling with just a hint of Class 3 toward the summit. This impressive adventure is often lost in a sea of 14ers in the area, meaning you'll likely have the entire route to yourself.

Primary route: Mount Hope, 13,933 feet
Optional summits: Quail Mountain, 13,461 feet
Difficulty rating: Medium–hard; Mount Hope's east ridge spurs off a beautiful section of the Colorado Trail (Class 2). The Class 2+/3 ridge is along mostly solid rock without much exposure. Hands-on scrambling sections are brief, fun, and give character to the ridge.
Class rating: Class 2+/3
Round-trip distance: 7.0-mile lollipop loop
Elevation gain: 4,070 feet
Round-trip time: 6–8 hours; full day

Finding the trailhead: The trail starts at Sheep Gulch Trailhead along CR 390 near Buena Vista. It is passable by passenger cars. Take US 24 20 miles south of Leadville or 15 miles north of Buena Vista to Chaffee CR 390. Turn west onto CR 390 and follow it 9.4 miles to the Sheep Gulch Trailhead on the right (north) side of the road. Parking is allowed along the road.

Trailhead GPS: N38 59.700' / W106 24.246'

The Hike

Mount Hope lives "next door" and across the valley from a collection of 14ers, including Huron Peak, Mount Belford, and Missouri Mountain. Because it isn't a 14er, it sees much less traffic than its lofty neighbors. Mount Hope's approach along Hope Pass/Colorado Trail is wonderful, especially as it breaks tree line.

Unlike a lot of Sawatch Range hikes, the forests fade into open alpine meadows rather than shrubby krummholz. Hope Pass is a destination hike in itself and is an incredible sight to behold during autumn's changing colors, but it's only the beginning of the fun. Mount Hope's east ridge is an aesthetically pleasing line that hovers between Class 2+ and Class 3. Climbers can downclimb the ridge or detour down steep Class 2 slopes to wrap up the day. Quail Mountain is a ranked 13er to the east of Mount Hope, and it's the perfect peak for people who love bland summit slogs.

Miles and Directions

0.0 From the Sheep Gulch Trailhead, take the Colorado Trail north. This is also the Hope Pass Trail and is signed. There is nothing tricky about this section of the hike. Follow the trail as it climbs up through a beautiful pine forest and breaks tree line into a series of switchbacks leading up to the saddle of Hope Pass.

Top: Mount Hope standing above Hope Pass
Bottom: Mount Hope's east ridge offers the most direct way to the summit. The south slopes avoid scrambling but are a slog to chug up.

2.7 Hope Pass tops out at 12,550 feet. The east ridge awaits. It is 0.9 mile to the top. The first portion of the ridge consists of Class 2 terrain along the wider lower shoulder. Halfway up, the ridge narrows and shifts to Class 2+ terrain with light scrambling. The best terrain on the ridge alternates between the ridge proper and below the ridge on the south side of the peak. At 13,580 feet are a few rock sections (the crux) that are passed with easy Class 3 scrambling moves. Beyond this, an easy, flat walk concludes at the well-earned summit.

3.6 Hope's summit is decorated with a cairn, and the views are astounding—Colorado's highest mountain, Mount Elbert (14,443 feet) is the king of the northern horizon. Besides a bevy of 14ers to the north, west, and south, the underrated 13er Rinker Peak (13,783 feet) can be seen to the northwest.

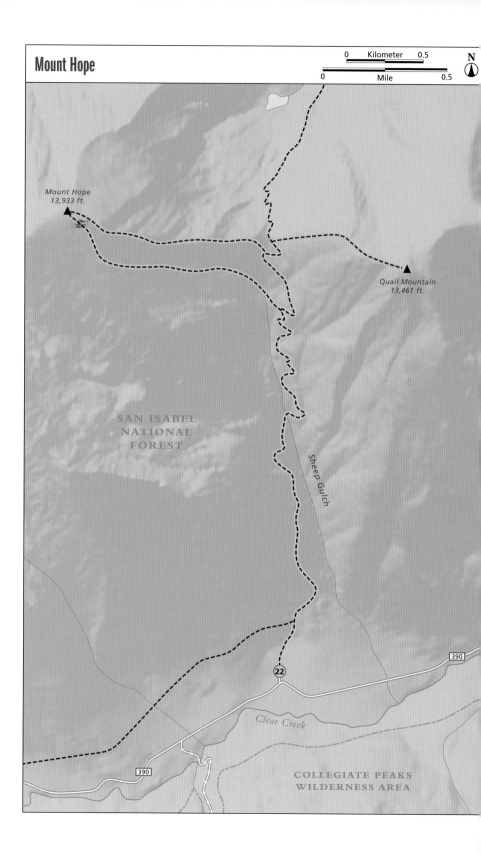

Mount Hope

Mount Hope
13,933 ft.

Quail Mountain
13,461 ft.

SAN ISABEL
NATIONAL
FOREST

Sheep Gulch

390

22

Clear Creek

390

COLLEGIATE PEAKS
WILDERNESS AREA

Looking down on Twin Lakes Reservoir from the summit of Mount Hope

There's no easy way to descend Mount Hope. The obvious way is to return back down the ridge, which has become my preferred route in recent years. If you brought along hiking poles and have sturdy knees, you can potentially save time by going south off the summit (steep Class 2) and edging west toward the "Grass Wall" that heads back to the Colorado Trail. Most years these slopes hold snow, which can actually make the descent easier if it is soft enough to plunge, step, or glissade out. I've come to prefer the East Ridge direct return, but the descent south off the summit is the standard descent, so it is included for those who want to avoid scrambling on the way back down. This route description takes the east ridge back to Hope Pass, but the mileage is about the same either way.

4.5 You can contour south to regain the Colorado Trail and avoid returning to the top of Hope Pass. Once you are back on the trail, it's smooth sailing to the parking area.

7.0 Arrive back at the Sheep Gulch Trailhead.

Optional Routes

Quail Mountain shares a saddle with Mount Hope. It is a ranked 13er, but it plays Art Garfunkel to Mount Hope's Paul Simon—very much a second banana. It's 0.5 mile up a grindy Class 2 slope from the saddle to reach its nice-enough summit.

Final Thoughts

Mount Hope is a great introduction to easy Class 3 terrain and off-trail navigation. In geological terms, Mount Hope put up quite a fight in resisting glacial erosion in contrast to some of its mountainous neighbors. Most of the Sawatch peaks are rounded domes. Mount Hope is made of more rugged stuff, and the end result is a peak that has more crags, cliffs, and cracks than most of its counterparts.

23 | Mount Silverheels

Mount Silverheels is a prominent giant, cutting an impressive profile from Hoosier Pass and the surrounding areas. Because the adventure starts high on Hoosier Pass at 11,539 feet, most of the hiking is done above tree line.

Primary route: Mount Silverheels, 13,822 feet
Difficulty rating: Medium; this route combines Class 2 ridgewalking along the Continental Divide with a walk up Silverheels's massive dome.

Class rating: Class 2
Round-trip distance: 8.7 miles out and back
Elevation gain: 3,625 feet
Round-trip time: 5–7 hours; full day

Finding the trailhead: This route starts at the parking lot off the paved Hoosier Pass (passable for all vehicles). From Breckenridge, take CO 9 south out of town. From the intersection of CO 9 and Boreas Pass Road, it is 9.6 miles to the large parking area on the west side of the road. The hike begins across the street to the east.

Trailhead GPS: N39 21.702' / W106 03.750'

The Hike

After touring along a scenic (and often windy) section of the Continental Divide, traverse down into a vast basin where the true girth of Silverheels reveals itself. While there is no formal trail, the broad slopes have excellent footing and offer a technically easy walk up to the top. Because of its unique position between the Tenmile and Mosquito Ranges, there are spectacular views of the valleys and plains to the east and miles of mountains to the west—you can see the high plains kick up into the Rocky Mountains from the summit!

There are a few ways up Mount Silverheels. The route described here is perhaps the most scenic and provides a nice full-day hike, as well as has an easy-to-reach trailhead. If you're looking for a shorter, easier route accessible via a modest 4x4 road, check out the optional route from FR 569.

Miles and Directions

0.0 From the parking area, cross the street and pass a gate to access a 4x4 road. Don't worry, you won't be hiking the road for long. Its main purpose is to get you through the last stand of pine trees and into the open tundra of the Continental Divide.

0.5 When the road cuts off left to the north, go off-trail and head up the accommodating tundra slopes of Hoosier Ridge. There are no formal trails from here. Mount Silverheels can't be missed to the south. Rather than making a beeline down into the valley toward Silverheels, continue northeast on the high ridge.

Mount Silverheels

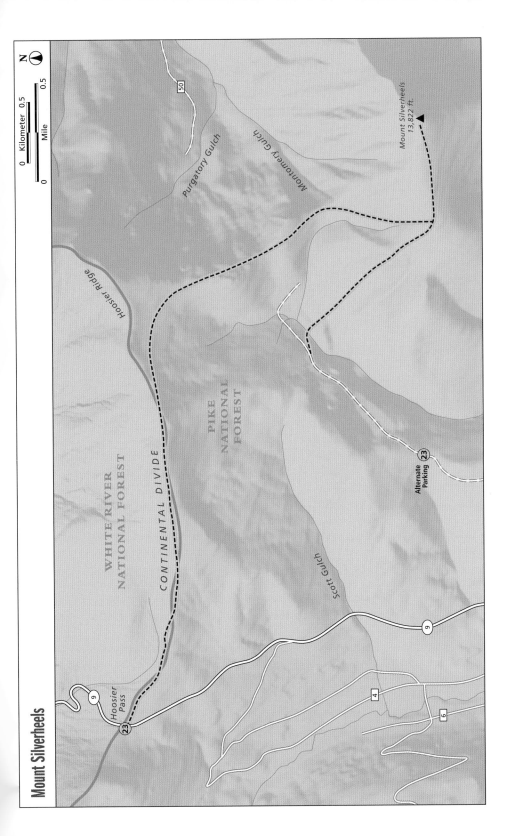

N

0   Kilometer   0.5

0   Mile   0.5

50

Purgatory Gulch

Montomery Gulch

Mount Silverheels
13,822 ft.

Hoosier Ridge

WHITE RIVER
NATIONAL FOREST

PIKE
NATIONAL
FOREST

CONTINENTAL DIVIDE

Alternate
Parking   23

Scott Gulch

9

Hoosier
Pass

9

23

4

6

Spectacular views await from the top of Mount Silverheels

1.7 At Point 12,814, start contouring downhill (!) southeast to connect with the north spur. The goal is the saddle where a set of power lines seem out of place in the open alpine slopes.

2.8 At the saddle's low point at 12,378 feet, Mount Silverheels's enormous north slopes beckon. The scale and distance from here are tricky—it's one heck of a big mountain! Thankfully, the slopes are gradual with solid footing and even a few patches of wildflowers. That doesn't change the fact that a 1,440-foot vertical push awaits. Hiking poles are a very good idea.

4.0 The north slope's natural path of least resistance ends up on the west shoulder below the summit at around 13,570 feet. Incredible 360-degree views reward hikers as they approach the large wind shelter on the summit itself. Like everything else with this hike, it looks closer than it actually is.

4.4 A well-earned summit! Soak in the stunning views from the flat, spacious summit area. You can see the way back, which includes one more big push back up to Hoosier Ridge. When you are ready, head back down to the saddle (which should go quickly on the descent).

5.8 Back in the saddle again! It's ok to cheat and contour northwest rather than strike out directly for the highest connecting point of Hoosier Ridge.

6.8 At about 12,710 feet, reconnect with the ridge. You still have to roll over or around Point 12,814, then it is a straight shot west to the finish.

8.7 Arrive back at the parking area.

Optional Routes

An easier route up Silverheels is possible. It is 3.6 miles round-trip, has 1,900 feet of elevation gain on easy Class 1/2 terrain, and features great car camping potential. This option starts west of the peak along Beaver Ridge. A stock SUV will have no problem getting up here. SUCs with good clearance and a good low gear can also make it.

To get there, take either US 285 or CO 9 to the quirky town of Fairplay. Off CO 9, turn onto Fourth Street. Turn left onto Beaver Lane (which has signs saying "National Forest Access") and follow this level but heavily washboarded road about 2.9 miles to a right turn (there is another forest access sign here). Note that somewhere along the way, Beaver Lane turns into Beaver Creek Road—it's the same road. After turning right, continue a few hundred feet to the winter trailhead and a cattle gate. This is FR 659. Open the gate, pass through, and please close the gate before continuing. The 4x4 road gets (oddly) nicer here and continues for 6.5 miles to the road closure. There is good camping all the way up to mile 6.0, but I'd suggest the sheltered spots off the left of FR 441 (marked). They are only a few hundred feet down the road. The only tough part of the road is a rocky hill, a bouncy but non-technical steep climb that I barely pushed up in normal 4x4 (though low might have been a good idea).

Park in the open meadows at 6 miles in (near the power towers). Past this the road becomes a true shelf road with sketchy turnarounds. Hike the road as it curves northeast and jump off onto Silverheels's north or northwest slopes wherever you like—it's all above tree line, so the navigation will be easy.

The 4x4 road that you detour off goes all the way to a mine marked as Iron Mine on the map. It's an interesting side trip if you have the time and the legs.

The parking lot at the top of Hoosier Pass serves as the launch point for the popular hike up North Star Mountain (13,614 feet), a ranked 13er to the west.

Final Thoughts

Silverheels's enchanting name is in honor of a mysterious "dancing girl" known for her silver-heeled shoes. She was already a favorite of the local miners at the outpost town of Buckskin Joe when an epidemic of smallpox hit the area in 1861. While most of the other women left to escape, Silverheels stayed behind to nurse those afflicted with the disease. She contracted the disease herself but survived. Legends say that after her recovery, she wore a mask to hide the scars on her face from smallpox. Shortly after this, she left the area and never returned. The men who remained felt that naming the mountain Silverheels for her was a fitting tribute.

24 Mount Solitude

Mount Solitude is a challenging 13er summit that is typical of Gore Range Peaks: a mix of on-trail hiking, dense bushwhacking, steep slopes, and ultimately, staggeringly gorgeous summit vistas. Despite the various terrain shifts, the difficulty stays at Class 2 and the off-trail navigation isn't overly difficult. Bring your A-game fitness for this one!

Primary route: Mount Solitude, 13,090 feet
Optional summits: Climbers Point, 13,005 feet; Vista Peak, 13,075 feet
Difficulty rating: Hard; while the rating stays firmly at Class 2+, this is a tough day. A long intro on the Pitkin Creek Trail leads to a burly bushwhack, followed by a steep push up to an incredible summit plateau.
Class rating: Class 2+
Round-trip distance: 10.8-mile lollipop loop
Elevation gain: 4,850 feet
Round-trip time: 6–8 hours; full day

Finding the trailhead: This is the easiest part of the hike! Any vehicle can make it to the paved trailhead in Vail. Take exit 180 off I-70. If coming westbound, take a right at the end of the exit onto North Frontage Road. If coming eastbound, take a left off the exit and continue under the I-70 bridge. Pass the westbound exit and then take the right onto North Frontage Road. It is 0.2 mile to the Pitkin Creek Trailhead, with parking for 10 to 12 vehicles. This trailhead is close to a condo complex—please park in the designated spots, not the ones reserved for residents of the condos.

Trailhead GPS: N39 38.598' / W106 18.216'

The Hike

The multifaceted climb up to Mount Solitude begins along the scenic Pitkin Creek Trail. Pass through dense forests and alpine meadows along the 3.5-mile on-trail warmup. Then the adventure begins! Pass through a gateway of willows and trees en route to a gorgeous open basin, whose steep—but hikeable—walls guard the upper ring of summits, the tallest of which is 13,090-foot Mount Solitude.

Mount Solitude is the only ranked 13er among the trio that share the ridge. Unranked Vista Peak is a short detour to the north, while Climbers Point is more-or-less required hiking since it leads to the easiest descent line. Rewarding views of the jagged, jutting Gore Range landscape is a terrific reward for a hard-won summit.

Miles and Directions

0.0 Begin your hike in by crossing a wooden bridge and following the well-established trail. The hike up to Pitkin Lake is a popular one, especially for Vail locals. Don't worry, you'll see why the peak is named "Mount Solitude" in a few more miles. Enjoy the gradual ascent that parallels Pitkin Creek. For most hikers, the start of this hike goes quickly.

Vista Peak from the summit of Mount Solitude. PHOTO BY JON BRADFORD

3.0 There are good dispersed camping sites here. Even though it's about a half mile from the spot where you'll go off-trail, it's better than the swampy ground closer to the spot where you'll begin bushwhacking.

3.5 Pass through a marshy portion of the trail and keep an eye out for the impressive waterfall along Pitkin Creek to the east. The Solitude Basin finally comes into view to the right (east), above the waterfall. You won't be able to see Mount Solitude's summit from here, but you will have a good look at most of the route ahead.

At a low point in the trail (before it begins gaining elevation again), hop off-trail and head toward the open basin. Before reaching it, there is a little matter of bushwhacking to attend to. There is something of an improvised trail through the willows that is just right of a small waterfall that splits the basin (not the Pitkin Creek Waterfall). The best footing is to the right of the willows and bushes, along a hill that has stands of high-altitude pine trees. If it has been raining or there is a lot of morning dew, you may get soaked in this section! Keep pushing up until you get into the clearing of the basin. This portion is only about 0.3 mile, but it will be some work.

3.8 Arrive in the beautiful, open basin. The obvious line to the ridge is right of center in the basin, up a wide slope that cuts between Climbers Point and 12,620-foot Skiers Point. This will be your descent line. The best line to get to Mount Solitude is along the steep, grassy slopes on the left (north/northeast) side of the basin. This slope follows a drainage through the last high stands of pine trees and a few rocky outcrops, and eventually just

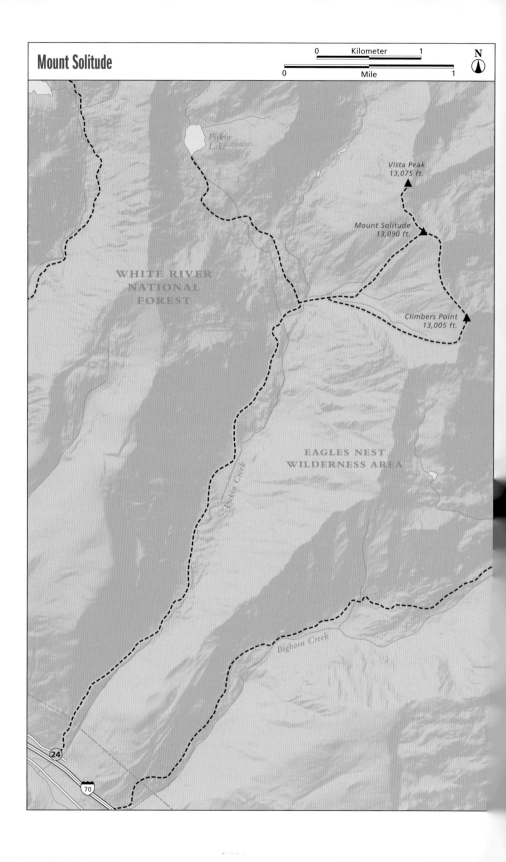

0   Kilometer   1

0   Mile   1

N

Pitkin Lake

Vista Peak
13,075 ft.

Mount Solitude
13,090 ft.

Climbers Point
13,005 ft.

WHITE RIVER
NATIONAL
FOREST

EAGLES NEST
WILDERNESS AREA

Pitkin Creek

Bighorn Creek

24

70

Fog shrouds the mountains en route to Mount Solitude. The off-trail portion of the hike follows the low saddle into the upper basin, then blasts directly up the semi-steep grassy slopes.

grinds up along grassy/rocky slopes with mostly good footing. In less than a mile, you will go from 11,100 to 13,000 feet. That's close to 2,000 feet of elevation gain. Pace yourself (and bring poles if you have them!). The terrain stays Class 2, or 2+ if you opt for more direct options.

4.5 Depending on your line, you will top out very close to the summit or a few hundred feet to the west. Vista Peak to the north looks impressive from here! But for Mount Solitude, head southeast to its wonderful summit.

It's possible to simply retrace your path back into the basin. However, it's worth the 0.4-mile walk south over Climbers Point and then descending into the basin via the saddle between Climbers Point and Skiers Point. It has the best footing, the lowest angle, and will ultimately be the quickest way down.

4.9 Climbers Point has a very interesting summit feature! It will be a surprise when you reach it. Carry on south to the saddle and drop into the basin. Again, poles are helpful here and the terrain stays Class 2. Once in the basin, bushwhack west back to the trail. Do not trend too far south as a shortcut—you will get cliffed out.

7.3 Around this mileage, regain the Pitkin Creek Trail. There are still 3.5 on-trail miles to go, but after all the work you've done, they will feel much easier! Continue south back to the parking area.

10.8 Arrive back at the Pitkin Creek Trailhead.

A good look at the bushwhacking terrain that blocks access into the upper basin

Optional Routes

Vista Peak is a Class 2+ walk-over that is 0.5 mile one-way, so it adds an extra mile of overall hiking to your day. The 500 vertical feet gained going out and back from Mount Solitude's summit will put your overall vertical gain over 5,000 feet—a monster day!

To the northwest, you can see another ranked 13er in the area, 13,057-foot East Partner Peak. There's no reasonable way to tack it on to this outing, but note that its standard route does follow the Pitkin Creek Trail to Pitkin Lake and then goes up from there. Its counterpart is the ranked 13er West Partner Peak (13,041 feet).

Final Thoughts

There are other Gore Range peaks in this guide (Red Peak B, chapter 30, and Snow Peak, chapter 33), but Mount Solitude is a better example of a typical Gore Range summit hike. If anything, it's a little easier. Gore summits like 13,213-foot Peak L (aka "Necklace Peak") have a longer approach, hard Class 4 scrambling, and a wickedly exposed razor-blade ridge that makes the knife-edge portion on the popular 14er Capitol Peak look like child's play. The point being that Mount Solitude will give you a good idea if you want to explore deeper into the Gores (I personally think they are some of the most enjoyable mountains in Colorado).

Pitkin Lake is a great destination in its own right. But after the trip up and down Mount Solitude, you likely won't want to tack on the extra work to see it (and the weather may be closing in).

Finally, if you have 12 seconds to spare, check out my video of a very close lightning ground strike I saw from the back of my truck at the Pitkin Creek parking lot after one of my climbs up Mount Solitude. It's worth manually typing into your browser— www.youtube.com/watch?v=-8fSLOf6Sdo.

25 Mount Spalding–Gray Wolf Mountain

Dive into the Mount Evans Wilderness with this pair of 13ers. A shared trail is the gateway to both peaks, which can be reasonably hiked in a single day. The optional summits add value to your adventure that includes a drive on America's highest paved road.

Primary route: Mount Spalding, 13,842 feet; Gray Wolf Mountain, 13,602 feet
Optional summits: Mount Warren, 13,307 feet; Rogers Peak, 13,391 feet
Difficulty rating: Medium; the combo of Mount Spalding and Gray Wolf Mountain is an excellent pairing of nontechnical 13ers, thanks to Class 2 terrain, great views, and easy access.
Class rating: Class 2
Round-trip distance: 4.7 miles out and back
Elevation gain: 2,340 feet
Round-trip time: 3–5 hours; half day

Finding the trailhead: From Idaho Springs, take exit 240 off I-70 to CO 103. Follow this road south for 13.5 miles to the entrance to the Mount Evans Scenic Road (CO 5) at Echo Lake. There is a fee to drive the road as of 2020 (a National Parks Pass will grant you passage on the road without the fee). Drive up this spectacular, paved road 9 miles to the Summit Lake parking area. Passenger cars can make it to the trailhead. Mount Evans Road is the highest paved road in North America. It may surprise drivers not familiar with the area to see many people cycling the road. Please drive with caution and share the road.

Trailhead GPS: N39 35.856' /W105 38.340'

The Hike

Most hikers who set off from Summit Lake are headed to 14,258-foot Mount Evans. This route shares the trail to Mount Spalding, then splits off to the north along a pleasant tundra walk to Gray Wolf Mountain (one of the better-named peaks in Colorado). This is an excellent introduction to off-trail hiking, thanks to the easy terrain. Enjoy gazing down onto broken cliffs from the safety of unexposed alpine slopes as you traverse the duo. It's interesting to note that only the lower of the two peaks, Gray Wolf Mountain (13,602 feet) is a ranked 13er. Mount Spalding (13,842 feet) is a sub-summit of Mount Evans.

Two ranked 13ers (Mount Warren and Rogers Peak) can be hiked from the same trailhead at Summit Lake. They offer more scrambling and a bigger day than the Gray Wolf/Spalding combo. It's not unreasonable for strong hikers to hike all four in a single day, though there's a lot of up and down to contend with—I suggest breaking them up into two adventures.

Mount Spalding–Gray Wolf Mountain

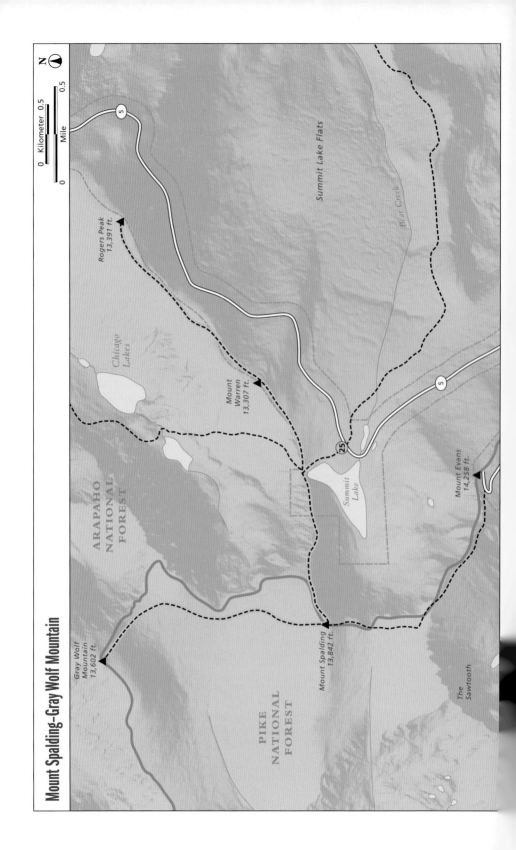

Mount Spalding's summit block

Miles and Directions

0.0 At the Summit Lake parking area, take the Mount Evans Trail from the west side of the parking lot. This fun trail hikes up the east ridge of Mount Spalding. There is light scrambling that can be voluntarily made into Class 3 climbing, but most hikers just stay the course on the well-worn trail.

0.7 At the top of the shoulder at 13,552 feet, it's a short walk to Mount Spalding's nifty summit block to the southwest. Humble Mount Spalding is dwarfed by Mount Evans from this perspective.

1.0 After topping out on Spalding, return to the junction of the east ridge. Go off-trail to the north and follow the big slopes along Class 1 tundra toward Gray Wolf Mountain. Prepare to lose 800 vertical feet on the walk over—you'll have to make it up on the way back.

1.8 The saddle at 13,042 feet is the lowest point along the connecting ridge and offers nice views of the Chicago Lakes to the northeast. Carry on back uphill to Gray Wolf's summit.

2.6 The second summit of the day, Gray Wolf Mountain! Though the mileage is low, the rolling elevation gains give you a great workout. Check out the steep, gnarly cliffs to the west and northwest. At the base is the semi-famous area known as the Hells Hole, which lives up to its devilish name if you ever try to snowshoe or hike through its dense willows (this is an alternate way to ascend Gray Wolf Mountain). Head back the way you came to return to the parking area at Summit Lake.

4.0 Return to the east ridge and the trail back down.

4.7 Arrive back at the Summit Lake parking area.

Optional Routes

Mount Warren and Rogers Peak could just as well be the primary route for this chapter. The total out-and-back distance for this pair is 3.3 miles with 1,140 feet of elevation gain. Start on the wide road/trail at the north end of Summit Lake. The lower part of Mount Warren has some fun Class 2+ scrambling along an improvised social trail. From the summit of Mount Warren, it's a Class 2 tundra walk across rocky slopes over to Rogers Peak. If you combine all four summits, it's roughly 8 miles and 3,350 feet of elevation with a whole lot of up and down!

An interesting variation that makes for a different day is to park at Summit Lake and bring along your bike. Cycle up to the upper Mount Evans parking area, lock up your bike, and make the very short walk up to the summit. From there, walk downhill to Spalding, over to Gray Wolf, then return to your car and drive up to grab your bike. This strange duathlon nets a ranked 14er, a ranked 13er, and the bonus summit of Mount Spalding.

Navigating the boulders on the traverse to Gray Wolf Mountain

Final Thoughts

Writing up this chapter presented an interesting challenge: It was easy to misspell the peak names! The peaks are "Spalding," "Gray Wolf" and "Rogers," not "Spaulding," "Grey Wolf," and "Rodgers." Also of note is the spelling of "Hells Hole," which uses the USGS standard in Colorado of not using apostrophes in any official names.

The Mount Evans Road is open May to September most years, depending on the snow conditions. You may see cars with crazy zebra stripes or bizarre colorations en route. Many car manufacturers use the high-altitude conditions along the road to test prototype features. They often "disguise" their cars with wild patterns that can obscure body designs or other innovative features.

Finally, the "Evans" name is one of the many Colorado titles whose names come packed with controversy. First off, Mount Evans was originally named "Mount Rosalie" after Rosalie Bierstadt, wife of the famous painter Alfred Bierstadt. Alfred met Rosalie while she was married to his friend and traveling companion, Fitz Hugh Ludlow. Rosalie found her way to Alfred's arms following her divorce from Ludlow in 1866. Interestingly, it was Bierstadt who named the peak after Rosalie while she was still married to Ludlow.

All that got thrown out the window when the peak was renamed to honor Colorado's second governor, John Evans. His is a complicated legacy. Evans was a champion of education and development in the West, but his reputation has been tarnished by his role in the Sand Creek Massacre in 1864.

Mount Spalding was named for Denver bishop John Franklin Spalding. Spalding's son, Franklin Spencer Spalding, is remembered by history as being part of the team that recorded what is believed to be the first ascent of the Grand Teton in 1898 via the Owen-Spalding route. To his credit, Spalding firmly believed his team of four was not the first to reach the top, insisting another party turned the trick in 1872. But, because Spalding's climb was a verified ascent, the title still stands today.

26 Mount Parnassus

Colorado's Mount Parnassus is over 5,000 feet higher than its more famous namesake located in Greece. Despite easy access from the Front Range and very accommodating slopes, Mount Parnassus is another overlooked 13er that deserves a little love. It can be combined with the nearby 13er Bard Peak or a nice ring of 12ers to the west.

Primary route: Mount Parnassus, 13,574 feet
Optional summits: Bard Peak, 13,641 feet; Robeson Peak, 13,140 feet; Engelmann Peak, 13,362 feet
Difficulty rating: Medium; Class 2 slopes, semi-steep at times but always on solid footing

Class rating: Class 2
Round-trip distance: 6.5-mile lollipop loop
Elevation gain: 3,510 feet
Round-trip time: 5–7 hours; full day

Finding the trailhead: Start from the Herman Gulch parking area. From I-70 west of Denver, take exit 218. If exiting westbound, take a sharp right at the end of the exit ramp into the large parking area. Eastbound, take a left, go under I-70, and then turn right just past the westbound exit ramp. This area gets very busy on summer weekends, primarily from people hiking to Herman Lake.

Trailhead GPS: N39 42.186' / W105 51.204'

The Hike

Love vertical hill hiking? Mount Parnassus is your peak. This Class 2 giant is a great out-and-back hike (the primary route) but also can be linked with several other peaks for a fun day out. An optional walk over to Bard Peak is possible, though I prefer a different route (see chapter 5) to reach this nearby summit. A better loop option involves snagging a couple of 12ers along an excellent, descending ridge toward the Jones Pass Trail.

Miles and Directions

0.0 Start along the Herman Lake Trail. In a few hundred feet, the trail splits. Go right on the less-traveled Watrous Gulch Trail. Follow it as it climbs up into Watrous Gulch. This is a wonderful start to the day, as the tree line gradually gives way to open meadows and spacious hillsides.

2.0 Decide if you want the direct route up Mount Parnassus (the west slopes) or the longer, more gradual northwest slopes. This route uses the west slopes to ascend and the northwest slopes to descend, but either way works. The direct route is steeper but shorter—did I mention it passes through a ghost forest? To start the direct route up the west slopes, go off-trail, hop the creek, and head left (east) anytime after reaching the initial clearings off the Watrous Gulch Trail. While the hill is steep, the footing is quite good.

Mount Parnassus

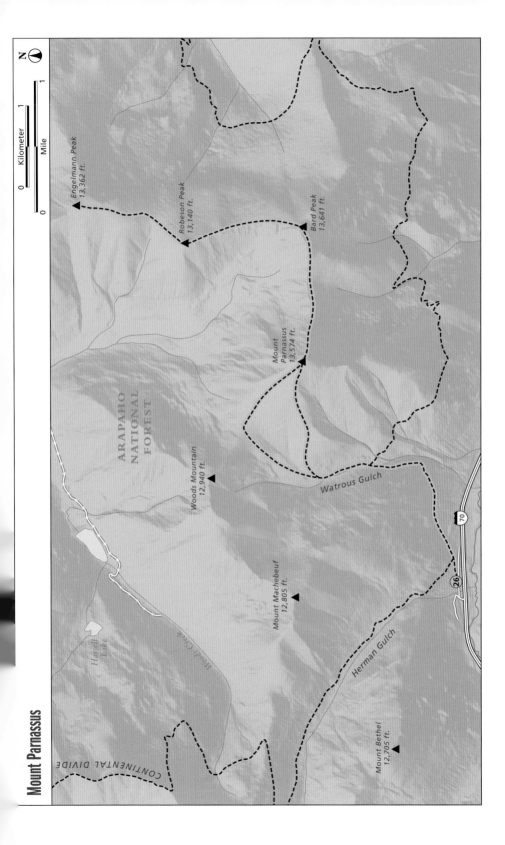

Mount Parnassus from Bard Peak

2.6 At around 11,800 feet, the ghost forest of Mount Parnassus awaits. Old, twisted zombie trees give a haunted vibe to the hillside. A few defiant bristlecone pines still live among their fallen flora brethren. Keep pushing east and toward the direct highest point. From here it's a beautiful grind to the top. There are plenty of spectacular views to take in when you stop to catch your breath.

3.3 When you summit Parnassus, you'll have gained about 2,000 vertical feet in roughly 1.3 miles. There are a few options from here, including tacking on Bard Peak to the east, a mere 67 feet taller than Parnassus. (Read the Optional Routes section for more information on Bard Peak.) For this route, descend via the northwest slopes toward a saddle between 12,940-foot Woods Mountain and Mount Parnassus. This is the best way down in terms of secure footing.

4.1 At the saddle, either descend into Watrous Gulch or . . . make a quick summit detour to Woods Mountain. It's hard to pass up another close-by peak! When you descend into Watrous Gulch, keep an eye out for the Watrous Gulch Trail. It fades out at the north end of the gulch. If you can't initially find it, stay close to the creek and you'll eventually cross it. Once back on the trail, follow it back to the parking area.

6.5 Arrive back at the parking area.

Optional Routes

Tacking on Bard Peak (13,641 feet) from Parnassus is the easiest way to summit the 13er, but it's not the most interesting (see chapter 5). An out-and-back, Class 2 walk from the summit of Parnassus will add 2 total miles and 1,160 feet of elevation gain. Beyond Bard, two more Class 2 13ers (13,140-foot Robeson Peak and 13,362-foot Engelmann Peak) are within striking distance to the north—from Bard, that out-and-back trek will add 3.6 total miles and close to 1,600 feet more vertical feet to the day.

Less taxing is a loop that summits Parnassus, then continues over to Woods Mountain, southwest to Point 12,805 (aka "Machebeuf Peak"), and down the west ridge to the Jones Pass Trail. This is my favorite route in the area because it makes a huge loop and returns via the Herman Gulch Trail. It's about 10.3 miles total, but the lion's share of the hard work will be getting up Parnassus. From there the ridges roll up and down to Point 12,805, adding another 980 feet of total elevation gain. From Point 12,805 a trail goes south to Jones Pass Trail and then reconnects to the south to the Herman Gulch Trail. Just make sure you don't accidentally head north on the Jones Pass Trail toward Jones Pass!

Final Thoughts

Mount Parnassus's huge dome really stands out when seen from I-70. Despite its obvious hiking allure, it has no formal trail to its summit.

Even though the primary route is only 6.5 miles, give this one a full day. If the stiff climb up doesn't wear you out, the potential to tack on more summits makes this outing an excellent option for hikers who want to extend their day in the mountains.

27 Petroleum Peak

Petroleum Peak and its neighbor Anderson Peak, both ranked 13ers, are unofficial names that correspond to the respective lakes on their eastern flanks, two of the most stunning lakes in Colorado. This basin is truly one of Colorado's best-kept secrets, rich with wildflowers, streams, lakes, and solitude.

Primary route: Petroleum Peak, 13,505 feet
Optional summits: Anderson Peak, 13,631 feet
Difficulty rating: Medium; enjoy a Class 1 trail en route to a brief, steep Class 2 hill climb.

Class rating: Class 2
Round-trip distance: 5.4 miles out and back
Elevation gain: 2,207 feet
Round-trip time: 4–6 hours; half day

Finding the trailhead: Lincoln Creek Road is a bouncy, rutted 4x4 road that has a few steep sections. It is best driven in an SUV, though a carefully driven SUC with high clearance (like a Honda CRV) can at least make it to Grizzly Reservoir and Portal Campground. Beyond that, the rutted road requires good clearance.

Lincoln Creek Road is accessed off CO 82 (Independence Pass), about 10 miles east of the town of Aspen or 9.5 miles from the top of Independence Pass. (**Note:** Independence Pass is closed from late October to May.) Turn south onto Lincoln Creek Road (listed on some maps as FR 106 or CR 23). It is 9.9 miles to the trailhead, but expect the drive to take a solid hour—this is another 13er trailhead access road with an identity crisis. It goes from jarringly rough to sandy smooth and back again.

Drive downhill on a somewhat steep dirt road, bypassing the Lincoln Creek camping area on your right. The first 4 miles of this road are riddled with ruts. There are also a couple of narrow sections and a few steep hills, though nothing a stock SUV cannot handle. For overnight campers, there are some numbered dispersed camping sites here, but it makes more sense to ignore them and camp closer to the trailhead.

Around 4 miles in, the road becomes oddly passenger-car smooth. A stretch of avalanche debris is worth a closer look as you drive by. This ocean of flattened trees looks like the work of giants. Stay on this road 2.7 more miles to Grizzly Reservoir and the first-come, first-served Portal Campground. It may be a surprise to see so many vehicles here, but chances are they aren't here to hike—the area is popular with ATVs, horseback riders, and other more casual outdoor enthusiasts. There are a few vault toilets available.

Beyond Grizzly Reservoir it is 3.5 miles to the trailhead. There are continual pullouts for free dispersed camping sites along the way, which are great for car camping. It's slow going to the trailhead. The road has exaggerated ruts, a few stream crossings, and plenty of bumpy boulders. Stock SUVs will do fine as long as you take your time. About 9.9 miles in, there is a signed turnoff for "Anderson/Petroleum Lakes Trail" to the right. A few hundred feet down this road is a river crossing. If it is running high you can park before it but . . . if you drove this far, you might as well take the plunge, cross the creek, and park at the official trailhead about a hundred feet past the river. The trail heads west on an obvious path from here.

Trailhead GPS: N39 01.854' / W106 36.984'

Petroleum Peak as seen just above Petroleum Lake

The Hike

Petroleum Peak is tucked away behind a collection of high 13ers, including Colorado's highest-ranked 13er, the talus pile known as Grizzly Peak A (13,988 feet). Anderson Peak is an especially aesthetic mountain from below, but it's Petroleum Peak that is the more enjoyable ascent. Because neither peak sports an official USGS name, this secret garden is destined to stay relatively anonymous. The two lakes leading up to Petroleum Peak are among my very favorites in Colorado. There are a few old mining cabins to see at the start of the hike, and beyond that is pure, pristine, Rocky Mountain beauty.

Miles and Directions

0.0 Start your adventure in the shady woods along a good trail. Pass a few mining cabins and carry on toward your first destination of the day, Anderson Lake. Anderson Peak's jagged summit is an attention-grabbing feature in the distance.

1.0 Anderson Lake often has a silty greenish haze. Anderson Peak cuts an impressive profile. Despite its craggy ridges and broken rock faces, it has an inviting presence. Staying on the formal trail can be a little tricky, as it is marked by a very small cairn. The correct trail goes by the north lakeshore about a hundred feet before turning right, where the established trail is once again easy to see. If you turn too early (at a junction-like section about 25 feet before the lake), it's not a big deal—you can navigate up to the Petroleum Lake basin without any major difficulties, it just won't be on the trail. There is a brief swamp section to negotiate this way, so if you can, stick to the established trail. Wildflower blooms here can be bonkers if you time it right.

1.8 Petroleum is a dark, inky black lake that is far more beautiful than its oil-based name suggests. The 12er Larson Peak stands out to the north. The formal trail ends here, but a wispy social trail continues up higher toward your next goal, Petroleum Peak's east ridge.

Petroleum Peak

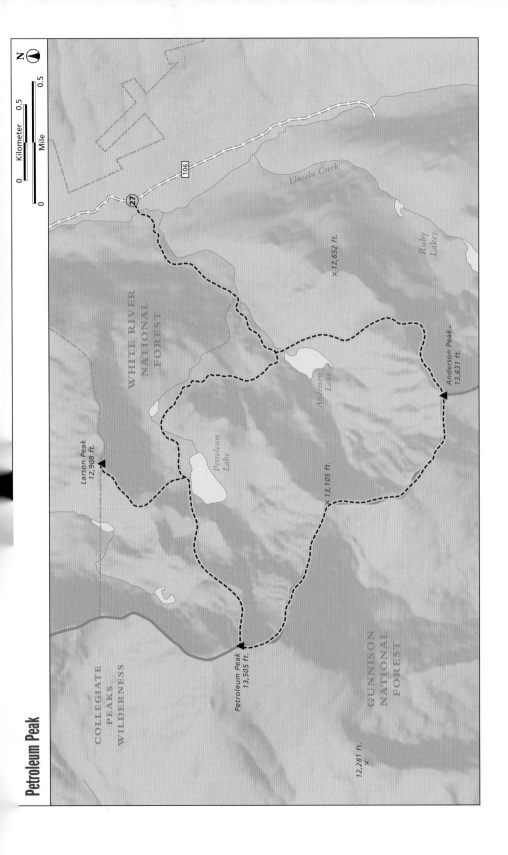

COLLEGIATE
PEAKS
WILDERNESS

Larson Peak
12,908 ft.

WHITE RIVER
NATIONAL
FOREST

Petroleum
Lake

Petroleum Peak
13,505 ft.

12,281 ft.
x

x 13,105 ft.

Anderson
Lake

Anderson Peak
13,631 ft.

GUNNISON
NATIONAL
FOREST

x 12,652 ft.

Lincoln Creek

Ruby
Lakes

106

27

N

0   Kilometer   0.5

0   Mile   0.5

Petroleum Peak with Petroleum Lake in the foreground

2.4 After climbing up a few smaller hills, you'll be at the base of a grassy ramp at 12,750 feet that goes directly up to the summit. The bottom section is grassy, as is the last saddle before the final push. Toward the very top, the terrain is rocky, steep, and a bit loose (Class 2). You can either chug right up or veer left, creating a switchback that follows the better natural terrain.

2.7 Great views of Anderson Peak, Larson Peak, and Truro Peak (to the north) can be seen from the summit. To the east the unspectacular summit of Colorado's highest 13er, Grizzly Peak, stands out as a high point along the distant ridge. Perhaps the most beautiful scenery is directly below you along the path you ascended. Petroleum Lake and a few smaller unnamed lakes add sparkle to the grassy alpine tundra.

   When you are ready to descend, simply go back the way you came. Because this is a short day, it leaves open options to grab additional peaks. However, you may just want to lounge around the shore of Petroleum Lake among the flowers and soft grass!

5.4 Arrive back at the trailhead.

Optional Routes

Normally I try to avoid descriptions to non-13er linkups, but 12,908-foot Larson Peak is only 92 feet shorter, so let's give it an honorary mention. If you want to add it to your day, the easiest way to hike it is to go directly below the low saddle between Petroleum and Larson. The ridge to the northwest of the saddle that connects the two is tempting, but the rock is rotten, loose, and crumbly. Gain the saddle from the slopes below and head northeast to the summit. Petroleum Peak looks very impressive from the top of Larson Peak!

Connecting to Anderson Peak is an interesting adventure. It is 1.5 miles and 900 vertical feet one-way from Petroleum Peak along the ridge that runs south from Petroleum's summit. It's a relatively straightforward route, with Class 2/2+ rock. Pass over Point 13,105 and Point 13,503 before making the final push up a boulder field to Anderson's summit.

Here's where things get interesting. Even though Anderson Lake looks so close, the descent off Anderson Peak that would close a loop (to the northeast) is a major pain. There is a tower that forces a long detour off the southeast of the ridge, with a few Class 3 downclimb sections. This can be kept as Class 2 on shifty boulder fields by skirting even farther out to the right of the ridge. The rock is loose and is just begging to twist an ankle. It will get you there, but it's a slow journey.

The better way down for most climbers is to retrace the ridge back toward Petroleum Peak. Either drop into the steep, sandy gully just northeast of Point 13,105 (Class 2 sand surfing) or suck it up and go all the way back to Petroleum's east ridge.

Final Thoughts

This is one of my absolute favorite weekend adventures in Colorado. The camping beyond Grizzly Reservoir is perfect car camping—flat spots galore and good access to water. The sheer beauty of the two lakes really has to be seen in person; photos just don't do the area justice. If you have friends who aren't peakbaggers, they can tag along to hang out at the lakes among the wildflowers (and the goats that frequent the area). Petroleum Lake is one of the very best secret spots within a reasonable day's drive from the Front Range.

The 13,282-foot Tabor Peak is also accessed off Lincoln Creek Road, around 3 miles in. I struggled to pick which of the peaks should make it into this guide—they are very near to one another. If you have a three-day window of time, consider hiking Tabor Peak via the Tabor Trail in the same visit. It features a view of Colorado's most amazing alpine shelf lake, Tabor Lake, and has an exciting, narrow, knife-edge ridge just before the summit.

If you happen to have an online mapping program, check out the crazy wilderness boundary for White River National Forest in this area. It was designated to cleanly include both 13ers and half of Larson Peak. Never fear, the other, northern half of Larson is in the Collegiate Peaks Wilderness and still on public land.

28 Pettingell Peak

Pettingell Peak's east ridge is an exciting scramble that reveals its third-class nature as it progresses toward the summit—from a distance, parts of the ridge look much harder than Class 3. This route is very similar to the popular Class 3 line Kelso Ridge on 14,267-foot Torreys Peak.

Primary route: Pettingell Peak, 13,553 feet
Optional summits: UN 13,215 (aka "Hassell Peak")
Difficulty rating: Hard; an on-trail approach leads to a challenging but fair ridge scramble on solid Class 3 rock

Class rating: Class 3
Round-trip distance: 8.9-mile lollipop loop
Elevation gain: 3,260 feet
Round-trip time: 5–7 hours; full day

Finding the trailhead: From I-70 west of Denver, take exit 218. If coming off I-70 westbound, take a sharp hairpin turn right at the end of the exit ramp to the dirt parking lot. From I-70 eastbound, take the exit then go left at the bottom of the ramp (under the highway bridge) and then right after the westbound exit ramp. There is parking for 40-plus cars here, but the lot still fills up by around 8 a.m. on summer weekends.

Trailhead GPS: N39 42.180' / W105 51.222'

The Hike

The primary route covers the Class 3 option, which is the spiritual equivalent of the popular Kelso Ridge route on Torreys Peak. The navigation is slightly tougher on Pettingell, though there are no distinct knife-edge sections like on Kelso Ridge. Like many Class 3 ridgelines, there are sections that look intimidating and technical from a distance, but reveal their secret passages on closer inspection. Simply gaining the ridge may be the hardest part of the day, thanks to steep slopes with sections of loose dirt.

It's worth noting that the Class 2 option listed makes the hike a pure walk-up with no scrambling required. It's an easier route thanks to the trail that leads to Herman Lake, which is well above tree line. From there an off-trail saunter up the grassy (or snowy) slopes leads to the summit.

Miles and Directions

0.0 Herman Gulch has gotten very popular over the years, with the majority of hikers going to Herman Lake. The peaks in this area don't see a lot of traffic, despite the easy access. Start on the signed trail at a sign kiosk and follow the route toward Herman Lake.

0.2 Go left at the trail split toward Herman Lake. This is a busy trail and a nice warm-up for the day ahead.

Starting the adventure along Pettingell Peak's east ridge

3.0 Just before reaching Herman Lake, leave the main trail and take a right to the Jones Pass Trail. You have two options here: bully up an off-trail spur to gain the ridge just right of a pronounced ridge notch or follow the Jones Pass Trail to the ridge. The spur is roughly 0.7 mile to the ridge on Class 2+/3 slopes, while the Jones Pass Trail is easy Class 1 but longer at 2.2 miles to the ridge. The mileage on this route follows the spur.

There are good reasons for each line. Fit hikers who want to get the Class 3 party started early can save time by charging up the spur. Alternatively, the Jones Pass route gives access to the optional 13er in this chapter, UN 13,215 (aka "Hassell Peak"). Hassell is only 0.5 mile (one-way) and 400 vertical feet from the Jones Pass saddle along an easy Class 2 ridge.

3.7 Pick your way up the spur to the main ridge at 12,930 feet. The rest of the ridge is only 0.7 mile but will likely take about an hour or so due to the route-finding. Near the summit, a "foreboding fin" looks to be a problem from this perspective (it turns out to be not bad at all). There's plenty of work to do at the start of the ridge. Carefully scramble down into the narrow saddle on the ridge and continue west along the ridge. Grassy/rocky ledges on the left (south) side avoid the airy, Class 4 terrain on the ridge proper. Most of the rock is solid, but check every hold.

4.0 There's a lull in the action after the initial scrambling. The ridge mellows into a brief but welcome Class 2 hike, complete with a social trail. Class 3 terrain reintroduces itself as you near a small bump on the ridge just in front of the foreboding fin.

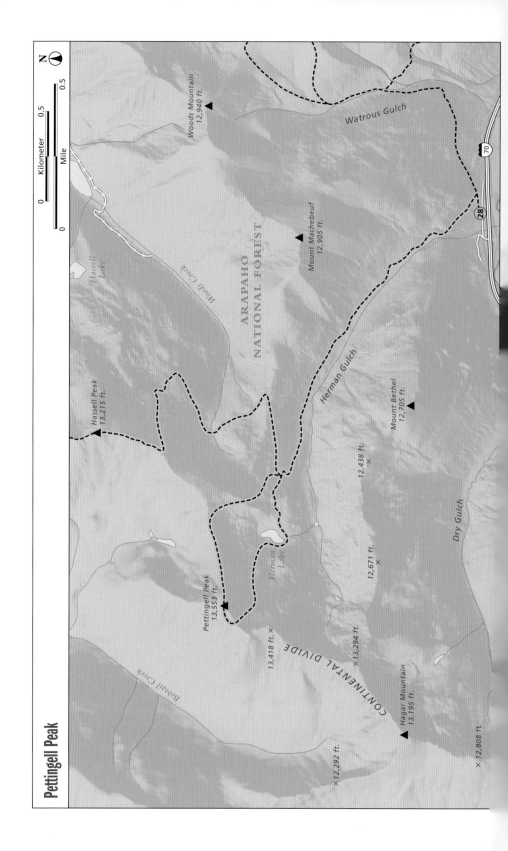

Pettingell Peak

4.3 From the small bump on the ridge, the fin reveals itself to be totally manageable. Good Class 3 lines go directly through the fin or to its left side. It's a bit of a relief that this section isn't more trouble. Past the fin/notch, the final walk to the summit is surprisingly easy Class 2 terrain.

4.5 Pettingell's summit is quite a perch. It's also the highest point in Grand County. The Class 2 slopes down to Herman Lake await. While the way down is only about a mile, be aware there are sections that cliff out above Herman Lake. Following the streams is the cleanest line, though it's possible to stay farther west and trudge down the more gradual slopes there.

5.5 Regain the Herman Lake Trail, where tourists have likely been watching you come down off Pettingell for a while. Take the trail back to the parking area from here.

8.9 Arrive back at the Herman Gulch parking area.

The heavily used Herman Lake Trail begins and ends your hike but only reaches as far as the small lake at the foot of Pettingell Peak.

Optional Routes

Pettingell Peak South Slopes

This route simply takes the descent line mentioned in the primary route and uses it to climb the south slopes to the top of Pettingell Peak. It's all Class 2 with a bit of route-finding and a nice option for hikers who aren't in a Class 3 frame of mind.

Hassell Peak Combo

If you're looking to hike just Hassell Peak, you're looking at an 11.4-mile day as an out-and-back. Doing only Hassell Peak is actually a fun hike and a good all-day outing. Pairing it with Pettingell's east ridge makes for roughly a 12.2-mile trip—a nice combo for fit hikers, but be certain you have the weather window. Getting caught in a storm on the east ridge would be a nightmare.

Final Thoughts

If you're looking for a fun Class 2 day out, Hassell Peak is more enjoyable than Pettingell Peak's Class 2 option. It's also possible to link up to the peaks in Watrous Gulch (see chapter 26, Mount Parnassus) for an epic ridgewalk loop.

Fourteener fans will find the east ridge very similar to Kelso Ridge. It's a touch easier but perhaps with more challenging route-finding.

29 Weston Peak-Ptarmigan Peak

These two summits can be chained together with their parent peak, Horseshoe Mountain (see chapter 13), though they make for a good outing on their own. There are no established trails for these mountains via Weston Pass, but the way up will be obvious (and steep!)

Primary route: Weston Peak, 13,572 feet; Ptarmigan Peak, 13,739 feet
Difficulty rating: Medium; a Class 2 hike with a big push at the start to ascend the grassy slopes that grant access to both peaks

Class rating: Class 2
Round-trip distance: 4.2 miles out and back
Elevation gain: 2,305 feet
Round-trip time: 3-5 hours; half day

Finding the trailhead: Weston Pass is a maintained dirt road that can be driven by passenger cars. It connects the towns of Leadville and Fairplay and can be accessed from either location. The Leadville side is easier. Take US 24 south out of Leadville. From the intersection of US 24 and CO 300 just out of town, it is 3.5 miles to the signed turnoff left (east) for Weston Pass (CR 10/CR 7). Follow the signs for Weston Pass as the road initially climbs through the Massive Lakes community, then gradually to the well-marked top of the pass in 9.8 miles. Park at the top of the pass.

If coming from Fairplay, follow US 285 south out of town roughly 4.7 miles, then take a right onto CR 5. Follow the signs for Weston Pass 15.8 miles to the top. Note that this side of the pass is a little easier on passenger cars; the Leadville side is a bit bumpier near the top of the pass.

Trailhead GPS: N39 07.866' / W106 10.902'

The Hike

Weston Peak and Ptarmigan Peak get a "medium" rating relative to 13ers—it's still going to be hard work to punch up the Class 2 slopes that lead to the high plateau that connects the peaks. This is the only route in this guide that focuses on two unranked but officially named 13ers. The parent peak of these two is Horseshoe Mountain (chapter 13), which can be added to this adventure via a long tundra walk with very moderate grades.

The western views along this portion of the Mosquito Range are amazing. Wildflowers regularly coat the slopes and, once you've gained the high ridge, wandering on the alpine plateaus is a real pleasure.

Miles and Directions

0.0 Start the hike by heading northeast past power lines along one of several improvised trails, all of which disappear as you reach the steeper flanks of the ridge. Your first goal is to hoof it up the big, grassy slopes that lead up to the ridge. The work for this hike is front-loaded at the start—you will gain 1,350 vertical feet in the first 0.7 mile, topping out at 13,315

Enjoying a traverse to Ptarmigan Peak from Horseshoe Mountain

feet. Thankfully, this slope is often covered with flowers to help lift your spirits if your lungs are burning.

0.7 The views in all directions make the initial push up worth it! Before heading north, it's time to climb up Weston Peak, a short distance to the east. Follow the ridge east to a defined high point.

1.2 Weston Peak's summit narrows a bit along the ridge but doesn't feature any significant exposure. To the far north, the 14er Mount Sherman looms, as does Horseshoe Mountain midway between Weston Peak and Mount Sherman.

1.7 Return to the ridge shoulder and proceed north toward Ptarmigan Peak. The rest of your day will be relatively easy tundra walking with stunning views of many of Colorado's highest peaks to the west among the Sawatch Range.

2.2 Pass over Point 13,525. Ptarmigan Peak is not far off, but there is still one more hill to hike up to reach the top.

2.6 The wide-open summit of Ptarmigan Peak is marked with a cairn. This is a great place to soak in the vast majesty of Colorado's mountains. This vantage point is one of the very best views of Mount Elbert and Mount Massive, Colorado's two highest peaks. Head back the way you came off the summit of Ptarmigan Peak. You'll save mileage on the descent by going directly down the ridge versus the slight detour you took to Weston Peak.

3.5 Back at the high shoulder, it's time to descend the grassy slopes. Hiking poles are a great help here. Your vehicle is only 0.7 mile away, but it's very steep!

4.2 Arrive back on Weston Pass.

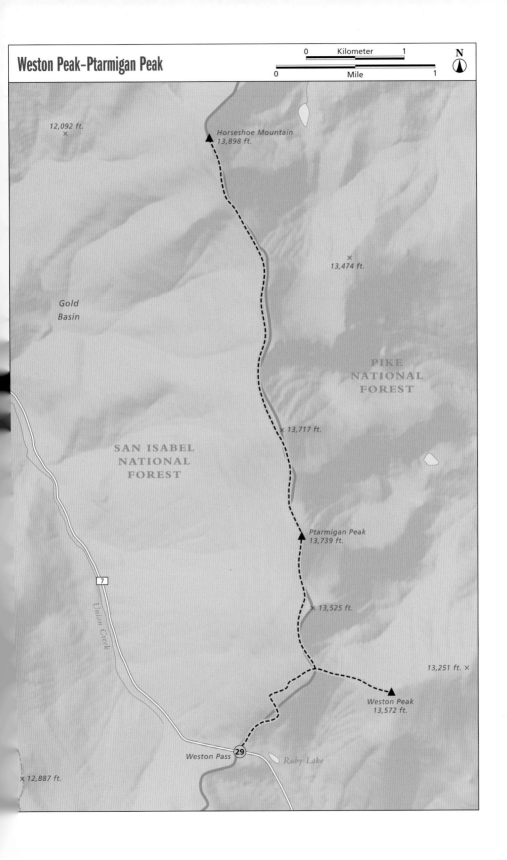

12,092 ft.
×

Horseshoe Mountain
13,898 ft.

×
13,474 ft.

Gold
Basin

PIKE
NATIONAL
FOREST

SAN ISABEL
NATIONAL
FOREST

× 13,717 ft.

Ptarmigan Peak
13,739 ft.

7

Union Creek

× 13,525 ft.

13,251 ft. ×

Weston Peak
13,572 ft.

Weston Pass   29   Ruby Lake

× 12,887 ft.

After a steep push up grassy slopes, the walk over to Weston Peak is pretty mellow

Optional Routes

If you're itching for more adventure, the trek over to Horseshoe Mountain is 2.6 miles one-way from the summit of Ptarmigan Peak, with 902 feet of vertical gain. This option turns a moderate day into a long one, so make sure you have the weather window to safely return—this entire hike is above tree line.

Looking for a bigger adventure via a point-to-point outing? Consider traversing from the Leadville side, from Mount Sherman from Iowa Gulch all the way to Weston Pass! This route is 11.3 miles with 4,700 feet of vertical gain, with most of the day spent above 13,000 feet. The car shuttles can take a while to set up. Strong hikers looking for a monster hike that tags a 14er, two ranked 13ers (Horseshoe Mountain and Sheridan Mountain), and several unranked summits will enjoy this one!

That said, don't underestimate the low mileage of the primary route described here. It's a robust half day out. This area is a great place to take fit mountain dogs, as the slopes are very open without dangerous cliff faces—just keep an eye out for mountain goats.

Final Thoughts

Colorado has three officially named Ptarmigan Peaks—this one is the highest of the group and the only 13er in the bunch.

Weston Pass is named for Bert Weston, a blacksmith and former postmaster of a small outpost town called Los Sisneros. In 1892 the town was named for Weston as well.

The collection of summits visible to the immediate south of Weston Pass do not reach 13,000 feet. The highest of this group is South Peak at 12,892 feet, which is an enjoyable hill walk. A bit farther south, the boundary of the unique Buffalo Peaks Wilderness Area begins. The marquee peaks in this small but special wilderness area are two ranked 13ers, 13,300-foot East and 13,326-foot West Buffalo Peaks (these hikes almost made this guide, so they deserve an honorable mention here). They are too far away to reach from Weston Pass, but if you're looking for a 12er playground, the unnamed summits south of Weston Pass will give you solitude, spectacular views, and a sense of remote wilderness.

Touch the sky on the high, rolling meadows that connect Weston Pass to Horseshoe Mountain.

30 Red Peak B

Despite some really big numbers in terms of elevation gain and distance, this is still a reasonable day hike for fit hikers as 12.6 of the 15 miles are on-trail, and the off-trail hiking is along an easy-to-navigate ridge.

Primary route: Red Peak, 13,189 feet
Difficulty rating: Medium; on-trail access leads to a fun, nontechnical Class 2+ ridge scramble
Class rating: Class 2+

Round-trip distance: 15.2 miles out and back
Elevation gain: 5,100 feet
Round-trip time: 7–9 hours; full day or overnight

Finding the trailhead: Start the hike at the Meadow Creek Trailhead, accessible by passenger cars. Take I-70 west of Denver to exit 203 in Frisco. If coming westbound, go right at the end of the exit ramp into the roundabout and take the second right onto a flat dirt road. Follow it 0.5 mile to the trailhead. If coming eastbound, take a left off the exit ramp onto Summit Boulevard. Continue to the roundabout, passing the westbound exit ramp and then taking the second right 0.5 mile to parking.

Trailhead GPS: N39 35.328' / W106 06.348'

The Hike

Red Peak is set in the eastern Gore Range, offering some of the best western views of the Gores. The eastern views to the Front Range and southern views to the Tenmile Range are excellent as well. The approach trail goes up and over Eccles Pass into one of the most beautiful basins in Colorado. Camping on the northern side of Eccles Pass is an exquisite experience, especially when wildflowers are in bloom.

Miles and Directions

0.0 Start on the Meadow Creek Trail at the large sign in the parking lot at 9,150 feet. The first phase of this hike is following the trail 5 miles to the top of Eccles Pass. Elevation gain is gradual and the trail is in tip-top shape. Aspen forests gradually give way to pine groves, and the din of I-70 slowly fades. Open alpine meadows appear below Eccles Pass, decorated with small ponds and streams. This portion of the hike will go quickly for fit hikers.

4.4 The Meadow Creek Trail ends at the Gore Range Trail junction. Stay straight toward Eccles Pass and continue climbing up.

5.0 The top of Eccles Pass reveals the deeper beauty of the hike. Besides getting a marquee look at Red Reak, the small lakes and abundance of flora make this basin especially charming. If you're camping for the night, this is a good vantage point to pick out a good spot in the trees. Continue down the trail and into the basin.

Top: *Red Peak from Eccles Pass*
Bottom: *Scrambling along Red Peak's ridge with Eccles Pass in the background*

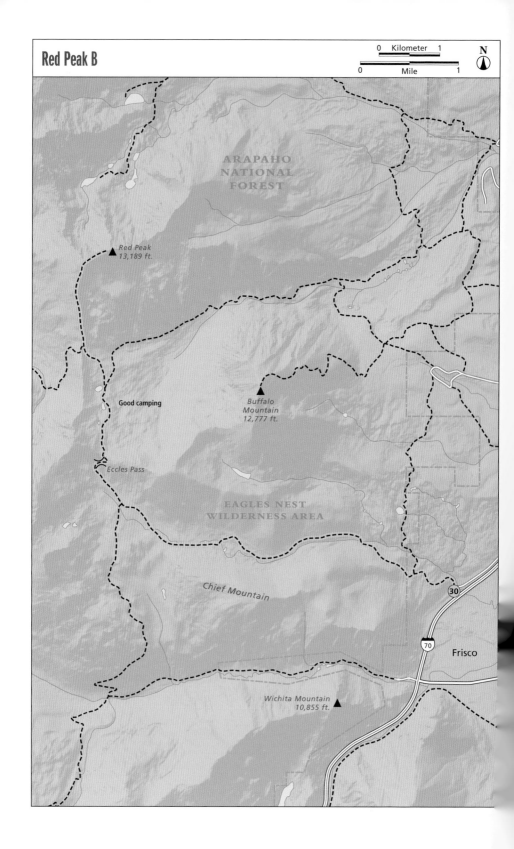

0   Kilometer   1

0   Mile   1

N

ARAPAHO
NATIONAL
FOREST

Red Peak
13,189 ft.

Good camping

Buffalo
Mountain
12,777 ft.

Eccles Pass

EAGLES NEST
WILDERNESS AREA

Chief Mountain

30

70

Frisco

Wichita Mountain
10,855 ft.

5.8   Trails start to diverge in strange ways at the largest of the trio of lakes. An access trail to the left of the lake is the quickest way to your next goal, Red Buffalo Pass. Technically, you will take the Gore Creek Trail up to Buffalo Pass, though it is not signed. The main trail also gets around to reaching Red Buffalo Pass, it just takes longer.

6.3   At Red Buffalo Pass the off-trail portion of the day begins. Follow the ridge north. Exposure is minimal for a ridge. Several social trails appear and disappear on the way up, and the scrambling is easy.

7.3   Most of the climbing is behind you by the time you reach the false summit at 13,005 feet. From here it's tough to tell if the true summit is dead ahead or on the far side of a dangerous-looking notch. Good news! It's on the closer side of the notch (something that becomes more apparent as you close in on the top).

7.6   Red Peak's hard-won summit. Views in all directions are spectacular. Return the way you came. Even though you have a long hike back, it tends to go fairly quickly. There is still the matter of gaining an additional 500 feet of elevation on your way back up Eccles Pass.

10.2 Back at the top of Eccles Pass. It's all downhill from here!

15.2 Arrive back at the Meadow Creek Trail parking lot.

Optional Routes

Red Peak is a straight shooter—there aren't a lot of options to tack onto an already big day. If you're camping in the area, there are excellent 12,000-foot peaks off Eccles Pass including Eccles Peak (12,313 feet), Deming Mountain (12,902 feet), and Buffalo Mountain (12,777 feet).

Final Thoughts

Thinking of climbing Longs Peak? Red Peak is a fantastic training day for the famous 14er. The mileage and elevation gain is similar to Longs, though scrambling on the upper part of Longs is Class 3 versus the Class 2+ stuff on Red Peak. Nonetheless, it's a good primer to help gauge your fitness level and how you perform at altitude. It can also help you dial in your nutrition and get you used to an early start (I wouldn't start a day hike for Red Peak any later than 5 a.m.).

Red Peak B is the lower of two "Red Peak" 13ers. The other is off Hoosier Ridge and gets a mention in chapter 3, Bald Mountain A–Boreas Mountain. Red Peak B is very accessible by Gore Range standards—many Gore Range summits involve off-trail bushwhacking, horribly loose rock, and difficult navigation.

31 Rio Grande Pyramid

Rio Grande Pyramid is an epic mountain experience like none other. If you can only do one hike in this guide, Rio Grande Pyramid is it. Hiking this remote San Juan 13er feels more like a quest than a climb, especially if you've seen the pyramid's awe-inspiring profile towering over the landscape like a beacon from afar.

Primary route: Rio Grande Pyramid, 13,821 feet
Optional summits: Fools Pyramid, 13,278 feet; Window Peak, 13,157 feet; Point 13,017
Difficulty rating: Medium; this exceptional adventure on the most epic of 13ers never exceeds Class 2+. Most of the route is on trails, with the exception of some final light scrambling through a stable boulder-covered slope to the finish.
Class rating: Class 2+
Round-trip distance: 17.0 miles out and back
Elevation gain: 4,346 feet
Round-trip time: 10–12 hours; overnight or very long, full day

Finding the trailhead: This adventure starts from the Thirty Mile Campground, roughly between Creede and Lake City—a big plus for those who have a long drive and want to build in a relaxing night before starting the adventure. From May to early September, you'll need to make reservations through www.recreation.gov or by calling (877) 444-6777. The 35-site campground stays open in the off-season without a fee, just without the amenities of a full-service campground as in the summer. I suggest late September, as the campground will be less busy and the autumn colors will be near their peak. Passenger cars can reach the trailhead.

If coming from Creede, take CO 149 north about 20 miles; if Lake City, take CO 149 south 30 miles to CO 18. Go west on this road and follow the signs for Rio Grande Reservoir. Stay on CO 18 (a spectacular drive in its own right) for 11.1 miles along a slightly bumpy dirt road. Turn left at the signed turn onto CO 18C to the Thirty Mile Campground and Thirty Mile Trailhead (this is before reaching the Rio Grande Reservoir). There is an overnight/day-use parking lot on the west side of the campground (parking there is free).

The trailhead is a little tricky to find. It is on the southwest side of the campground, just past a pavilion, and is well signed. Note that this route description encourages a night of camping at Weminuche Pass, which is the most logical place to set up for a night.

Trailhead GPS: N37 43.344' / W107 15.480'

The Hike

Rio Grande Pyramid's hike unfolds like a dream, starting under the canopy of a dense aspen forest then gradually climbing up to a shelf trail with fantastic views of the Rincon La Vaca valley below. When Rio Grande Pyramid finally reveals itself, it becomes apparent how it earned its mystical name. Before topping out, there is one final secret—a high, flat saddle that looks like the surface of Mars is the last stop before an exceptionally fun scramble up to the remarkable summit.

Rio Grande Pyramid stands towering on the horizon.

The adventure is perfectly set up for an overnight backcountry camping trip, but strong hikers can definitely get this one as a day hike despite the long mileage. There is a big vertical push at the start, then a very long section of gradually inclined trail. Most of the hard stuff is found only in the last mile.

Miles and Directions

0.0   Find the trailhead on the southwest side of the campground. It is marked with a sign for the Weminuche Trail and Big Squaw Trail. Take the Weminuche Trail. If you're backpacking in, the first mile of the hike is where you'll do the lion's share of the work, though it's not terrible—about 700 feet of vertical gain on an excellent trail. The grunt work is offset by great views of the Rio Grande Reservoir and the shady aspen forest.

1.1   After a push up a few steep hills, the trail shifts to a lower, more comfortable grade. The trail maintains this accommodating character for the next 2.8 miles, all the way to the premier camping spot.

3.8   At Weminuche Pass, the Weminuche Trail splits into two trails just after crossing Weminuche Creek: the Pine River Trail to the south and the faint Skyline Trail to the west. You want to take the Skyline Trail (marked with a series of cairns).

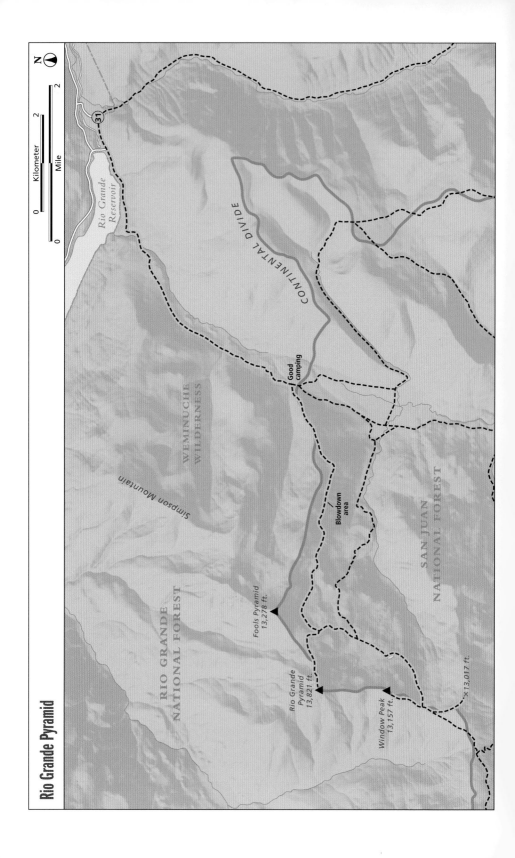

Rio Grande Pyramid

This junction is a great place to camp. For one, the hike back out with heavy packs will be fairly easy from here. Secondly, you have a reliable water source in Weminuche Creek. I suggest setting up camp on the west side of the Weminuche Trail (or to the left of the Skyline Trail, if you go up a hundred feet or so). There are some camping spots to the east of the trail as well, but they are situated in a throng of dead or near-dead pine trees with a lot of blowdown potential. Beyond this point the camping potential is poor, due mostly to dense willows and steep slopes.

The Skyline Trail looks very faint for a few hundred feet, but rest assured if you are heading west on a trail marked with cairns, you are going the correct way. The trail gets more defined after passing through a forested area. From this spot it is 4.6 miles one-way to the top.

4.0 As you bend west to run parallel with the stunning valley below, you'll encounter the trickiest part of the trail. The trail runs through a collection of blowdown trees—some of them very large! As a result, there are a few different side trails. This section is short, only a few hundred feet, but it can be easy to pick up the wrong trail again. Stay right (north) when you can, and do not be tempted to follow "mistake" trails that go steeply down to the south. (**Note:** Rangers I spoke with said this trail section will likely be cleaned up. As of autumn 2019, the blowdown was still there.) When you regain the trail, it again becomes well-defined and follows a thrilling approach as the shelf slowly morphs into a willow patch. Around this point, you get your first real look at Rio Grande Pyramid—and it looks *big!*

6.6 Reach a flat opening in the willows. If you start to lose the trail in the willows, keep looking down. It's also easy to see it in the distance if you get a bit off-track. The large rock gap you can see along Rio Grande's south ridge is known as "The Window." It looks more like a feature out of the desert scenery of Moab, Utah, than high in the Colorado mountains!

7.5 The Skyline Trail continues south at 12,260 feet. Get off it and head west up a direct slope to the base of Rio Grande Pyramid. This trail isn't signed, but it is *very* obvious and well worn. It pushes up a pair of sandy slopes to the west—the better footing is actually on the rocks to the left of the trail. The gashed trail has been formed from descending hikers and isn't necessary to stay on as you climb up.

8.1 After bullying up the two sandy hills, you will arrive at one of the most incredible saddles in the Rocky Mountains. The mountain instantly changes character, transforming from sandy and loose to a solid boulder field of dark rock. The final scramble to the top earns this hike its Class 2+ rating. The easiest rock is left of center, but the entire face is made up of mostly solid boulders. There are plenty of fun opportunities to mix in an optional Class 3 move here and there. A faint climber's trail appears from time to time, though isn't necessary to follow.

8.4 The flat summit reveals some of the most breathtaking mountain vistas in Colorado. The Grenadier Range to the west cuts a particularly stunning profile. The peaks off Carson Pass (see chapter 6, Bent Peak–Carson Peak–UN 13,580) can be seen to the north, which is a satisfying change of position if you've seen Rio Grande Pyramid from Carson Peak or the Colorado Trail in the area. Enjoy your time on this most special summit—it is one of the absolute best hikes in the Rocky Mountains. When you are ready, return the way you came.

12.8 You'll have to contend with the blowdown section of the Skyline Trail one more time. It's a bit easier to track the trail on the return.

13.0 Back at Weminuche Pass.

17.0 Arrive back at the trailhead in the campground.

Once out of treeline the way to the summit of Rio Grande Pyramid has a worn trail that flickers out at the start of the last scramble to the top.

Optional Routes

Fools Pyramid (13,278 feet) is the connecting summit to the northeast of Rio Grande Pyramid and is a ranked 13er. It's a nice Class 2 walk-up. When you get up the first sandy slope after the split from the Skyline Trail, you can target it from the flattish, sandy saddle. It is about 0.6 mile and 550 feet one-way from this point. If you've camped, the extra mileage here makes more sense than on a single-day push for the pyramid.

The two other ranked 13ers here are 13,157-foot Window Peak and Point 13,017. The best strategy for getting these two is to do them as their own outing. A second night of camping at Weminuche Pass makes sense, even if you have to do some back-tracking. As mentioned before, there is no good camping and few good water sources beyond the pass. To reach them stay south on the Skyline Trail at the spot at 12,260 feet where the unnamed trail splits west up the sandy slope toward Rio Grande Pyramid. From here, follow the Skyline Trail south 2.2 miles as it bypasses a lake and connects with the Continental Divide Trail. Follow it southwest to a saddle between the two 13ers at 12,617 feet. From here, go off-trail north 0.6 mile to Window Peak and 0.5 mile south to Point 13,017.

Final Thoughts

Rio Grande Pyramid is a wonderful experience, even if it is a far-off adventure for folks who live in the Front Range. It is worth the time and logistics. It has all the ingredients of a great mountain hike: a good trail, few crowds, great scenery, and a summit with a cool name! If you happen to hike during peak autumn colors, this climb is downright magical. For all the thousands of mountain hikes I've done in Colorado, this one has something special—many other hikers who have climbed it agree.

32 Rosalie Peak

Rosalie Peak showcases an ancient side of the Rockies, manifested in 1,000-year-old bristlecone pines, old-growth forests, and defiant pegmatite rock outcrops. There is no technical terrain, but it's still a big day, thanks to the gradual elevation increase on the approach.

Primary route: Rosalie Peak, 13,575 feet
Optional summits: Epaulie Peak, 13,530 feet
Difficulty rating: Medium; a Class 1/2 trail heads up to open alpine tundra followed by enjoyable walking along flowery slopes through an ancient region of the Rocky Mountains.

Class rating: Class 2
Round-trip distance: 10.5 miles out and back
Elevation gain: 4,370 feet
Round-trip time: 5–7 hours; full day

Finding the trailhead: From the town of Bailey, take US 285 south. Turn north onto CR 43 (this is about 4 miles from the town of Pine Junction and 2.7 miles from the center of Bailey). There is a traffic light and a gas station at this junction. It's 9 miles to the Deer Creek Trailhead from here. Follow CR 43 until a fork in the road about 7 miles in. Take the left fork (CR 43), not the right (CR 47). The road becomes dirt and will bypass the Deer Creek Campground, which is a left-hand fork—stay right (there is a microscopic sign for Deer Creek Trailhead at the fork). In about 5 more minutes, you'll reach the large parking lot, which has a sign for no overnight camping. The entire road (dirt and pavement) is passable by passenger cars. The trail begins through a gap in the fence in the upper left part of the parking lot.

Trailhead GPS: N39 30.636' / W105 34.002'

The Hike

Starting from the deep woods at Tanglewood Creek, enjoy a climb up to tree line, where some of Colorado's oldest living trees greet you. Continue up to vast, open tundra, where wildflowers add splashes of color among the rocks and grasses. The views are especially spacious and wide open. As you near the summit of Rosalie Peak, the paved road up Mount Evans can be seen in the distance. This hike is a peaceful hill walk and an excellent tour of several mountain ecosystems.

Miles and Directions

0.0 From the Deer Creek Trailhead, follow the Tanglewood Creek Trail, an easy-to-follow, shady trail that parallels the humble flow of Tanglewood Creek most of the way. At the very start, there is a signed split. Stay right toward the Rosalie Trail and Tanglewood Creek.

1.0 Here is another split with the Rosalie Trail going left and the Tanglewood Trail going right. Oddly, stay on the Tanglewood Trail. The Rosalie Trail circumnavigates the bottom of Rosalie Peak and offers a *long* way to the summit via the west slope—skip it! As the trail begins

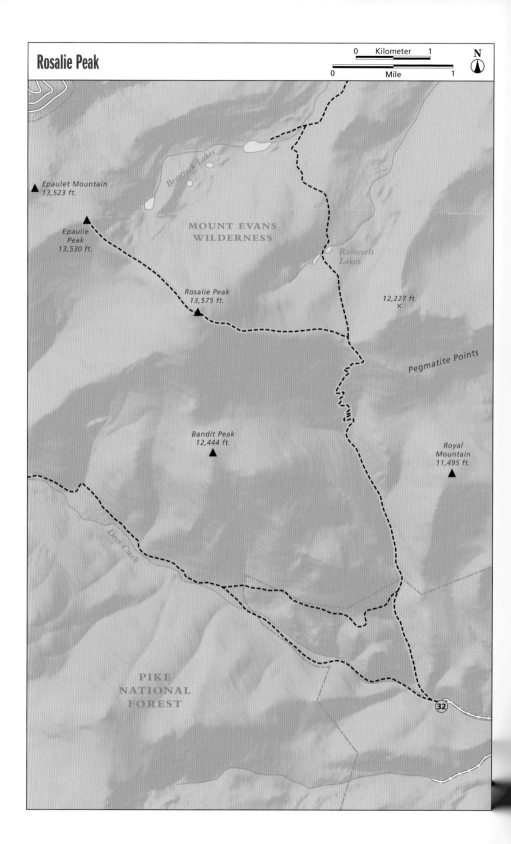

0   Kilometer   1

0   Mile   1

N

▲ Epaulet Mountain
13,523 ft.

Beartrack Lakes

**MOUNT EVANS
WILDERNESS**

▲ Epaulie
Peak
13,530 ft.

Roosevelt
Lakes

▲ Rosalie Peak
13,575 ft.

12,227 ft.
×

Pegmatite Points

Bandit Peak
12,444 ft.
▲

Royal
Mountain
11,495 ft.
▲

Deer Creek

**PIKE
NATIONAL
FOREST**

32

to climb in earnest, you'll pass through a duff-strewn forest and high willows, and finally breach tree line in a series of switchbacks. Old, twisted bristlecone pines lie about like living ghosts. The transition to tree line is one of the highlights of this adventure.

3.8 Reach the saddle between Rosalie and the Pegmatite Points. The trail continues on to the Roosevelt Lakes below. The rest of the hike is simple, at least as far as navigation goes. Get off-trail at the saddle and head directly to Rosalie's summit via its broad eastern slopes. I call this section the "pleasant grind," as it is still 1.5 miles and 1,600 vertical feet to the top. These slopes are known for their vast blooms of alpine wildflowers that tend to stick around until late summer.

4.6 Enjoy watching the Mount Evans Road and Mount Evans's summit block come into view the higher you get. Chances are you'll have the entire place to yourself despite the proximity to the popular 14er.

5.3 Rosalie's rocky summit is topped by a cairn. There is a calm dreaminess to the views here. The landscape is rounded, curved, and gentle rather than being craggy and coarse. On the far east shoulder of Rosalie Peak, the Pegmatite Points can be seen. (***Note:*** These rocky blocks make for an interesting detour from the saddle.) The hike down goes quickly. Rumble down the slopes, back to the Tanglewood Creek Trail, and return the way you came.

10.5 Arrive back at the Deer Creek Trailhead.

Optional Routes

UN 13,530, known informally as Epaulie Peak, is a ranked 13er (#234) 1.1 miles northwest of Rosalie Peak. It's a straightforward Class 2 walk over, but note that the out-and-back to Rosalie's summit tacks on 1,200 more vertical feet to an already big day. Interestingly, its sub-summit, 13,523-foot Epaulet Mountain, has an official USGS name but isn't a ranked 13er.

If you want to get creative with car shuttles, it's possible to start or finish a point-to-point hike at Mount Evans Road (the road has a fee to drive). If you're feeling lazy, start by getting dropped off on the Mount Evans Road just north of Epaulet Mountain and hike downhill roughly 7 miles back to the Deer Creek Trailhead and your second vehicle!

Final Thoughts

While Rosalie Peak isn't a thrill-a-minute mountain climb, it's still a hearty day out. Most 13ers start below tree line and work their way up through changing flora, but there is something extra special about this approach's transformation into tundra. Perhaps it's the energy of the still-living bristlecone pines, some of which may be over 1,500 years old. Thick yellow sunflowers and assorted pops of color from smaller flowers make the final push to the summit a lot more decorative than on most mountains. Just as a reminder: Keep a vigilant eye out for storms, as there is nowhere to hide above tree line. The push up to the summit from the saddle can take longer than some hikers expect.

Wildflowers bring vibrant color to the slopes of Rosalie Peak.

Rosalie is named for the wife of the famous Western painter Alfred Bierstadt. The two used to be joined in mountain eternity: Mount Evans (which shares the famous Sawtooth Ridge with Mount Bierstadt) used to be called Mount Rosalie, but that union ended when the Colorado legislature renamed the original Mount Rosalie for Governor John Evans and bumped the Rosalie Peak name south to its current location.

33 Snow Peak

Snow Peak is a bona fide Class 3 scramble and one of the few 13er summits in the Gore Range that is relatively easily won ("relatively" being the key word). It's also got one of the most distinct profiles in the Vail area. Snow Peak is a memorable, classic 13er that should be on every adventurer's list.

Primary route: Snow Peak, 13,024 feet
Optional summits: Grand Traverse Peak, 13,041 feet; Mount Valhalla, 13,180 feet
Difficulty rating: Medium-hard; a long Class 2 trail leads to a semi-stable boulder field, steep slopes, and a solid Class 3 scramble.

Class rating: Class 3
Round-trip distance: 9.6 miles out and back
Elevation gain: 4,200 feet
Round-trip time: 6–8 hours; full day or overnight

Finding the trailhead: From I-70 west of Denver, take Vail exit 180. If coming from I-70 westbound, take a left at the end of the exit ramp onto Big Horn Road (under the highway bridges). From I-70 eastbound, simply take a right at the exit ramp to get on Big Horn Road. Follow Big Horn Road 2 miles east to the Deluge Lake Trailhead/Gore Creek Campground. Be sure to park in the spots along the road, not in the campground.

Trailhead GPS: N39 37.638' / W106 16.488'

The Hike

The on-trail approach to Deluge Lake is more demanding than it looks on the map, mostly due to the sustained elevation gain. It's possible for fit hikers to knock off Snow Peak in a single outing. Overnight camping in the forest just below Deluge Lake is a real treat and is a great way to hike Snow Peak or its neighboring summits.

Snow Peak is best attempted in late summer or early autumn. True to its name, it can hold snow year-round, especially on the north-ridge route written up here. It's a good idea to bring crampons and an ice axe—and even a short rope and pickets—if going for Snow Peak anytime other than late July through mid-September (and even then, it's a good idea to pack them in).

Miles and Directions

0.0 Start at the Deluge Lake Trailhead. A few hundred feet in, stay left at the trail split toward Deluge Lake. It's 4 miles to Deluge Lake, so settle in and enjoy the hike. Watch your footing through the patches of boulder fields en route. Though the trail is well traveled, pay attention if there are snow patches on the ground—it can be easy to lose the trail in the shadowy parts of the forest about 3 miles in. As you near the open basin below Deluge Lake, there is a small stream crossing. Beyond this open field is the start of the good camping. If you do camp, be sure to find a spot sheltered from the wind.

The saddle and final scramble up Snow Peak

4.0 The Deluge Lake Trail ends at the dark, mysterious waters of Deluge Lake. Here you are in the company of giants. Snow Peak beckons to the southeast. Trend southeast toward the flat saddle between Mount Valhalla (on the left) and Snow Peak (on the right). From here it's less than a mile to Snow Peak's summit, but there's a lot of work to be done.

The first challenge is navigating a dense boulder field of mostly stable rock. These rocks tend to hold snow most of the year, so be extra careful where you step. You may notice a thin ribbon of trail twisting up the steep grass slopes beyond the boulder field. Reaching this improvised trail is your next goal, though the footing on the lower part of this trail may be worse than on the actual grassy slopes. Hiking poles are a very good idea on this route! Slug up the slopes as they finally ease up a bit approaching the saddle.

4.5 Snow Pass. This broad saddle is a welcome resting point, especially if you're tackling Snow Peak as a single-day outing. Snow's summit ridge is directly south, only 0.3 mile away. When this ridge is snow free in late summer, it's a scrambler's dream—good rock, clean lines, interesting route-finding, and a good Class 3 "hero scramble" to the summit block. When there is snow, you'll want crampons and an ice axe. Follow the ridge to the summit, staying left to avoid unnecessary exposure. A series of ledges just below the summit block will require a bit of navigating (stay left for the best terrain).

4.8 Snow Peak's impressive summit block. I've felt that Gore Range summits evoke a unique set of emotions—you'll have to experience it for yourself to test this theory. There is some-

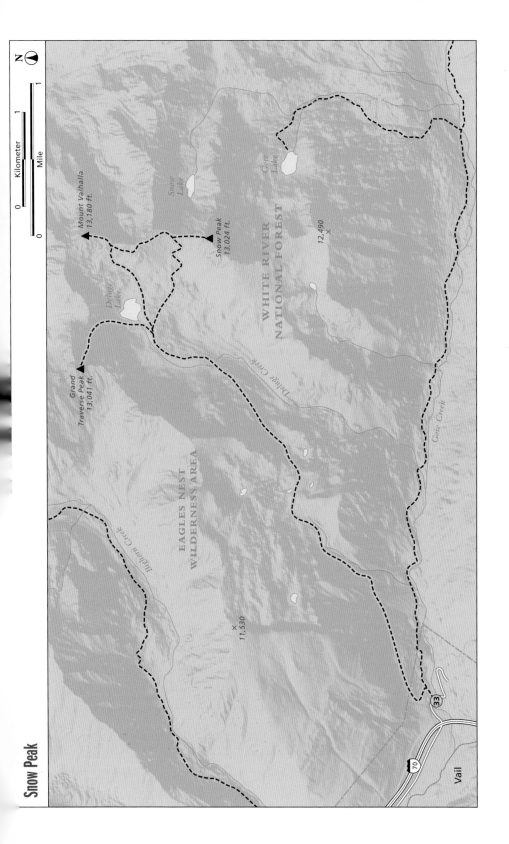

Snow Peak

thing raw, untamed, and wild about this area. Snow Lake blazes below in a diluted aqua hue when it isn't completely frozen over. Carefully pick your way back down the ridge and the access trail to Deluge Lake. Again, be cautious through the boulder field and stay on the higher ground to avoid the swampy terrain closer to the east side of the lake.

5.6 Back at Deluge Lake, the lion's share of the work is over. Regain the trail and follow it back to the parking area.

9.6 Arrive back at the Deluge Lake Trailhead.

Optional Routes

Mount Valhalla

It's possible to link all three peaks in a day, but it's very demanding in terms of physical fitness and route-finding. It's possible to link Snow to Valhalla via Class 3+ terrain by staying left of the main ridge, then navigating through a matrix of loose rock towers and sloped grassy ledges. The route-finding is very difficult, and it's easy to get in trouble if you're not careful. If you're aiming to combine Valhalla and Snow, start by hitting a semi-direct line up the broken western slopes of Valhalla first (steep Class 3+

Snow Peak often lives up to its name. Late summer is a good time to go for this bold 13er.

Goats congregate in the open tundra near Deluge Lake.

with the potential for Class 4 moves), then traverse to Snow. There is no easy way up Valhalla, though it can be a lot of fun for expert route-finders. It's worth noting that Valhalla is very typical of Gore Range summits: long approaches, hard route-finding, exposed ledges, and lots of crumbling rock.

Grand Traverse Peak

Grand Traverse Peak can be traversed from Valhalla, though it's better done by itself as a Class 2 walk-up. If you're camping in the area and want to tag two peaks, I'd suggest Snow Peak one day, Grand Traverse the other. Doing Grand Traverse as a single peak is a straight-up grind fest: Go to the bottom of the mountain and chug up the steep, grassy slopes.

Final Thoughts

Weather can move in fast here, so be extra vigilant about getting off the summits by 11 a.m.

There is a privately owned cabin south of Deluge Lake that is falling into disrepair. Each year that I return to the area, the cabin seems worse for wear. As of 2019 the windows were mostly broken and the inside seems to have been trashed by a bear. There is a *lot* of animal poop in the cabin as well. Maybe someday the owner will repair it, as it is in a brilliant location and would be a welcome shelter in colder months.

Backpackers often access Snow Pass via Snow Lake and the Gore Lake Trail from the east. Gore Lake is a nice place to camp and can be viewed as an alternate route to hike Snow Peak.

34 South Arapaho Peak–North Arapaho Peak

If Colorado had "best in class" awards, both of the Arapaho Peaks would make strong cases in their respective categories. South Arapaho is a dramatic but attainable Class 2 hike, while extending the adventure to North Arapahoe Peak adds in one of the best Class 3 traverses in the Rocky Mountains.

Primary route: South Arapaho Peak, 13,397 feet; North Arapaho Peak, 13,502 feet
Optional summits: UN 13,038 (known informally as "Old Baldy" or "Bald Mountain")
Difficulty rating: Medium (South Arapaho); hard (North Arapaho). South Arapaho as an out-and-back is a pleasant Class 2 hike with a little thrilling scramble near the summit. Traversing from South to North Arapaho ups the ante on a Class 3+ ridge with tricky route-finding and several moves that could classify as Class 4. If you're hiking with dogs, do not attempt the traverse both for the safety of your pup and other hikers on the route.
Class rating: Class 3+
Round-trip distance: South Arapaho only, 8.0 miles out and back; South and North Traverse, 9.4 miles out and back
Elevation gain: 3,650 feet (traverse)
Round-trip time: 6–8 hours; full day

Finding the trailhead: Begin at the 4th of July Trailhead, a very popular destination on summer weekends. Carefully driven passenger cars can navigate this semi-maintained dirt road, but it's better to have a vehicle with a bit of ground clearance. From Nederland, take CO 119 south out of town and go right onto the signed Eldora Road toward the Eldora Ski Area/town of Eldora. From this junction it is 4 miles to the town of Eldora. Stay straight on Eldora Road when it splits left toward the Eldora Ski Area and proceed to the town. At the west end of town, the road turns to dirt.

Reset your odometer at the start of the dirt road. Pass the hectic Hessie Trailhead and, at mile 0.8, follow the signed road to the 4th of July Trailhead, 3.8 miles farther. This dirt road has some thrill shelf sections and narrows in a few places but is passable by passenger cars. If you do have a car, park below the upper trailhead just past the Buckingham Campground—parking along the road is allowed and it's only a few hundred feet to the trailhead. SUCs/SUVs can push up a needlessly rocky little hill to the main lot where the trail starts. There is a restroom here and parking for about a dozen cars.

Trailhead GPS: N39 59.712' / W105 38.034'

The Hike

Hikers are rewarded with a wealth of wilderness beauty en route to the base of South Arapaho Peak, including meadows of wildflowers, an elegant waterfall, and mesmerizing views of neighboring peaks to the west.

Pass rust-hardened mining ruins and begin an excellent Class 2 hike up South Arapaho Peak. Just below its summit pyramid, get a glance at the impressive Arapaho Glacier before reaching the summit via a fun Class 2 scramble. From here a bold

Top: The crux slab near the start of the traverse to North Arapaho Peak
Bottom: Midway through the Arapaho Peaks traverse

Pulling through the notch that grants access to North Arapaho Peak's broad summit

Class 3+ traverse scales rock slabs, tiptoes along an exposed catwalk, and presents a matrix of chutes and gullies before topping out on one of Colorado's most memorable summits.

This traverse is among the very best in Colorado. In addition to the daring terrain, it requires quite a bit of creative route-finding. Downclimbing skills are required. Careful navigation will yield solid footing on mostly good rock. The final ramp to North Arapaho Peak leads to a protected notch that opens up the broad summit, complete with an enormous cairn.

Miles and Directions

0.0 Begin the hike at the signed Arapaho Pass Trail at the north side of the lot. This well-defined trail is a nice warm-up for the adventures to come.

1.2 Stay on the Arapaho Pass Trail at the junction with the Diamond Lake Trail.

2.0 After passing below a rolling waterfall, reach a flat section decorated with alpine pools and grassy tufts. Views to the west to Mount Neva and Arapaho Pass are astounding, especially when illuminated by early morning light.

2.1 An old boiler and other mining ruins serve as good markers to turn off the Arapaho Pass Trail. At a sandy section, turn right (north) and follow a makeshift trail over a stream crossing and through a thicket of willows. Don't worry if you're not exactly on the trail; it rematerializes past the willows. Continue on the trail as it ascends toward the pass between South Arapaho Peak and Old Baldy.

3.6 Gaze north down to the rock-strewn Arapaho Glacier at the saddle. Old Baldy is an optional 13er 0.4 mile east and is a good add-on now if you're going only for South Arapaho Peak. If doing the full traverse, you may want to make sure you have the legs (and the weather) for it on the way back. South Arapaho looms to the northwest, its steep south-facing walls striped with layers of grayscale rock. The trail up forks a bit, but both arms head to the same place. There is some exposure if you stay close to the ridge, but it's easily avoided by nudging over to the left.

4.0 The summit of South Arapaho Peak. If this is your goal, turn around when you're ready and enjoy the walk down. If you're up for North Arapaho, it's only 0.7 mile away, but oh, what an adventure it will be to get there! You can see the entire ridge from here, but the difficulties don't reveal themselves until you're upon them. When you're ready to roll, go west off South Arapaho's summit.

The traverse begins on easygoing Class 2 terrain and follows a hiker's trail. Decades ago this trail was marked with orange paint. Some faint marks remain, but don't count on them. They are also easily confused with patches of orange lichen. Follow the trail to a cairned notch and scramble right. Ahead is a move that some consider the crux, a 10-foot slab that regains the ridge from a very tight notch. There is significant exposure to the east at the slab. The move up the slab will be easy for tall climbers, but even my 5 foot, 4 inch hiking partner was able to get up the slab without trouble. Whether it's a Class 3 or 4 move is a point of contention, but the point is you don't want to blow it here. The slab is well featured, and for my two cents, it didn't feel like the crux of the route.

Once past the slab, you begin the traverse on an airy catwalk slab. Past the slab the route-finding work begins in earnest. The challenge here is to skirt left of the ridge along good rock or scramble close to the ridge as you progress. Be cautious not to drop down too far, as the footing gets loose and steep the lower you go. The crux of the route may be in this section, as it requires finding Class 3 downclimb chutes that are hard to see until you're right on top of them. These can be descended face-out for the most part, but may require a move or two face-in.

Carry on back to the ridge proper en route to the last approach section. North Arapaho's south face has a significant chockstone in the middle, with gullies up to the left and the right. From a distance the left gully looks better, but ultimately it's not the best line up. Take the ridge toward the base of the left line. At the split, a surprisingly welcome ramp of light-colored rock goes right toward the shadowy right gully. Follow this rock to the base of

Now that's a big summit cairn! North Arapaho Peak's east face drops abruptly to the Arapaho Glacier 1,000 feet below.

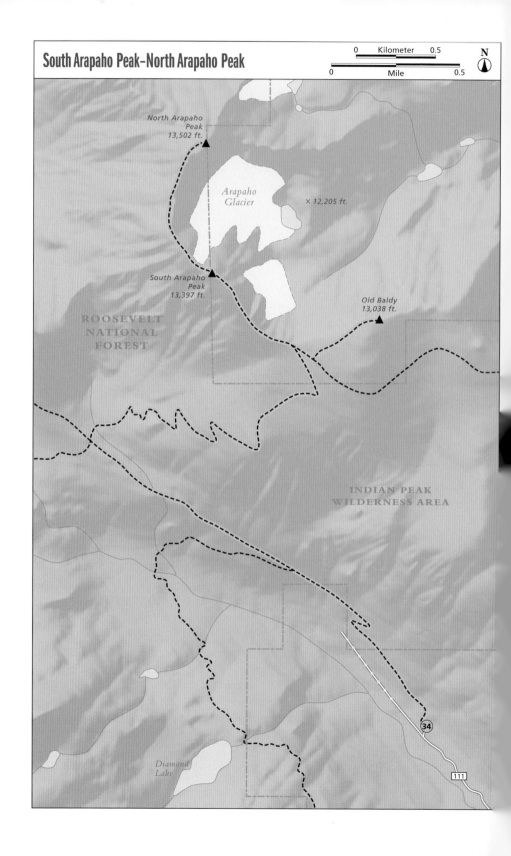

0   Kilometer   0.5

0   Mile   0.5

N

North Arapaho
Peak
13,502 ft.

Arapaho
Glacier

× 12,205 ft.

South Arapaho
Peak
13,397 ft.

Old Baldy
13,038 ft.

ROOSEVELT
NATIONAL
FOREST

INDIAN PEAK
WILDERNESS AREA

34

111

Diamond
Lake

the gully. A single, gutsy step over a low fin of rock into a chalky, slightly off-camber step is required to enter the chute. The chute itself is well protected—quite a change of pace from the rest of the traverse. The rock is solid and the climb up is fun. I'd put the top-out from this gully up there with the most exhilarating finishes in Colorado.

4.7 North Arapaho's broad, flat summit is a wondrous place. An enormous cairn marks the summit. Cliffs drop off to the east with dizzying views of the Arapaho Glacier. North Arapaho's summit is the highest point in the Indian Peaks.

The traverse back to South Arapaho is slightly easier but still demands your full attention. Drop the summit chute, step over the chalky fin, and head back. One advantage of going north to south is that the Class 3 chutes you had to downclimb are much easier to find—and easier to go up than down. Return to the airy catwalk and downclimb the crux slab. Below the slab, be sure not to hug the ridge too much or you'll be momentarily cliffed out just before the easy section of the ridge. It's not a big deal if you do, but you'll have to backtrack about 100 feet to the easier downclimbing back to the notch where the climber's trail ends. Once you're back on the climber's trail, the lion's share of your work is done. Enjoy the walk back to South Arapaho and descend the way you came.

9.4 Arrive back at the 4th of July Trailhead.

Optional Routes

The only other 13er in the area is Old Baldy, which is a ranked 13er (the 616th highest mountain in the state and 563rd of the 13ers). Strong hikers can get all three in a day.

Final Thoughts

This is one of my very favorite traverses in Colorado. It's not terribly long but is feature-rich and packed with all kinds of daring moves, though it never gets desperate. Popping out of the chute below the summit to the vast tundra at the top never gets old.

South Arapaho Peak is an excellent single-summit day hike and one of the more accommodating 13ers in terms of trail quality and access. It also has an exciting finish thanks to the light scrambling near the top.

It's possible to access these peaks from the Arapaho Glacier Trail, but it adds mileage on the approach and descent. You'll want as much pep in your legs for this traverse as possible.

Looking north from North Arapaho's summit are two "forbidden" 13ers, 13,150-foot Arikaree Peak and 13,276-foot Kiowa Peak. Both are in the protected Boulder Watershed, a sectioned-off pocket of the Indian Peaks where the public is not legally allowed.

35 Stewart Peak–Baldy Alto

This pair of ranked 13ers are often climbed with 14,014-foot San Luis Peak—it's almost inevitable given the relative ease of topping out on the 14er along the way. Add in the remote location (it's a long drive from almost anywhere) and chances are you'll be going for a triple-header in this beautiful and isolated part of Colorado's Rocky Mountains.

Primary route: Stewart Peak, 13,983 feet; Baldy Alto, 13,698 feet
Optional summit: Organ Mountain, 13,801 feet
Difficulty rating: Medium; this route is predominantly Class 1 hiking, with some Class 2 terrain surrounding the summit of Baldy Alto. Despite the long distance and beefy elevation gain, this is a surprisingly tame outing that is great for fit hikers looking for an exquisite mountain tour without technical terrain or challenging navigation. It's also a great route for experienced mountain dogs, thanks to the open terrain and abundance of water on the approach. For a more relaxed experience, consider an overnight backpacking trip to split up the mileage.

Class rating: Class 2
Round-trip distance: 14.3-mile lollipop loop
Elevation gain: 5,170 feet
Round-trip time: 7–9 hours; full day or overnight

Finding the trailhead: This trailhead features a long, lonely drive, but no technical dirt roads. SUCs/SUVs are advised as there are two water crossings along the maintained dirt roads. Both have concrete drainages, so they aren't "normal" 4x4 water crossings, but 2WD cars with low clearance could have trouble when the creeks are running high.

Driving directions here start at the intersection of US 50 and CO 114 E, which is 7.8 miles east of downtown Gunnison. I'd highly suggest getting a full tank of gas in Gunnison before setting out, even if it means a bit of backtracking. From the junction it's 47.4 miles to the trailhead, a lot of it on maintained but washboarded dirt roads. It will be about a 2-hour drive.

Take CO 114 E (which goes directly south). Follow this road for 20 miles, then turn onto CR NN14. Now on dirt roads, this area feels very remote. Continue on NN14 for 6.9 miles, then turn right on CR 15GG. Follow this road for 4 miles, then stay straight onto CR 14DD (also called FR 794). In 12.7 miles, stay on 14DD/FR 794, following the signs for Stewart Creek Trailhead. Arrive at the small trailhead in 4.3 miles. If the lot is full, 0.25 mile down the road is the Eddiesville Trailhead, which has more parking and an outhouse (and is the better of the two lots to car camp).

Google Maps does a good job navigating to the trailhead. You can put "Stewart Creek Trailhead, Creede, CO" as the destination. I'd suggest downloading offline maps in Google Maps before driving out if you're using GPS.

Trailhead GPS: N38 01.482' / W106 50.658'

Looking east to 13,801-foot Organ Mountain from the saddle between Baldy Alto and San Luis Peak

The Hike

This route focuses on the two 13ers with a nod to bagging 14,014-foot San Luis Peak as well. These summits are in the San Juan Mountains. This pocket of wilderness feels unique given the burly nature of the majority of the San Juans. The lower elevations are a mix of pristine alpine meadows, gently flowing creeks, and vast basins. Baldy Alto has a bit of gratuitous Class 2 rock that leads to a Class 1 slope walk up to Stewart. Nearby Organ Mountain is a fine optional peak in the area that is also a ranked 13er.

Miles and Directions

0.0 Start at the Stewart Creek Trailhead. For all the long driving to get here, the hike itself is very straightforward! The Class 1 trail is surprisingly well maintained and easy to follow. It goes all the way to the top of San Luis Peak, though that is not our goal. This is an excellent trail for mountain runners!

Stewart Peak (center) and Baldy Alto (right)

Stewart Peak–Baldy Alto

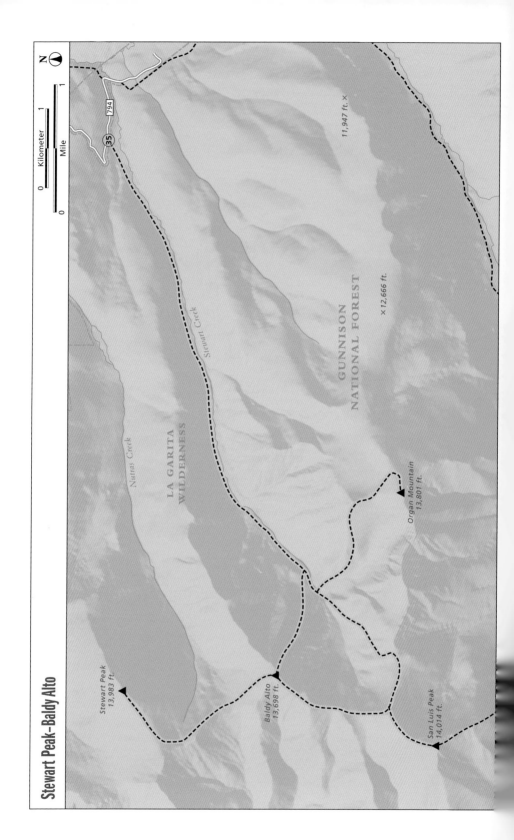

4.8 After a nice cruise into the lush valley, the Stewart Creek Trail splits off at 13,100 feet. Stay on the well-worn path up to San Luis Peak instead (which will be very obvious).

5.4 At the high saddle between San Luis Peak and Baldy Alto, it makes perfect sense to make a quick detour to summit San Luis along that sweet Class 1 trail (see the Optional Routes section). For our purposes, leave the trail at the saddle and walk along the tundra north to Baldy Alto. From here Stewart Peak looks far away, but it's a fast 2.7 miles from the saddle along easy tundra. As you approach Baldy Alto, you'll have a bit of Class 2 hiking thanks to the crumbly boulder near its summit.

6.4 The chunky summit of Baldy Alto has great views of San Luis Peak and Organ Mountain to the south. Continue north, dropping elevation toward Stewart Peak. The terrain morphs back into nice Class 1 tundra for your final approach.

8.1 Finally, the summit of Stewart Peak! Views east onto the flat valleys are incredible. To return, head back toward Baldy Alto but don't re-summit. Instead, contour to the northeast of the summit block.

9.7 The quickest way down to the Stewart Creek Trail is to descend the steep, grassy southeast slopes of Baldy Alto. Hiking poles are a big help. Descend the slopes, using the creek as a

Low-angle talus is standard issue on the ridges and slopes surrounding Stewart.

guide if the trail is hidden by willows. The footing is mostly good the whole way back to the trail. (**Note:** You also have the option to simply revisit the saddle near San Luis and regain the trail there, but it adds miles to an already long day.)

11.0 Around 12,060 feet, rejoin the Stewart Creek Trail and head northeast on the Class 1 trail back to the parking area.

14.3 Arrive back at the Stewart Creek Trailhead.

Optional Routes

San Luis Peak (14,014 feet) is about 0.3 mile (0.6 mile out and back) from the high saddle at mile 5.4 and adds about 700 vertical feet to the day.

Organ Mountain is an impressive chunk of rock! It looks rough from a distance, but it's possible to keep an ascent from Stewart Creek at Class 2. Leave the Stewart Creek Trail at 12,100 feet and head southeast up Organ's northwest slopes. The easiest path to the summit is on the east-facing slope. This detour is 1.2 miles one-way (2.4 miles as an out-and-back from the Stewart Creek Trail) and cranks up 1,720 vertical feet from when you leave the trail.

Final Thoughts

The peaks in this area of the San Juans are in the La Garita Wilderness, one of the most remote backcountry areas in Colorado. Besides gearing up for the backcountry, make sure your vehicle's spare tire is inflated and you have what you need for minor auto repairs.

Backcountry camping in the area is allowed, though it requires some strategy. The trailhead is at 10,475 feet (as is the Eddiesville Trailhead). The better backcountry sites along the trail are around 11,000 feet. This can make for rough sleep if you are coming from Front Range–type elevations of 5,000 feet or so. If you're going for a two-day adventure, I'd suggest sleeping as low as possible near the trailhead and getting as early a start as you can muster. Most of this hike is well above tree line, and storms could be a real problem if you are caught up high.

If you have the time, a three-day adventure can make the hiking more pleasant. Backpack in, rest a little, and save the drive home for a different day than the hiking.

36 Treasury Mountain

Treasury Mountain is an exciting adventure into the Ragged Wilderness area of the Elk Range. Views from its airy summit offer spectacular vistas of the Maroon Bells and other Elk Range behemoths.

Primary route: Treasury Mountain, 13,462 feet
Optional summits: Point 13,407; Treasure Mountain, 13,528 feet
Difficulty rating: Medium; this Class 2+ hike has a hearty approach on a deftly carved trail through rocky slopes. The final summit block offers the first real exposure of the day, though the summit outcrop is wide enough to avoid being too close to the steep summit drops.
Class rating: Class 2+
Round-trip distance: 5.6 miles out and back
Elevation gain: 2,130 feet
Round-trip time: 5–7 hours; half day

Finding the trailhead: The trailhead can be easily reached by SUCs and SUVs. Tough passenger cars can also make the trailhead, though if they are weaker four-cylinder vehicles I'd recommend against it—there is one steep hill that will really tax small engines. That said, I made the trailhead (barely) in my old Honda Accord the first time I hiked in the area. Subsequent visits were much easier once I upgraded to a Toyota 4Runner.

Starting in Crested Butte, take CO 135 north to Gothic Road (FR 317). Gothic Road passes the Crested Butte ski area before turning to dirt. From this point it is 10.5 miles to the top of Schofield Pass. The drive passes the eerie townsite of Gothic, through a rich aspen forest, and eventually into alpine pine territory. At the top of the 10,707-foot pass, turn left (west) onto the signed Paradise Divide Road (FR 734). Reset your odometer here.

Follow this road down to Elko flats, then at 0.6 mile up the aforementioned steep hill. Stay on the main road at 1.6 miles, bypassing a 4x4 road. When you reach 2.3 miles, the road splits. One road goes downhill to the left and two roads go uphill to the right. Take the far right road (both uphill roads go to the Yule Pass Trailhead; the other is made for 4x4 traffic). There will be signs guiding you toward Yule Pass. In 2.5 miles reach the Yule Pass parking area at an unsigned lot near a small pond. A gate marks the start of the Yule Pass Trail to the west.

Trailhead GPS: N38 59.448' / W107 03.936'

The Hike

Despite relatively easy access from Crested Butte, Treasury Mountain has a feeling of remoteness that adds to the pristine wilderness setting. There is good car camping along Paradise Divide Road, making this hike a great weekend overnight outing.

Both Treasury Mountain and nearby Treasure Mountain A are ranked 13ers. Whereas Treasury Mountain is an accommodating adventure, there is no easy way to Treasure Mountain—thus its inclusion as an optional summit in this chapter. Keeping

Treasury Mountain's summit block

the traverse Class 2 means pounding down chunky, sharp talus to skirt Point 13,407 before a steep push up to this seldom-visited 13er.

Miles and Directions

0.0 Begin on the Yule Pass Trail. A lot of work went into building this sturdy footpath. Slate River Canyon drops off dramatically to the south as the trail gradually climbs through several rock fields. Some years there may be a few small drainage gullies that will have washed the trail out—take care to step lightly over these 2- to 3-foot gaps.

0.7 Leave the trail at a low point between Cinnamon Mountain and Treasury Mountain. From here the route is off-trail, but the navigation is easy. Head northwest up shrub-covered slopes to a broad, flat plateau on the shoulder of the peak.

1.8 After the initial big push, arrive at a nearly flat section at 12,500 feet. Elk Range views begin to open up the higher you hike. Keep heading up to the northwest—it may not be apparent where the true summit is just yet. This section is rocky in places, but the footing is mostly good, notably to the left of the ridge.

2.3 Welcome to the dreaded false summit at 13,125 feet! You don't have much farther to go, and the walk up to the summit from here is quite possibly the best part of the climb. Enjoy the moderate grade as the shoulder narrows into the summit bump.

Treasury Mountain

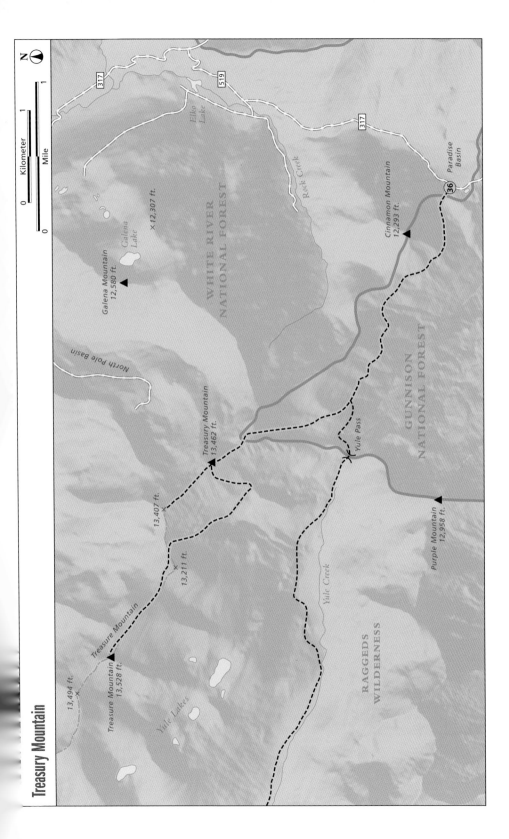

2.8 Light scrambling on a semi-exposed summit block leads to the top. Views from this pedestal gaze out on a fine collection of summits including Maroon Peak and Belleview Mountain. When you are ready, return the way you came, making sure not to stray too far west as you descend. As long as you are trending southeast, you will reconnect with the Yule Pass Trail.

5.6 Arrive back at the Yule Pass Trailhead.

Optional Routes

The walk northwest to Point 13,407 is along a broken ridge with a few Class 3 moves. This point is not a ranked or unranked 13er, but it's an exciting little add-on if you want to add some mileage to your day. Standing on its summit also reveals why traversing over to Treasure Mountain is no easy task—the ridge west of Point 13,407 is a Class 5 downclimb that would require ropes and climbing gear.

Treasure Mountain is a hard-won prize that requires skillful route-finding to connect with Treasury Mountain.

Treasury Mountain's accommodating summit ridge

However, if you are determined to hike over to Treasure Mountain, there is good news and bad news. The good news is that you can keep it Class 2+; the bad news is that you'll need to descend very loose, steep talus fields to skirt Point 13,407 to the south. Past that, a steep push up a grassy slope regains the east shoulder of Treasure Mountain.

The best way to do this is to drop off the dicey southwest slopes of Treasury Mountain and aim for an old mining road that cuts high into the hill. There are old mine openings that act like something of a waypoint. From there, cut west/southwest into a creek drainage around 11,960 feet, where you can begin to claw your way up to the grassy slope that regains the ridge. Head northwest on easy slopes after regaining the ridge to the top. From Treasury's summit it's about 2 miles and roughly 1,650 feet of gain (mostly making up what you dropped to bypass the dangerous section of the ridge). When you are ready to return, you can make it back to the access slope and simply follow the drainage down to the Yule Pass Trail (which may be faint, depending on where you reconnect). All told, it's roughly a 10-mile round-trip for this option. It's worth noting that there is no significantly easier way up Treasure Mountain, so if you're knocking off 13ers . . . this is a good opportunity.

Final Thoughts

Purple Mountain, just south of Treasury Mountain, is 12,958 feet—almost a 13er. It sure looks big enough to be a 13er from the Yule Pass Trail.

Treasure Mountain at 13,528 feet is the highest point of the Raggeds Wilderness. At 65,393 acres, the Raggeds are a smaller wilderness area, but it packs a ton of variety into a relatively small area. A collection of challenging 12ers awaits for the adventurous. The backpacking is amazing thanks to several notable waterfalls and amazing autumn colors courtesy of the many aspen stands.

North of Treasure Mountain are a collection of pillars known as the Chimneys of Treasure. Bold rock climbers ascend the towers, including the semi-popular moderate route on South Donkey Ear (5.7).

Finally, the backcountry camping along Paradise Divide Road is good beta for mountain bikers who might otherwise have a hard time finding an open camping spot along Schofield Pass.

The approach to Treasury Mountain is a perfect snapshot of the majority of the route.

37 UN 13,001

Colorado's lowest-ranked 13er is home to a fun, punchy scramble. The prelude to this highly underrated peak is a hike along the Lost Man Loop Trail. This well-maintained path wanders through willows and by streams, breaking tree line near Independence Lake.

Primary route: UN 13,001
Optional summits: Geissler Mountain, 13,301 feet; Twining Peak, 13,711 feet
Difficulty rating: Medium; a nice Class 2 trail leading to a fun ridge with Class 2+ or Class 3 options

Class rating: Class 2+/easy Class 3
Round-trip distance: 6.8 miles out and back
Elevation gain: 2,800 feet
Round-trip time: 6–8 hours; full day

Finding the trailhead: Start at the Independence Lake/Lost Man Pass Trailhead off CO 82 (Independence Pass). This trailhead is roughly 1.6 miles west of the parking lot at the top of Independence Pass or about 19 miles southeast of the town of Aspen. Independence Pass is closed from late October to May, so save this one for a summer or early autumn hike. There are about 8 parking spots at the trailhead and an auxiliary overflow parking area across the street.

Trailhead GPS: N39 07.482' / W106 34.890'

The Hike

The start of this hike is a reward in itself. Begin on the Lost Man Loop Trail as it gradually ascends through willows to tree line. Enjoy the shimmering waters of Independence Lake as the trail carries on over Lost Man Pass, where the rugged charm of Lost Man Lake decorates one of Colorado's most stunning basins. UN 13,001 stands in profile behind the lake, and the full ridge route will be visible. Scale the ridge to access a hidden side of the mountain, and finish the adventure with a fun summit block scramble.

Grabbing Geissler Mountain (and several of its sub-summits) is possible on the way back.

Miles and Directions

0.0 The adventure begins on the Lost Man Loop Trail. Simply follow this trail toward Independence Lake/Lost Man Pass, staying straight on the trail where it splits to Linkins Lake a few hundred feet in. For 2.5 miles you'll cruise on this trail as it breaches tree line and goes up and over Lost Man Pass. In autumn this approach is a glorious experience thanks to the blazing yellow and red colors of the flora and the fragile rims of ice lining streams and lakes.

1.5 Pass Independence Lake and continue up the switchbacked trail to Lost Man Pass.

UN 13,001 (center) from Lost Man Lake

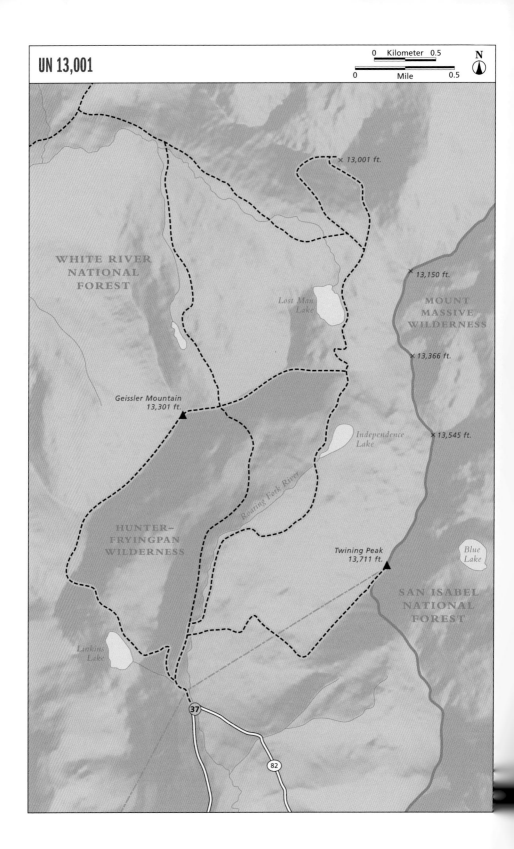

Stunning views from UN 13,001 looking back at Lost Man Lake and Lost Man Pass

2.0   The summit of Lost Man Pass. UN 13,001 finally comes into view, its great rounded spine rising to the northeast. Lost Man Lake dominates a postcard-worthy landscape as seen from the top of the pass. Stay on-trail down to the lake.

2.5   At Lost Man Lake, your warm-up is over. Continue down the trail past the northern end of the lake and get off-trail right (east). The goal is to scramble up the slopes to the saddle of UN 13,001 and Point 13,366. A few Class 2+ or easy Class 3 moves await on the upper part of this slope. There's no defined trail here.

2.8   Reach the saddle slabs. From here it's only 0.5 mile to the summit, but the scramble isn't entirely straightforward. Begin by following the ramps of rock north as the ridge narrows. Most of the terrain here is Class 2+, but mixing in a few Class 3 moves adds to the fun.

3.0   The crux of the summit ridge is a wall of rock that blocks progress on the ridge proper. There are two options. The less-enjoyable (but likely quicker) option is to go left along off-camber, grassy ledges until you can regain the ridge at the top of the rock wall. While not technical, footing here is sketchy and there aren't a lot of solid handholds for support. The better option is to go right, where a brief boulder field on the hidden side of the ridge gives way to easy, Class 2+ ramps back into the ridge.

Once you've regained the ridge, the rest of the route is obvious. A few Class 3 moves on semi-exposed terrain lead up to the summit block. Go left below the summit block and skirt up to UN 13,001's northwest ridge. A short, fun scramble east to the summit block wins this seldom-visited mountain.

3.3   The summit of UN 13,001. Below are deep valley troughs carved by ancient glaciers—a marvelous colosseum of rock and river. Views back to Lost Man Pass are especially stunning. There are two viable options to descend. One is to return the way you came, which

The author on the final blocks guarding the summit of UN 13,001

is the quickest option if you are solid at route-finding and can move at a good pace along the Class 3 sections of the ridge. The other option, which should take about the same time, is to descend starting from the northwest ridge down the Class 2 south slopes back to the Lost Man Loop Trail. The grassy terrain is steep, but not prohibitively so. A brief boulder field blocks the way back to the trail, but it can mostly be bypassed by staying left of the rock. This option will add about 0.2 mile to your overall day.

4.3 Back on-trail at Lost Man Lake. Head back on the Lost Man Loop Trail after one last push back up Lost Man Pass. It looks steep, but it's only about 400 vertical feet from the lake to the top of the pass.

6.8 Arrive back at the trailhead.

Optional Routes

Geissler Mountain

If the weather is good and you still have the legs for it, you can return to the trailhead by following the ridgeline of Geissler Mountain all the way to Linkins Lake and back to the parking lot via the Linkins Lake Trail. This ridgewalk is about 3.2 miles from Lost Man Pass to the parking lot (adding 1.2 miles to the overall day), but more importantly, it tacks on 1,100 feet of vertical gain. Dropping into the saddle between "East Geissler" and regaining Geissler Mountain is the most physical part of this route. The scrambling is a lot of fun (Class 2+).

Twining Peak

Twining Peak is the tallest mountain in this area. On the map it looks like it can be ascended from Lost Man Pass, which is technically true, but the ridge involves sustained Class 4 and even low Class 5 moves. A more direct route is to simply take the south/southwest slopes for a stiff Class 2 walk-up. Start on the Lost Man Loop Trail and break off as soon as you escape tree line. A straight shot of Twining is about 3.2 miles round-trip with 2,080 feet of vertical gain. It's not a bad option if you're short on time or have only a half day in the Buena Vista/Aspen area.

Final Thoughts

UN 13,001 is a fantastic scramble and considerably more fun than the tallest 13er in Colorado, Grizzly Peak A (13,988 feet). Griz A is just down the road from UN 13,001 and is also accessed from roads off Independence Pass. Hikers could make a novelty weekend by hiking them both, though Griz A is a loose, miserable pile of rock (but it is only Class 2).

UN 13,001 is the 637th highest ranked peak in Colorado and 584th among 13ers.

The Lost Man Campground is about 3.8 miles farther down Independence Pass and is a good place to crash either before or after your hike. It's also the other end of the Lost Man Trail Loop. Even if you stay there, I'd suggest driving up to the Independence Lake Trailhead to start your adventure rather than hiking the trail from the campground.

Gorgeous, wide-open views on the descent of UN 13,001

38 Vermillion Peak

This San Juan adventure begins with a tour of the waterfalls and streams propagated by the ghostly blue Ice Lakes. Beyond these iconic lakes are orange-hued summits that glow crimson in the setting sun, including the chunky, charming Vermillion Peak, the highest summit in San Juan County.

Primary route: Vermillion Peak, 13,894 feet
Optional summits: Fuller Peak, 13,761 feet; Golden Horn, 13,769 feet
Difficulty rating: Medium–hard; an exciting Class 2+ adventure to one of Colorado's most magical basins

Class rating: Class 2+
Round-trip distance: 10.3 miles out and back
Elevation gain: 4,060 feet
Round-trip time: 7–9 hours; full day

Finding the trailhead: Start from the town of Silverton at the junction of CO 110 and US 550. Go 2 miles south on US 550, then turn right onto Mineral Creek Road (FR 585). This dirt road is passable by 2WD cars. Follow it 4 miles to the South Mineral Campground. This is the Ice Lake Trailhead. Parking is across from the campground. (**Note:** Getting a camping spot along Mineral Creek is available, but it can be tough to claim an open spot—it's an RV-a-palooza from mid-spring to early autumn.)

Trailhead GPS: N37 48.402' / W107 46.434'

The Hike

Every section of this epic mountain adventure has a different flavor. Start on the popular Ice Lake Trail and ascend past walls of waterfalls and dense foliage along with a stiff 'n' steep trail. Break tree line into Ice Lakes Basin, where the namesake lakes glow electric blue. Grassy alpine tundra gives way to fields of red and orange boulders as you climb toward the scrappy saddle between Vermillion and Fuller Peaks.

The final push up to Vermillion Peak looks quite intimidating from a distance but reveals its true nature as you close in on the summit. Scrambling along a climber's trail is Class 2+ or easy Class 3 at its toughest spots.

Miles and Directions

0.0 Start at the signed Ice Lake Trail. This trail has exploded in popularity over the years, with the majority of foot traffic headed to Ice Lake. Be sure to stay on-trail in this lower section. There has been a lot of erosion from shortcutting the switchbacks.

0.7 At an old bridge, stay left on the worn trail that heads into the lower basin area.

2.0 Welcome to the land of waterfalls and streams! This is the Lower Ice Lakes Basin. The trail continues to efficiently gain elevation as you trend toward the higher basin and the show-

Vermillion Peak

piece namesake lake. The jagged bulk of Golden Horn is the centerpiece of this section of the hike in.

3.1 The formal trail ends at the upper Ice Lake (officially called "Ice Lake," not "Upper Ice Lake"). Point 13,230, a high point on the eastern shoulder of Golden Horn, looks a lot more important than it is, but you can see Vermillion Peak and Fuller Peak to the south. Your goal is to reach the saddle that connects them. The terrain gets rockier here. Follow the gradual slopes into the high basin, keeping Fuller Lake to your left. There's a mining cabin by the lake that seems to be standing the test of time, though it's not open for campers.

3.9 At the foot of the saddle, keep chugging up. Fuller is the more welcoming summit, as it doesn't protrude much higher than the saddle. Vermillion looks like a craggy mess, but don't worry, the way up is easier than it seems from this viewpoint. An improvised trail zigzags up the rocky, steep gully to the saddle.

4.2 At 13,460 feet, top out in the saddle. Thankfully, a climber's trail appears on the southwest side of Vermillion Peak. Even though it is loose and sketchy in places, it stays Class 2+. Follow it to a loose but welcome weakness just below the summit—a gully that scrambles up to Vermillion's airy summit.

4.7 Vermillion's summit is an exciting place! Dramatic exposure adds to the thrill—the summit area is small, but there is enough room to stay safely away from cliffs and ledges. The San Juan Peaks, notably the Wilson group, are amazing spectacles from here. Neighboring

Top: UN 13,230 is not the star of the show, but it sure looks impressive from the upper Ice Lakes B[...]
Bottom: Fuller Peak (left) with the ridge heading up Vermillion Peak (right)

Golden Horn and the broken peaks beyond are just as memorable. When you return, stay vigilant and be wary of the loose rock. Descend the saddle and backtrack to Ice Lake and the established trail to the parking area. If the weather is clear, this is a great area to linger before going down.

9.8 Arrive back at the trailhead. (**Note:** Your mileage may vary, depending on how much switchbacking/off-trail variations you choose. Final mileage will likely be between 9.8 and 10.3 miles.)

Vermillion Peak

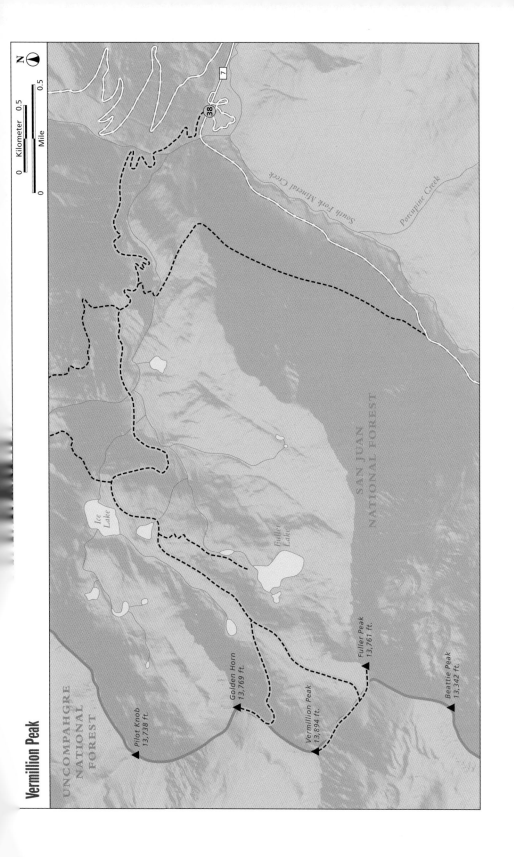

UNCOMPAHGRE NATIONAL FOREST

SAN JUAN NATIONAL FOREST

Pilot Knob
13,738 ft.

Golden Horn
13,769 ft.

Vermillion Peak
13,894 ft.

Fuller Peak
13,761 ft.

Beattie Peak
13,342 ft.

Ice Lake

Fuller Lake

South Fork Mineral Creek

Porcupine Creek

N

0   Kilometer   0.5

0   Mile   0.5

Lower Ice Lakes Basin

Optional Routes

Fuller Peak is a nice add-on, even though it isn't a ranked 13er. Adding on Fuller requires a 0.2 mile walk-up (only 0.4 mile out and back) from the saddle on the same loose rock as Vermillion.

Golden Horn's southwest ridge is an excellent Class 3 scramble, but connecting it from Vermillion is not advised. The ridge between the two requires downclimbing on Class 3+ (possibly Class 4) terrain on loose, awful rock. If you want to get up Golden Horn, the better route is to hike up Scarlet Pass (the saddle between Vermillion and Golden Horn) and go up from there. From my experiences, it's likely quicker to descend Vermillion back to the Vermillion/Fuller saddle and walk over to Scarlet Pass. Getting all three summits is a big day and requires a high level of fitness and endurance (there's over 5,000 feet of vertical gain if you combine them all).

Final Thoughts

Mining operations throughout the San Juans have left behind a lot of ruins. This area is no different. Rusted barrels, abandoned tools, and plenty of other relics are littered about the Ice Lakes Basin.

Pilot Knob sits to the northwest of Golden Horn and is a ranked 13er at 13,738 feet. Like Golden Horn, it's a decomposing pile of volcanic rock. Unlike Golden Horn, however, it's an absolute mess to climb and the most challenging 13er in the Ice Lakes region. I would classify it as "very uncomfortable Class 4," thanks to the poor rock quality and wicked exposure. If you're thinking of getting this elusive 13er, I'd highly suggest bringing ropes and climbing gear.

Like a lot of 13ers, Vermillion Peak is best hiked in mid- to late summer or early autumn. There's a lot of water here, so things can get muddy in spring and buggy in early summer.

39 West Spanish Peak

Looming large, West Spanish Peak was once thought to be the highest mountain in Colorado thanks to its impressive prominence. This hike is flush with interesting geology courtesy of its volcanic beginnings. The Spanish Mountains are distinct enough to warrant their own distinct sub-range.

Primary route: West Spanish Peak, 13,626 feet
Difficulty rating: Medium; an interesting ascent that stays Class 2 but has a few sections of loose rock as the formal trail ends and the ridgeline hike begins

Class rating: Class 2
Round-trip distance: 6.8 miles out and back
Elevation gain: 2,930 feet
Round-trip time: 4–6 hours; half day

Finding the trailhead: Start from the intersection of US 160 West and CO 12, about 7 miles west of Walsenburg. Go south onto CO 12 for 22.3 miles toward Cuchara Pass. Pass through the town of La Veta and drive along Cuchara Pass. At mile 22.3, turn left onto Cordova Pass (dirt, but passable by 2WD vehicles). Drive up for 6 miles to the top of the pass and the trailhead.

There is a nominal day-use fee for hiking in the Spanish Peaks Wilderness. There are also three first-come, first-served fee campsites. (**Note:** There is no water at the pass, so bring enough for your hike and for camping, if needed.)

Trailhead GPS: N37 20.898' / W105 01.458'

The Hike

West Spanish Peak is one of the most impressive looking 13ers, thanks to it having the highest "prominence" of all the 13ers and 12th overall in the state. (A simple definition of prominence is "the minimum height necessary to descend to get from the summit to any higher terrain"). One look at the massive mountain from the south near the town of La Veta might lead you to believe this is the tallest peak in the Rockies! Thanks to its volcanic past, there are a lot of amazing geological features to see, especially the tall igneous rock walls known as the Spanish Dikes that fan out at the foot of the mountain. It's also bone dry, in part due to its isolated profile.

If you use a metric state of mind, West Spanish Peak is the easternmost 4,000-meter peak in the United States. That translates to 13,123 feet in the imperial system.

Miles and Directions

0.0 Enjoy an easy start by taking the signed West Peak Trail north out of the parking lot. Pass through meadows, forests, and tundra along this nearly flat trail.

West Spanish Peak

Top: Dyke formations are seen from high on the ridge to West Spanish Peak.
Bottom: The aesthetic approach to West Spanish Peak

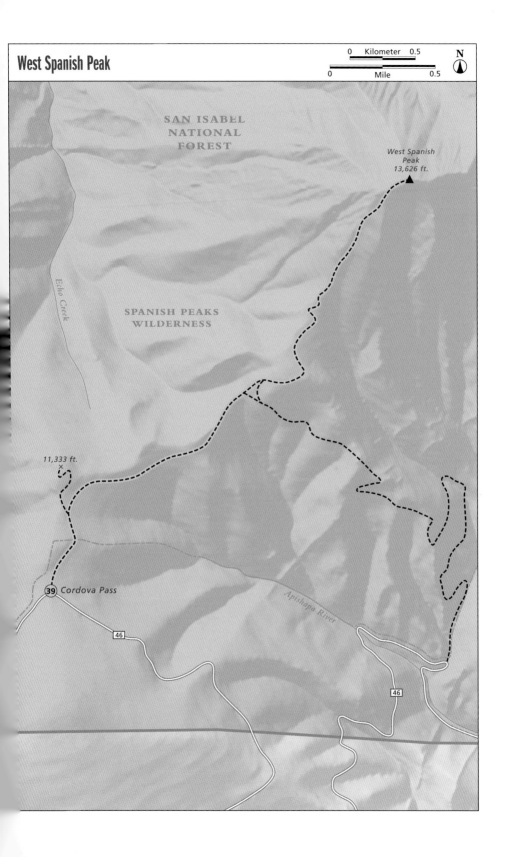

SAN ISABEL
NATIONAL
FOREST

West Spanish
Peak
13,626 ft.

Echo Creek

SPANISH PEAKS
WILDERNESS

11,333 ft.
×

39 Cordova Pass

Apishapa River

46

46

N

0   Kilometer   0.5

0   Mile   0.5

0.3 Stay straight on the Class 1 West Peak Trail at the junction with the barely there Salazar Trail.

1.5 The Apishapa Trail splits off from the West Peak Trail, which looks a little odd because it goes straight before turning right (southeast)—making it seem like it's the main trail. The split is marked, so stay left on the West Peak Trail.

2.4 The rocky flanks of West Spanish Peak absorb the easygoing, established trail. This is the start of the Class 2 trail. From this point it's about 1,500 vertical feet to the top. Though there is not a maintained trail, there are cairns and some worn stretches of pseudo-trail in the talus. The navigation is mostly straightforward, and the better footing is found to the left side of the ridge. About halfway up are a few random wind shelters.

3.1 You're at the top . . . of the false summit! Nonetheless, the views from here are incredible. This is a great place to see the Spanish Dikes far below, and the unheralded 11,573-foot Mount Mestas stands out to the north. Continue on a short distance to the true summit.

3.4 West Spanish's highest point is the first cairn on the broad summit area. There is a larger cairn a bit farther on (to be safe, why not visit both?). No matter which one you stand on, the other one is going to look taller—quite a trick of perception. When you are ready to return, pick your way down more or less the way you came up. Eventually reconnect with the West Peak Trail and head back to Cordova Pass.

6.8 Arrive back at the trailhead at Cordova Pass.

Final Thoughts

The impressive "Wall of 13ers" to the southwest are part of the Culebra sub-range of the Sangre de Cristo Mountains. There are a whole bunch of ranked 13ers in the group. The highest point of them all is the 14,049-foot Culebra Peak, a frustrating summit for many 14er enthusiasts because it is privately owned (as of 2020) and access is always in peril.

West Spanish Peak (and its 12,684-foot counterpart, East Spanish Peak) are known as "stocks." These are large masses of once-molten igneous rock that intruded into sedimentary rock, then were later revealed when the sedimentary rock eroded away. Perhaps the most famous igneous stock in the United States is Devil's Tower in Wyoming. West Spanish Peak is made of the same stuff.

The volcanic dikes were created in a similar fashion. Magma filled cracks in sedimentary rock that later were worn away, leaving the more resistant igneous walls. The dikes below West Spanish Peak extend in all directions, creating quite an impressive visual effect if you happen to see them casting shadows in the early morning or later afternoon. In the 1800s the dikes and the Spanish Peaks were major landmarks along the Santa Fe Trail.

40 Whale Peak

Whale Peak is a somewhat isolated Front Range 13er that is especially beautiful in late summer and early autumn. Besides its aesthetic charms, it's also a 13er whose access from the Denver/Boulder metro area does not require playing traffic roulette on I-70.

Primary route: Whale Peak, 13,078 feet
Difficulty rating: Medium; a Class 2 hike that starts on-trail and gets off-trail only at tree line
Class rating: Class 2

Round-trip distance: 6.8 miles (4x4 trailhead start) out and back; 9.2 miles (Hall Valley Campground) out and back
Elevation gain: 2,900 feet
Round-trip time: 5–7 hours; full day

Finding the trailhead: Take US 285 southwest of Denver to Park CR 60 (Hall Valley Road). This turnoff is 4.3 miles north of Kenosha Pass and 3 miles south from the center of the modest town of Grant. Turn onto Park CR 60 and follow this maintained dirt road 5.2 miles. Along the way you will pass Handcart Campground on your left. Go past it to a signed intersection at mile 5.2 and turn left toward Hall Valley Campground/Gibson Lake on FR 120.B. Passenger vehicles will have to park here. From this point it is 1.2 miles to the Gibson Lake Trailhead. (**Note:** Hall Valley Campground is only a few hundred feet from this juncture.)

Four-wheel-drive and high-clearance vehicles can take a right (westerly) turn onto FR 120.C just before the campground proper. This 4x4 road goes 1.2 miles to the Gibson Lake Trailhead. It's a rocky road with a few spots requiring high clearance, but it's not very difficult by Colorado standards. Sport-utility cars like Subaru Outbacks may have issues clearing some of the bigger rocks. There is a stream crossing 0.2 mile in. Go 1 more mile and the small parking area (4 to 5 vehicles) will be marked on the left-hand side of the road. The Gibson Lake Trail starts here.

Trailhead GPS: N39 29.532' / W105 49.440'

The Hike

A fun aspect of hiking Whale Peak is making a full tour above Gibson Lake by ascending the east slopes and descending the southeast slopes between Whale Peak and Point 12,733. This is an excellent adventure to gain off-trail experience with minimal navigational consequences.

Whale Peak's location gives it a nice overview of several Mount Evans Wilderness summits to the north and Lost Creek terrain to the south.

Miles and Directions

0.0 The mileage here starts from the Gibson Lake Trailhead. If you need to walk (or bike) up from the Hall Valley Campground, it's an extra 1.2 miles—but that distance goes by quickly. The start of this hike is simple: Get on the Gibson Lake Trail and follow it 1.9 miles. Enjoy the shade and the gently flowing creek as you ascend to tree line.

Top: Whale Peak
Bottom: Working up the approach to Whale Peak

Whale Peak

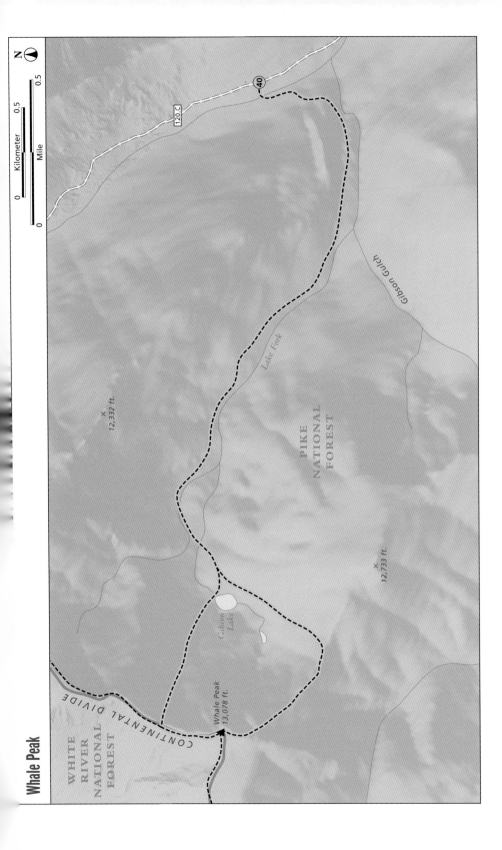

The summit of Whale Peak

1.9 Hop off the trail (before Gibson Lake) and head up the east slopes to the ridgeline north of Whale Peak. The off-trail work here is concentrated at the bottom of the slopes, where the hillside is off-camber—hiking poles are a good idea. Eventually the grade smooths out and the rest of the outing turns into a pleasant tundra walk. There is no significant exposure.

2.7 When you gain the ridge, Whale Peak will loom like a leviathan to the south. If you want to snag Whale's northern sub-peak, it's likely going to be only a few hundred feet from where you gained the ridge. It's 13,001 feet but not a ranked 13er (the lowest-ranked 13er is also 13,001 feet and is covered in this guide in chapter 37). Once you're on the ridge, it's a simple walk south to Whale's summit cairn. The Continental Divide Trail phases in and out along the ridge (as it tends to do everywhere it goes).

3.4 Whale Peak features an impressive summit cairn. From the summit you have two options down: Return the way you came or make a lollipop loop by heading southeast and dropping down the slopes to the south of Gibson Lake. Timewise, these are about the same. The loop route has better footing but is slightly longer, plus you get to see Gibson Lake up close. From the lake, regain the trail and head home.

6.8 Arrive back at the Gibson Lake Trailhead.

Final Thoughts

Gibson Lake does see hikers in the summer, but few of them head up the ridges to the peaks. Whale Peak seems to have escaped the brunt of mining damage that many other nearby peaks have sustained—especially those to the north.

This is great wildflower territory. There are a few other ways up Whale Peak (from Jefferson Lake and from Georgia Pass), but this one is my personal favorite.

Appendix: The 13ers

This list is a collected resource from the USGS, the Colorado Mountain Club, Gerry Roach's 13ers list (www.climb.mountains.com/Project_Island_files/CO_13ers.shtml), and the List of John 13ers elevations.

Mountains marked with "S" for an elevation are soft-ranked. Unnumbered 13ers are named/recognized but not ranked due to the 300-foot clearance rule. Highlighted rows are 13ers featured in this guide.

13er Name	Overall Rank	13er Rank	Elevation
"Sunlight Spire"			13,995
Grizzly Peak A	54	1	13,988
Stewart Peak	55	2	13,983
Columbia Point	56	3	13,980
"Pin Point"			13,980
"Prow, The"			13,980
Pigeon Peak	57	4	13,972
Ouray, Mount	58	5	13,971
"Kitty Kat Carson"			13,970
Ice Mountain	59	6	13,951
Fletcher Mountain	60	7	13,951
Gemini Peak			13,951
Pacific Peak	61	8	13,950
Cathedral Peak A	62	9	13,943
French Mountain	63	10	13,940
Hope, Mount A	64	11	13,933
"Thunder Pyramid"	65	12	13,932
Adams, Mount A	66	13	13,931
Gladstone Peak	67	14	13,913
Meeker, Mount EB	68	15	13,911
Casco Peak	69	16	13,908
Red Mountain A	70	17	13,908
Emerald Peak	71	18	13,904
"Drift Peak"	S2	S1	13,900
Horseshoe Mountain	72	19	13,898
"Phoenix Peak"	73	20	13,895
Vermillion Peak	74	21	13,894
Frasco Benchmark			13,876
Cronin Peak	75	22	13,870
Buckskin, Mount	76	23	13,865
Vestal Peak	77	24	13,864
Jones Mountain A	78	25	13,860
"North Apostle"	79	26	13,860
Meeker Ridge EB			13,860
Clinton Peak	80	27	13,857
Dyer Mountain	81	28	13,855
Crystal Peak A	82	29	13,852

13er Name	Overall Rank	13er Rank	Elevation
Traver Peak			13,852
Edwards, Mount	83	30	13,850
California Peak	84	31	13,849
Oklahoma, Mount	85	32	13,845
Spalding, Mount			13,842
Half Peak	86	33	13,841
Atlantic Peak	87	34	13,841
Hagerman Peak	88	35	13,841
Turret Peak A	89	36	13,835
Point 13,832	90	37	13,832
Holy Cross Ridge	91	38	13,831
Iowa Peak	S3	S2	13,831
Jupiter Mountain	92	39	13,830
"Tower One"			13,830
"Huerfano Peak"	93	40	13,828
Jagged Mountain	94	41	13,824
"Lackawanna Peak"	95	42	13,823
Silverheels, Mount TR	96	43	13,822
Rio Grande Pyramid	97	44	13,821
Teakettle Mountain	98	45	13,819
Point 13,811	99	46	13,811
Dallas Peak	100	47	13,809
Niagara Peak	101	48	13,807
American Peak	102	49	13,806
Trinity Peak	103	50	13,805
Arrow Peak	104	51	13,803
"Castleabra"	105	52	13,803
Organ Mountain A	106	53	13,801
"Obstruction Peak"	107	54	13,799
Arkansas, Mount	108	55	13,795
Point 13,795	109	56	13,795
"Column Ridge"			13,795
Rito Alto Peak	110	57	13,794
Square Top Mountain A	111	58	13,794
"Captain Bivwacko Tower"			13,790
Animas Mountain	112	59	13,786
Potosi Peak	113	60	13,786
Rinker Peak	114	61	13,783
Mosquito Peak	115	62	13,781
Golden Horn	116	63	13,780
Garfield Peak A	117	64	13,780
Sawtooth, The			13,780
McNamee Peak			13,780
Point 13,768	118	65	13,768
Ulysses S. Grant Peak	119	66	13,767
"West Trinity"	120	67	13,765
"Magdalene Mountain"	121	68	13,762
Deer Mountain A	122	69	13,761
Bull Hill A	123	70	13,761

13er Name	Overall Rank	13er Rank	Elevation
Fuller Peak			13,761
San Miguel Peak	124	71	13,752
Storm King Peak	125	72	13,752
Sheridan, Mount	126	73	13,748
Aetna, Mount	127	74	13,745
"East Trinity"	128	75	13,745
"West Dallas"	S4	S3	13,741
"West Eolus"	S5	S4	13,740
"South Windom"			13,740
Ptarmigan Peak			13,739
Sayres Benchmark	129	76	13,738
Grizzly Peak B	130	77	13,738
Argentine Peak	131	78	13,738
Pilot Knob A	132	79	13,738
Point 13,736	133	80	13,736
"T 0"	134	81	13,735
Vermejo Peak	135	82	13,723
"Animas Forks Mountain"	136	83	13,722
"Lightning Pyramid"	137	84	13,722
Pole Creek Mountain	138	85	13,716
Silver Mountain A	139	86	13,714
Point 13,712	140	87	13,712
Twining Peak	141	88	13,711
La Garita Peak			13,710
Grizzly Mountain	142	89	13,708
Point 13,708	S6	S5	13,708
Colony Baldy	143	90	13,705
Six, Peak	144	91	13,705
Thirteen, Peak			13,705
Glacier Point	S7	S6	13,704
Treasurevault Mountain	S8	S7	13,701
Grizzly Peak C	145	92	13,700
Fifteen, Peak	146	93	13,700
Baldy Alto	147	94	13,698
Monitor Peak	148	95	13,695
Gilpin Peak	149	96	13,694
"Kismet"			13,694
Rolling Mountain	150	97	13,693
Loveland Mountain			13,692
"Every Mountain"	151	98	13,691
Wheeler Mountain	152	99	13,690
"Cooper Creek Peak"	153	100	13,688
Point 13,688	154	101	13,688
Cirque Mountain	155	102	13,686
Bald Mountain A	156	103	13,684
Oso, Mount	157	104	13,684
White Ridge TR			13,684
Seven, Peak	158	105	13,682
Point 13,681	159	106	13,681

13er Name	Overall Rank	13er Rank	Elevation
Purgatoire Peak	160	107	13,676
"Quarter Peak"	161	108	13,674
Tweto, Mount	162	109	13,672
Jackson, Mount	163	110	13,670
White, Mount	164	111	13,667
"K 2"			13,664
Carbonate Mountain A	165	112	13,663
Lookout Peak	166	113	13,661
"Northwest Pole"	167	114	13,660
Point 13,660 A	168	115	13,660
Wood Mountain A	169	116	13,660
Point 13,660 B	S9	S8	13,660
"Purgatory Point"			13,660
Hamilton Peak			13,658
Carson Peak	170	117	13,657
Coxcomb Peak	171	118	13,656
Taylor Mountain A	172	119	13,651
Mamma, Mount	173	120	13,646
Champion, Mount	174	121	13,646
Redcliff	175	122	13,642
Bard Peak	176	123	13,641
"Electric Pass Peak"	177	124	13,635
Peak 10	178	125	13,633
"Anderson Peak"	179	126	13,631
Point 13,631	180	127	13,631
"South South Massive"			13,630
"Esprit Point"			13,630
Silex, Mount	181	128	13,628
White Dome	182	129	13,627
West Spanish Peak	183	130	13,626
Point 13,626	184	131	13,626
"Noname Needle"			13,620
Snowmass Peak			13,620
Guardian, The	185	132	13,617
Blaurock, Mount	186	133	13,616
Father Dyer Peak			13,615
North Star Mountain	187	134	13,614
"T 12"			13,614
Pico Aislado	188	135	13,611
Tijeras Peak	189	136	13,604
Jones Peak			13,604
Gray Wolf Mountain	190	137	13,602
"North Crown Mountain"			13,599
Electric Peak A TR	191	138	13,598
Cyclone Mountain A	192	139	13,596
"Lo Carb"			13,591
Matterhorn Peak	193	140	13,590
"Tower Two" aka "Light Tower"			13,590
One, Peak	194	141	13,589

13er Name	Overall Rank	13er Rank	Elevation
Cottonwood Peak A	195	142	13,588
Cosgriff, Mount			13,588
McClellan Mountain			13,587
Point 13,581	196	145	13,581
Emma, Mount	197	144	13,581
Powell, Mount A	198	145	13,580
Twin Peaks, North A	199	146	13,580
Clark Peak A	200	147	13,580
Point 13,580 A	201	148	13,580
Point 13,580 B	202	149	13,580
Point 13,580 C	S10	S9	13,580
"Rockfountain Ridge"			13,580
Chiefs Head Peak	203	150	13,579
Evans, Mount B	204	151	13,577
Point 13,577	205	152	13,577
Gravel Mountain A			13,577
Rosalie Peak	206	153	13,575
Greylock Mountain	207	154	13,575
Parnassus, Mount	208	155	13,574
Broken Hand Peak	209	156	13,573
Weston Peak			13,572
Crown Mountain			13,569
"West Apostle"	210	157	13,568
"Coffeepot" aka "S 1"			13,568
"Gudy Peak"	211	158	13,566
Point 13,565	212	159	13,565
Hayden Peak A			13,561
Hagues Peak	213	160	13,560
Wasatch Mountain	214	161	13,555
Point 13,555	S11	S10	13,555
Fluted Peak	215	162	13,554
McCauley Peak	216	163	13,554
Pettingell Peak	217	164	13,553
Gibbs Peak A	218	165	13,553
Tower Mountain	219	166	13,552
Point 13,550	220	167	13,550
Kuss Peak aka "Repeater Peak"	S12	S11	13,548
Point 13,546	221	168	13,546
Point 13,545	S13	S12	13,545
"T 2"			13,543
Whitecross Mountain	222	169	13,542
Point 13,541	223	170	13,541
White Rock Mountain TR	224	171	13,540
Point 13,540 A	225	172	13,540
Point 13,540 B	226	173	13,540
Eleven, Peak	227	174	13,540
"V 4"	228	175	13,540
"T 3" aka "Block Tops"			13,540
"T 4" aka "Block Tops"			13,540

13er Name	Overall Rank	13er Rank	Elevation
Emma Burr Mountain	229	176	13,538
Point 13,537	230	177	13,537
"K 49"	231	178	13,535
Point 13,535	232	179	13,535
Twin Peaks, South A			13,534
Ervin Peak	233	180	13,531
"Epaulie"	234	181	13,530
Treasure Mountain A	235	182	13,528
Boulder Mountain	236	183	13,528
Leviathan Peak	237	184	13,528
"V 3"	238	185	13,528
"Peak of the Clouds"	239	186	13,524
"Cataract Peak"	240	187	13,524
Browns Peak			13,523
Epaulet Mountain			13,523
Milwaukee Peak	241	188	13,522
Star Peak A	242	189	13,521
Trinchera Peak	243	190	13,517
Point 13,517 A	244	191	13,517
Point 13,517 B	S14	S13	13,517
Keefe Peak	245	192	13,516
Ypsilon Mountain	246	193	13,514
"Silver Peak"	247	194	13,513
Point 13,510 A	248	195	13,510
Point 13,510 B	249	196	13,510
Bridal Peak aka "T 11"	250	197	13,510
Telluride Peak	S15	S14	13,509
Eureka Mountain A	251	198	13,507
"Lake Point"			13,506
"Petroleum Peak"	252	199	13,505
North Arapaho Peak	253	200	13,502
Fairchild Mountain	254	201	13,502
Point 13,500	255	202	13,500
Iron Nipple			13,500
Needle Ridge			13,500
"The Butterknife"			13,500
Red Mountain B			13,500
Sixteen, Peak			13,500
"Blue Needle"			13,500
"Big Bear Peak"	256	203	13,498
Hunter Peak	257	204	13,497
Pagoda Mountain	258	205	13,497
Mears Peak	259	206	13,496
Whitehouse Mountain A	260	207	13,492
Point 13,490	261	208	13,490
Marcy, Mount	262	209	13,490
Graystone Peak	263	210	13,489
Cuatro Peak	264	211	13,487
Storm Peak A	265	212	13,487

13er Name	Overall Rank	13er Rank	Elevation
Three Needles	266	213	13,481
Canby Mountain	267	214	13,478
Three, Peak	268	215	13,478
"T 10"	269	216	13,477
Two, Peak	270	217	13,475
"V 10"	271	218	13,475
Point 13,472 A	272	219	13,472
La Junta Peak	273	220	13,472
Point 13,472 B	S16	S15	13,472
Eighteen, Peak			13,472
Silver Mountain B	274	221	13,470
Ridgway, Mount	275	222	13,468
Miranda Peak	S17	S16	13,468
"Big Blue Peak"	S18	S17	13,467
"Alamosito"	276	223	13,466
"Pear Peak"	277	224	13,462
Treasury Mountain	278	225	13,462
Point 13,462	279	226	13,462
Quail Mountain	280	227	13,461
Point 13,460 A	281	228	13,460
Point 13,460 B	282	229	13,460
Sleeping Sexton	283	230	13,460
San Joaquin Ridge	284	231	13,460
"East Windom"	S19	S18	13,460
"East North Star Mountain"			13,460
"Tower Three"			13,460
Ute Ridge	285	232	13,455
Hanson Peak	286	233	13,454
"Campbell Creek Peak"	287	234	13,454
Kendall Peak	288	235	13,451
Horn Peak	289	236	13,450
"Tundra Top"	290	237	13,450
Hurricane Peak			13,447
Apache Peak	291	238	13,441
"S 6"	292	239	13,441
"T 5"	293	240	13,436
"Punta Serpiente"			13,436
Taylor Peak A	294	241	13,435
"Mascot Peak"	295	242	13,435
"Mountaineer Peak"	296	243	13,434
Point 13,433	297	244	13,433
Twin Sisters, East	298	245	13,432
Jenkins Mountain	299	246	13,432
"Sundog"	300	247	13,432
"Oscars Peak"	S20	S19	13,432
Gray Needle			13,430
Vallecito Mountain	301	248	13,428
Grizzly Peak D	302	249	13,427
Point 13,427	303	250	13,427

13er Name	Overall Rank	13er Rank	Elevation
Mummy Mountain	304	251	13,425
Spread Eagle Peak TR	305	252	13,423
"Siberia Peak" TR	306	253	13,420
Eagles Nest A aka "Peak A"	307	254	13,420
Ten, Peak	S21	S20	13,420
Index, The			13,420
Rowe Peak			13,420
"T 1"			13,420
"Spencer Peak"			13,420
Twin Thumbs, North			13,420
"SoSo, Mount"	308	255	13,417
Little Giant Peak	309	256	13,416
Cleveland Peak	310	257	13,414
"Heisshorn"	311	258	13,411
Four, Peak	312	259	13,410
"S 3"			13,410
Hilliard Peak	313	260	13,409
Navajo Peak A	314	261	13,409
Finback Knob			13,409
Wilcox, Mount	315	262	13,408
Mariquita Peak	316	263	13,405
Nine, Peak	317	264	13,402
Point 13,402	318	265	13,402
Rhoda, Mount	319	266	13,402
White Benchmark TR	320	267	13,401
Point 13,401	321	268	13,401
Baldy Chato			13,401
Bartlett Mountain	322	269	13,400
South Arapaho Peak			13,397
Bent Peak	323	270	13,393
Parry Peak A	324	271	13,391
Rogers Peak	325	272	13,391
"East Pole Creek Mountain"	S22	S21	13,391
Chicago Peak aka "T 6"	326	273	13,385
Prize Benchmark	327	274	13,384
Point 13,384	328	275	13,384
Baldy Cinco	329	276	13,383
Williams Mountain	330	277	13,382
Gold Dust Peak	331	278	13,380
Precarious Peak TR	332	279	13,380
Geissler Mountain, East	333	280	13,380
South Lookout Peak	334	281	13,380
"Triangle Peak"	335	282	13,380
Music Mountain	336	283	13,380
"S 5"			13,380
Italian Mountain	337	284	13,378
Point 13,377	338	285	13,377
Lakes Peak TR	339	286	13,375
Point 13,374	340	287	13,374

13er Name	Overall Rank	13er Rank	Elevation
Twin Sisters, West	341	288	13,374
Guyot, Mount	342	289	13,370
Buckskin Benchmark	343	290	13,370
Dome Mountain A	344	291	13,370
Monumental Peak	345	292	13,369
Sultan Mountain	346	293	13,368
"Little Pikes Peak"			13,363
De Anza Peak A	347	294	13,362
Pearl Mountain	348	295	13,362
Englemann Peak	349	296	13,362
"T 7"	350	297	13,359
"Silverthorne, Mount"`	351	298	13,357
"North Summit"			13,357
Hoosier Ridge	352	299	13,352
Herard, Mount	353	300	13,350
Hermit Peak A	354	301	13,350
Malamute Peak	355	302	13,348
Peerless Mountain			13,348
"Finnegan Peak"	356	303	13,346
"Tincup Peak"	357	304	13,345
Point 13,342	358	305	13,342
Beattie Peak	359	306	13,342
Point 13,340 A	360	307	13,340
Owen, Mount A	361	308	13,340
Point 13,340 B	362	309	13,340
Kendall Mountain	363	310	13,340
Twin Thumbs, South			13,340
Ships Prow EB			13,340
Glacier Ridge EB			13,340
Brown Mountain A	364	311	13,339
Point 13,336	365	312	13,336
Maxwell, Mount			13,335
Coney Benchmark	366	313	13,334
Venable Peak	367	314	13,334
De Anza Peak B	368	315	13,333
Twin Peaks B			13,333
"East Thorn"			13,333
"Proposal Peak"	369	316	13,330
Cinnamon Mountain A	370	317	13,328
McHenrys Peak	371	318	13,327
West Buffalo Peak	372	319	13,326
Storm Peak B			13,326
"East Storm"	373	320	13,325
"Lake Fork Peak"	374	321	13,322
Leahy Peak			13,322
Sunshine Mountain A	375	322	13,321
Trico Peak aka "T 9"	376	323	13,321
Palmyra Peak aka "T 14"			13,319
Point 13,317	377	324	13,317

13er Name	Overall Rank	13er Rank	Elevation
"Ski Hayden Peak"			13,316
"T 8"	378	325	13,315
"Baldy no es Cinco"	379	326	13,313
William Benchmark	380	327	13,312
"Booby Prize"	381	328	13,312
"C.T. Peak"	382	329	13,312
"Oyster Peak" aka "West Pearl Mountain"	383	330	13,312
Alice, Mount	384	331	13,310
Aztec Mountain	385	332	13,310
Point 13,310	386	333	13,310
Emery Peak			13,310
"V 2"	387	334	13,309
Echo Mountain			13,309
Point 13,308	388	335	13,308
Warren, Mount	389	336	13,307
"P 2"	390	337	13,302
Geissler Mountain, West	391	338	13,301
Summit Peak	392	339	13,300
Middle Peak	393	340	13,300
Daly, Mount A	394	341	13,300
Point 13,300 A	395	342	13,300
Point 13,300 B	396	343	13,300
"P 3"	397	344	13,300
"Tellurium Peak"	398	345	13,300
East Buffalo Peak	399	346	13,300
Point 13,300 C	400	347	13,300
Galena Mountain A	401	348	13,300
"El Punto"	402	349	13,300
Point 13,300 D	403	350	13,300
Point 13,300 E	S23	S22	13,300
Point 13,300 F	S24	S23	13,300
"Middle Point"	S25	S24	13,300
"Tigger Peak"			13,300
"Gibraltar Mountain"			13,300
Point 13,295	404	351	13,295
James Peak	405	352	13,294
"Citadel, The"	406	353	13,294
Electric Peak B	407	354	13,292
Sheep Mountain A	408	355	13,292
Waverly Mountain			13,292
Dolores Peak	409	356	13,290
Bonita Peak	410	357	13,286
"Wayah Peak"	411	358	13,284
Five, Peak	412	359	13,283
Truro Peak	413	360	13,282
"Tabor Peak"	414	361	13,282
Grizzly Peak E	415	362	13,281
Lady Washington, Mount EB	416	363	13,281

13er Name	Overall Rank	13er Rank	Elevation
"Fools Pyramid"	417	364	13,278
Comanche Peak A	418	365	13,277
Ruby Mountain A	419	366	13,277
Kiowa Peak	420	367	13,276
Whitney Peak	421	368	13,276
Mendota Peak			13,275
Seigal Mountain	422	369	13,274
"Crestolita"	423	370	13,270
Twin Peaks B Northeast			13,270
Pecks Peak			13,270
"The King"			13,270
Antora Peak	424	371	13,269
Wildhorse Peak	425	372	13,266
Geneva Peak	426	373	13,266
Marble Mountain A	427	374	13,266
Knife Point	428	375	13,265
Heisspitz, The	429	376	13,262
Point 13,261	430	377	13,261
"Peak G"	431	378	13,260
Darley Mountain	432	379	13,260
"Golden Tops"	433	380	13,260
Point 13,260	434	381	13,260
"V 9"	435	382	13,260
Whitehead Peak			13,259
Broken Hill	436	383	13,256
"Sheep Rock Mountain"	437	384	13,255
Henry Mountain	438	385	13,254
"Van Wit"			13,254
Point 13,253	439	386	13,253
"Point 13,253 South"			13,253
"S 8"	440	387	13,252
Bancroft, Mount			13,250
"P 1"			13,250
Point 13,248	441	388	13,248
"Peak Z"	442	389	13,245
Spring Mountain	443	390	13,244
Point 13,244	444	391	13,244
"S 4" aka "Wolcott Peak"	445	392	13,242
"Fortress Peak" aka "U 3"	446	393	13,241
Landslide Peak			13,238
Notch Mountain			13,237
Point 13,235	447	394	13,235
Sniktau, Mount	448	395	13,234
Turner Peak	449	396	13,233
Belleview Mountain A TR	450	397	13,233
Hesperus Mountain	451	398	13,232
"Cassi Peak"	452	399	13,232
Point 13,232	453	400	13,232
Point 13,230 A	454	401	13,230

13er Name	Overall Rank	13er Rank	Elevation
"Peak Q"	455	402	13,230
Point 13,230 B	S26	S25	13,230
"Peak F"			13,230
"Tower Four" EB aka "Mr. Stubbs"			13,230
Red Mountain C	456	403	13,229
Point 13,229	457	404	13,229
Eight, Peak	S27	S26	13,228
Audubon, Mount	458	405	13,223
Point 13,222 A	459	406	13,222
Point 13,222 B	460	407	13,222
Macomber Peak			13,222
"Weminuche Peak"	461	408	13,220
"Peak C"	462	409	13,220
Greenhalgh Mountain	463	410	13,220
"S 7"	464	411	13,220
Lavender Peak aka "L 1"	465	412	13,220
Hagar Mountain	466	413	13,220
Ellingwood Ridge	S28	S27	13,220
Point 13,220	S29	S28	13,220
California Mountain	S30	S29	13,220
King Solomon Mountain	S31	S30	13,220
"Peak E"			13,220
"Kurzhorn, The"			13,220
Little Finger			13,220
Keyboard of the Winds			13,220
Jones Mountain B	467	414	13,218
Irving Peak	468	415	13,218
Engineer Mountain A	469	416	13,218
Point 13,216	470	417	13,216
"Hassell Peak"	471	418	13,215
Red Peak A			13,215
Fairview Peak A	472	419	13,214
"Hardrocker"			13,214
"Peak L" TR	473	420	13,213
Thirsty Peak			13,213
Campbell Peak			13,213
Point 13,212 TR	474	421	13,212
Homestake Peak	475	422	13,209
Gladstone Ridge	476	423	13,209
Lambertson Peak			13,209
Teocalli Mountain TR	477	424	13,208
Powell Peak	478	425	13,208
Hayden Mountain, South	479	426	13,206
Point 13,206	480	427	13,206
Jacque Peak	482	429	13,205
Eagle Peak A	481	428	13,205
Nebo, Mount	483	430	13,205
Lenawee Mountain	484	431	13,204

13er Name	Overall Rank	13er Rank	Elevation
Bennett Peak	485	432	13,203
Tuttle Mountain	486	433	13,203
Point 13,203	487	434	13,203
"Leaning South Peak"	488	435	13,203
Point 13,202	489	436	13,202
Point 13,201	490	437	13,201
"Mountain Boy Peak"	491	438	13,198
Peak 9	492	439	13,195
London Mountain	493	440	13,194
"Black Mountain"			13,193
"Fancy Peak"	494	441	13,192
Moss, Mount	S32	S31	13,192
Red Peak B	495	442	13,189
Sheep Mountain B			13,188
Valois, Mount	496	443	13,185
Beaubien Peak	497	444	13,184
Rowe Mountain			13,184
Bullion Mountain			13,182
"Valhalla, Mount"	498	445	13,180
Babcock Peak	499	446	13,180
Point 13,180 A	500	447	13,180
Santa Fe Peak	501	448	13,180
Grand Turk	502	449	13,180
Point 13,180 B	503	450	13,180
"Southwest Lenawee"	S33	S32	13,180
Point 13,180 C	S34	S33	13,180
Point Pun			13,180
"Point Giesecke"			13,180
"Tower Six"			13,180
"Tower Seven"			13,180
Yellow Mountain			13,177
Copeland Mountain	504	451	13,176
Conejos Peak	505	452	13,172
Point 13,169	506	453	13,169
Sheep Mountain C	507	454	13,168
Amherst Mountain	508	455	13,165
"Stony Pass Peak"	509	456	13,165
Kelso Mountain	510	457	13,164
Point 13,164	511	458	13,164
Helen, Mount			13,164
Point 13,162 A	512	459	13,162
Point 13,162 B	513	460	13,162
Point 13,159	514	461	13,159
Twilight Peak	515	462	13,158
Point 13,158	516	463	13,158
"Window Peak"	517	464	13,157
"V 5"	518	465	13,156
Point 13,155	519	466	13,155
Baldy Mountain A			13,155

13er Name	Overall Rank	13er Rank	Elevation
"Medano Peak"	520	467	13,153
Taylor Peak B	521	468	13,153
Point 13,153	522	469	13,153
"Could Be"			13,152
Pomeroy Mountain A	523	470	13,151
Montezuma Peak	524	471	13,150
Arikaree Peak	525	472	13,150
South River Peak	526	473	13,148
Point 13,147	527	474	13,147
Flora, Mount	528	475	13,146
"Jackass Point" aka "No Name Peak"	529	476	13,145
Point 13,145	S35	S34	13,145
Precipice Peak aka "U 2"	530	477	13,144
Little Horn Peak	531	478	13,143
Willoughby Mountain	532	479	13,142
Point 13,140 A	533	480	13,140
Point 13,140 B	534	481	13,140
"West Virginia"	535	482	13,140
Twelve, Peak	536	483	13,140
"West Truro"	537	484	13,140
Point 13,140 C	S36	S35	13,140
Emerson Mountain	S37	S36	13,140
Point 13,140 D	S38	S37	13,140
Guyselman Mountain			13,140
Robeson Peak			13,140
"Dicker's Peck"			13,140
Savage Peak	538	485	13,139
Hayden Mountain, North	539	486	13,139
"North Point"			13,139
Ogalalla Peak	540	487	13,138
Hunchback Mountain	541	488	13,136
Francisco Peak	542	489	13,135
"S 9"	543	490	13,134
Sullivan Mountain			13,134
Point 13,132	544	491	13,132
Sewanee Peak			13,132
Eva, Mount	545	492	13,130
"Rain Peak"			13,130
Black Benchmark			13,129
Lomo Liso Mountain	546	493	13,128
"Pika Peak"	547	494	13,126
Kennedy, Mount			13,125
"Woods Peak"	548	495	13,123
Point 13,123	549	496	13,123
Spiller Peak			13,123
Peters Peak	550	497	13,122
Point 13,122	551	498	13,122
"Peak N"	552	499	13,121

13er Name	Overall Rank	13er Rank	Elevation
Point 13,121	553	500	13,121
Isolation Peak	554	501	13,118
"Cupid"	555	502	13,117
Lizard Head	556	503	13,113
Fitzpatrick Peak	557	504	13,112
Point 13,111	558	505	13,111
Cow Benchmark	559	506	13,111
"Hancock Peak"	560	507	13,111
Point 13,110	561	508	13,110
Point 13,109	562	509	13,109
Point 13,108	563	510	13,108
Thunder Mountain A			13,108
Point 13,106	564	511	13,106
Bushnell Peak	565	512	13,105
"Peak Twenty Two"	566	513	13,105
Point 13,100 A	567	514	13,100
Middle Mountain A	568	515	13,100
Point 13,100 B	569	516	13,100
"Baldy Lejos"	570	517	13,100
"Corbett Ridge" aka "Chipeta Peak" or "Sultan Peak"	571	518	13,100
Point 13,100 C	S39	S38	13,100
South Twilight Peak			13,100
"Peak H"			13,100
"Leaning North Peak"			13,100
"Gore Thumb"			13,100
"C Prime"			13,100
Kreutzer, Mount	572	519	13,095
"Tomboy Peak"	573	520	13,095
Point 13,093	574	521	13,093
Point 13,091	575	522	13,091
"Solitude, Mount"	576	523	13,090
Point 13,090	577	524	13,090
Paiute Peak	578	525	13,088
Virginia Peak	579	526	13,088
Spencer Peak			13,087
Keller Mountain TR	580	527	13,085
"Ribbed Peak"	581	528	13,085
"Peak X"	582	529	13,085
"Peak Twenty One"			13,085
Boreas Mountain	583	530	13,082
"Huerfanito"	584	531	13,081
"North Traverse Peak"	585	532	13,079
Whale Peak	586	533	13,078
Point 13,078	587	534	13,078
Snowdon Peak	588	535	13,077
Winfield Peak			13,077
Florida Mountain			13,076
Point 13,075	589	536	13,075

13er Name	Overall Rank	13er Rank	Elevation
North Twilight Peak	590	537	13,075
"Vista Peak"			13,075
"West Tellurium"	591	538	13,074
Garfield, Mount A	592	539	13,074
Blackwall Mountain	593	540	13,073
"Son of Corbett"			13,072
Hunts Peak	594	541	13,071
Sheep Mountain D	595	542	13,070
Point 13,070	596	543	13,070
"Devils Playground Peak"			13,070
Point 13,069	597	544	13,069
Chiquita, Mount	S40	S39	13,069
Kendall No 2 Benchmark	S41	S40	13,066
Point 13,062 A	598	545	13,062
Point 13,062 B	599	546	13,062
West Needle Mountain	600	547	13,062
Centennial Peak	S42	S41	13,062
Point 13,060 A	601	548	13,060
Point 13,060 B	602	549	13,060
Point 13,060 C	S43	S42	13,060
"Igloo Peak"	S44	S43	13,060
Point 13,060 D	S45	S44	13,060
Saint Sophia Ridge			13,060
Silver Mesa			13,060
Middle Mountain B			13,060
"Little Wasatch Mountain"			13,060
"Palomino Point"			13,060
Owen, Mount B	603	550	13,058
"East Partner Peak"	604	551	13,057
"Chalk Rock Mountain"	605	552	13,055
Point 13,054	606	553	13,054
Houghton Mountain	607	554	13,052
Point 13,051	608	555	13,051
Point 13,050	609	556	13,050
"Dead Man Peak"	610	557	13,050
Green Mountain A			13,049
West Dyer Mountain			13,047
"Peak D"			13,047
"N 2"	611	558	13,046
Eagle Peak B			13,043
"V 7"	612	559	13,042
"West Partner Peak"	613	560	13,041
"Grand Traverse Peak"	614	561	13,041
Wolcott Mountain			13,041
Point 13,039	615	562	13,039
"Old Baldy"	616	563	13,038
United States Mountain			13,036
West Elk Peak	617	564	13,035
Point 13,034	618	565	13,034

13er Name	Overall Rank	13er Rank	Elevation
Point 13,033	619	566	13,033
Organ Mountain B	620	567	13,032
Point 13,030	S46	S45	13,030
Point 13,028	621	568	13,028
Point 13,026	622	569	13,026
"Snow Peak"	623	570	13,024
Van Wirt Mountain	S47	S46	13,024
Niwot Ridge			13,023
"Yellow Boy"			13,023
"Unicorn, The"	624	571	13,020
Point 13,020 A	625	572	13,020
Point 13,020 B	626	573	13,020
Point 13,020 C	627	574	13,020
Point 13,020 D	S48	S47	13,020
Point 13,020 E	S49	S48	13,020
"The Hand"			13,020
"North Irving"			13,020
"The Thumb"			13,020
Cuba Benchmark			13,019
Point 13,017	628	575	13,017
Point 13,016	629	576	13,016
Point 13,015	630	577	13,015
Chief Mountain A	631	578	13,014
Twin Sisters, North	632	579	13,012
Hope Mountain			13,012
Point 13,010	633	580	13,010
"Golden Bear Peak"	634	581	13,010
"Dorothy Peak"			13,010
Pennsylvania Mountain	635	582	13,006
"Climber's Point"			13,005
"Yahoo Mountain"			13,005
"Cooper Peak"			13,004
Point 13,003	636	583	13,003
Ruffner Mountain			13,003
Point 13,001	637	584	13,001

Peaks in This Guide

Point (13,017 feet), 150
Point (13,407 feet), 181
Ptarmigan Peak (13,739 feet), 141
Quail Mountain (13,461 feet), 108
Red Mountain (13,229 feet), 13
Red Peak (13,189 feet), 146
Red Peak A (13,215 feet), 13
Rio Grande Pyramid (13,821 feet), 150
Robeson Peak (13,140 feet), 24
Rogers Peak (13,391 feet), 121
Rosalie Peak (13,575 feet), 157
Ruby Mountain (13,277 feet), 1
Santa Fe Peak (13,180 feet), 77
Snow Peak (13,024 feet), 161
South Arapaho Peak (13,397 feet), 166
Stewart Peak (13,983 feet), 174
Sullivan Mountain (13,134 feet), 77
Traver Peak (13,852 feet), 35

Treasure Mountain (13,528 feet), 181
Treasurevault Mountain (13,701 feet), 82
Treasury Mountain (13,462 feet), 181
Tundra Top (13,450 feet), 29
Twining Peak (13,711 feet), 187
UN 13,001, 187
UN 13,038 ("Old Baldy"), 166
UN 13,215, ("Hassell Peak"), 136
UN 13,546, 87
UN 13,580, 87
UN 13,580A, 87
UN 13,581, 29
Vermillion Peak (13,894 feet), 194
Vista Peak (13,075 feet), 116
West Spanish Peak (13,626 feet), 199
Weston Peak (13,572 feet), 141
Whale Peak (13,078 feet), 205
Window Peak (13,157 feet), 150

About the Author

James Dziezynski is the best-selling author of *Best Summit Hikes in Colorado, Best Summit Hikes: Denver to Vail,* and *The Best Indian Peaks Wilderness Hikes.* James has worked as a professional writer and editor for over twenty years and is currently the senior editor at RootsRated.com and contributing editor at *Elevation Outdoors Magazine.* His work has appeared in *National Geographic Adventure, Outside, Backpacker,* the *Denver Post,* the *Boulder Weekly,* the *Boulder Daily Camera, Elevation Outdoors, Women's Adventure, The Bark, Discover Magazine,* and many more outlets, both print and online.